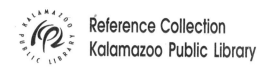

AN ENCYCLOPEDIA OF
CELTIC MYTHOLOGY

AN ENCYCLOPEDIA OF
CELTIC MYTHOLOGY

BOB CURRAN

CB

CONTEMPORARY BOOKS

The publisher thanks Mary Evans Picture Library for permission to publish photographs on pages: 19, 20–21, 24, 35, 38–39, 40, 42–43, 44, 46, 49, 50, 52, 57, 59, 69, 78, 80, 82, 91, 103, 104, 109, 113, 116, 122, 124, 126–127, 128–129, 130–131, 156, 161, 166, 171, 178–179, 187, 188–189, 206, 209, 213, 218, 220, 228–229, 231, 232, 237 (Saint Vincent).
The publisher thanks Collections for permission to publish photographs on pages: 96–97, 102, 103 (Giant's Causeway), 106.
The publisher thanks e. t. archive for permission to publish photographs on pages: 22, 46 (Queen Boudicca), 58, 64, 66–67, 72–73, 74–75, 78, 85, 100, 105, 108, 174–175, 195, 210, 214, 237, 238.
The publisher thanks The Ancient Art & Architecture Collection Ltd. for permission to publish photographs on pages: 10, 13, 14, 16, 146–147, 165, 176, 192–193, 197, 207, 234, 235.
The publisher thanks Fortean Picture Library for permission to publish photographs on pages 11, 134, 158, 164.

First published in 2000 by Appletree, the Old Potato Station, 14 Howard Street
South, Belfast BT7 1AP,
Tel: +44 (0) 28 90 243074
Fax: +44 (0) 28 90 246756
Website: www.irelandseye.com
E-mail: reception@appletree.ie

This edition first published in 2000 by Contemporary Books
A division of NTC/Contemporary Publishing Group, Inc.
4255 West Touhy Avenue, Lincolnwood (Chicago), Illinois 60712-1975 U.S.A.
Copyright © 2000 by the Appletree Press Ltd.
Photographs and illustrations copyright © Mary Evans Picture Library; e.t. archive,
The Ancient Art & Architecture Collection Ltd.; Fortean Picture Library; the Appletree
Press Ltd.
Printed in China
International Standard Book Number: 0-8092-2330-9
00 01 02 03 04   20 19 18 17 16 15 14 13 12 11 10 9 8 7 6 5 4 3 2 1

CONTENTS

INTRODUCTION

Celtic Mythology

Warhorse on Celtic coin, AD 20

The Celts were, and have remained through the ages, a people of mystery.

We speak of the Celtic Race but there never, really, existed such a race in the way that we understand the term today. Rather, they were a loose amalgam of tribes, communities and disparate groups that had, at some point in history, come together for shared purposes such as defence, worship, trading and hunting.

Compared with the great Mediterranean cultures – Greece and Rome – we know relatively little about the Celts. Unlike the Classical civilisations, they left exceptionally little behind them that scholars today can classify with any degree of certainty. We do not really know what they thought of themselves, or how they viewed the rest of the world; we don't know their political views and they left no real translatable written texts behind them to give us a picture of their day-to-day lives.

They have, however, left us some records because, although a people with a primarily oral tradition, they did have a form of writing. This was known as Ogam, or Ogham, taking its name from Ogma, the Irish god of eloquence and literature. Much of it is in the form of stylised lines, mainly drawn on oak-bark or stone. It had probably gone out of common use, however, by the eighth century. However, although an

Ogam alphabet has been worked out, there is no real linguistic context in which to put it.

Even the name Celt is only a nickname, given to them by other races with which they came into contact. The word 'keltoi' was taken from their own tongue and it meant 'secret' or 'hidden'. It was a description aptly applied to them as a 'secretive or hidden people' – a term first used by the Greek Hectaeus in approximately 517 BC – as they never gave away too much concerning themselves. We have, therefore, to rely on what other peoples have said about them – not that such accounts can, in any way, be considered impartial as many of the more 'civilised' peoples looked down on the Celts considering them mere barbarians and savages and were anxious to portray them as such.

The Celts are mentioned in recorded and formal history in about the third or second millennium BC although their exact origins are not known. It is known that they crossed the Alps from lands further to the north and that they were probably one of the first of the ancient peoples to do so. It is possible that they may have come from the Central Steppes of Russia and were nomadic peoples who had been displaced from their lands by the expansion of other tribes. They first came to the attention of history when they settled in the valley of the River Po in northern Italy, driving out another more settled, agricultural, people known as the Etruscans.

Introduction

In their earliest incarnation, they were a war-like, ferocious people, defeating all who opposed them and treating their captives cruelly and inhumanly but, once having settled in the Po Valley, the Celts gave up their nomadic existence and were content to turn to agriculture, becoming a settled, farming people.

They appear to have been polygamous and, perhaps, even polyandrous and soon the lands around the Po Valley could no longer contain the expanding population. The Celts therefore began to range further south, through Italy, where, of course, they came into contact with a Roman Republic keen to extend its conquests northward.

Ogham inscription on graveslab reads "Colman Bocht", Poor Colman, found in Clonmacnois, County Offaly, Ireland

Conscious of the Celts' war-like reputation, the Romans treated them warily and, though many northern settlements were attacked and taken, they judiciously hung back from any major confrontation. Even though, from time to time, individual Roman commanders might have engaged with, and sometimes even defeated, Celtic forces, for the most part, the legions gave the Celts a fairly wide berth.

The military turning point came in 225 BC at Cape Telamon on the Italian coast. This was a significant encounter between the Celtic armies and the Roman legions and was the place where the myth of Celtic invincibility was shattered for good. The battle turned into a Celtic rout and they fled back to the Po Valley to regroup. The victorious Roman legions followed them and within a matter of years had seized their lands and scattered their tribes.

Some of the Celtic peoples fled east, attacking the Delphic Oracle in Greece and besieging the ancient capital of Byzantium. Eventually they were to settle on the plains of Asia Minor forming Celtic societies on the borders of Turkey – Saint Paul's famous Epistle to the Galatians was to a Celtic church within the boundaries of modern-day Turkey.

Celtic Mythology

The majority of the Celts, however, fled west, settling the furthest reaches of Europe where Roman influence was either nominal or non-existent. They spread into Gaul (France), Iberia (Spain) and even North Africa and Egypt where we know of Celtic brigades in the Egyptian army.

A great number of tribes, however, settled in an area where the Romans traded for tin and consequently called the Tin Isles – these we now know as the British Isles. Here they either ousted, or intermarried with, the aboriginal inhabitants and began to put down roots, just as they had done in the Po Valley. Once again, they became a predominantly agricultural people.

Not that this means that the Celts had become a unified people in the accepted sense. They were still largely a hotch-potch of individual tribes and what we do know about them was that they were savagely territorial. Thus Scotland, Wales, Cornwall, Brittany and the offshore islands became a series of small kingdoms, each ruled by a territorial king who was little more than a tribal warlord. Frequently fighting with each other, or making alliances towards some shared goal or purpose, a kind of pecking order gradually began to develop within this ramshackle structure of localised kingships. A number of High Kings or Great Leaders emerged, coupled with provincial and local monarchs. But even at this stage the Celts do not appear to have been a unified or cohesive people.

We do not even know if all Celts spoke just one language. Historical linguists have detected at least two language-strands amongst them – the harsh-speaking *Gaidheal*, which is identified in linguistic terms as 'Q Celts' and the softer sounding Brythonic tongue spoken by tribes known as 'P Celts'. The *Gaidhlig* tongue formed the more guttural languages of Irish, Manx and Scots whilst the Brythonic emphasis gave rise to Welsh, Cornish and Breton. Another 'P' language, Gaulish, disappeared around the fourth or fifth century AD.

Julius Caesar depicted on a Roman coin

Nowadays, there are roughly sixteen million people living in Celtic countries with only about two and a half million of these speaking a Celtic-based language.

The Celts were both an exciting and inventive people, giving the lie to their description as barbarians as they were relatively sophisticated and civilised. They produced one of the first law systems and were the first people to develop a theory regarding the immortality of the soul. Many of the great philosophers of the Mediterranean world, such as Artistotle and Sotion, owe a debt to the Celts, influenced as they were by the thinking of the Celtic holy men – the druids.

Introduction

In religion and folklore, however, tribal divisions within the Celtic political and territorial structures continued to be manifest. There was little in the way of a common, coherent religious structure, although some common themes existed during the pre-Roman Celtic period. Much of their worship was parochial, being centred on local gods and sites. Certainly, some of the gods shared fairly common characteristics but they were known by so many differing names that it becomes almost impossible to establish any common link between them. Many gods reflected the elements and the geographical landscape of the area settled by their worshippers and it is possible, in common with the deities of other ancient peoples, that the Celtic gods developed out of a form of unsophisticated animism. This belief, that spirits abound everywhere in nature, continued to underpin even their most developed religious forms.

Although the Celts had established themselves securely in the west, the Romans were never far behind. The Roman empire was expanding at a tremendous rate at this time, stretching far beyond the shores of its native Italy. Roman legions had arrived in Gaul and conquered as far as the British island. The fractured structure of the Celtic political system had made such conquest relatively easy, enabling individual Roman commanders to exploit tribal animosities to their own advantage, siding first with one Celtic leader then another. Despite wars and insurrections, inevitably, Roman authority triumphed. Eventually Rome established a formal empire in the

west comprising most of the Celtic lands with the exception of Ireland, which the Romans did not consider worthy of their interest. An adaptive people, the Celts quickly fitted in with the new Roman political and administrative systems and fused Latinised beliefs, customs and folklore to their own, creating curious Romano-Celtic mythological hybrids.

The Romans, who believed that the Celtic deities were merely versions of their own gods under a different name, were happy to assist them in this endeavour. Consequently, they took over existing Celtic sites, turning them into formalised temples and shrines and adopted Celtic feast days as religious festivals of their own and these adapted beliefs continued long after Rome had withdrawn from the greater part of the western world.

Because the Celts wrote virtually nothing themselves, it was left to others to record accounts of their lives, mythologies and folklore. The first accounts were by historians such as Julius Caesar whose description of Celtic life in Gaul during the Gallic Wars is still one of the central sources of information for this early period. Other reports on Celtic folk life tend to be biased and untrustworthy, seeking to portray Celtic culture as both barbaric and savage.

Celtic tradition, itself, continued mainly in oral form. A small number of Celtic authors wrote in Latin but it was not until the eighth and ninth centuries that such traditions were collected into any cohesive and comprehensive form. But the authors were, again, far from unbiased.

These compilers were Christian monks and, like the Classic scribes before them, had their own agenda to follow. They wished to give order to these scattered, oral tales and to place them within a comprehensive – Christianised – world-view and began to adapt the original, oral stories they heard. They added to them, left sections out and changed names and places to fit in with the overall thrust of the tale they themselves wished to tell. Nevertheless, the result is the most coherent collection of tales we have and it forms the basis of many of the famous stories we know today.

These monks, writing in the remote monasteries of Ireland, Cornwall, Wales and Brittany, were able to draw together a large corpus of tales, which they then compiled into a number of manuscripts. Because of the coherence of these collections they became known as the Myth Cycles – a series of interlocking stories, many grouped around a central theme, detailing histories and events remote from the time in which their monkish compilers were writing.

These cycles have been passed down to us, as the traditional tales of the early Celtic peoples, in a series of medieval compilations, scattered throughout early British monastic literature. Some of these have become famous in their own right and

Ogham alphabet on stone in 12th-century church in Dingle, Ireland

include the *Irish Leabhar Gabhála* (*Book of Invasions*) which has survived in a number of ancient manuscripts such as *The Book of Leinster*. Since no Celtic creation myth appears to have survived, this epic tried to trace the history of Ireland, from earliest times, in the form of a series of invasions of ancient peoples. The lineage of kings continued down to the Irish High King, Malachi Mór (980-1002). Although some of the details which it contains are extremely suspect, the Book came to be regarded as Ireland's national epic and the Irish historian Micheál Ó'Cléirigh (1575-c.1645) compiled a version which reputedly drew upon a number of very ancient sources which were subsequently lost.

Another great Irish epic, considered in mythological terms as being comparable with Homer's *Iliad*, is the *Táin Bó Cuailnge* (*Cattle Raid of Cooley*). Its basic text is to be found in the 11th century *Leabhar na hUidhre*, *The Book of the Dun Cow* and also in *The Book of Leinster*, but both versions are incomplete and additions have to be found in *The Yellow Book of Lecan*. The compilation comprises a number of tales constructed around a war between Connacht and Ulster and concerning a famous bull. The famous Ulster hero Cú Chulainn is featured in this epic. *The Táin*, as it came to be known, is probably the most elaborate and powerful of all the Irish myths.

In the Welsh tradition, the 'Four Branches of the Mabinogi' have survived in the *White Book of Rhydderch* and the *Red Book of Hergest*, both collections culled from the mainstream of Welsh oral mythology.

Introduction

In addition to these are a number of other, less-well-known, books – such as the *Annals of Ulster*, the *Annales Cambriae* – which also draw on the rich tradition of the Celtic peoples all over western Europe. From these diverse sources, we can ascertain the depth and expanse of Celtic history, imagination and folklore. This literature has been coupled with the writings of other ancient scribes and archaeological evidence unearthed over the centuries. Although we must be very careful about romanticising these elements, they provide us with our clearest picture of a shadowy and enigmatic race which, from its secret past, continues to fascinate us even today.

THE DRUIDIC TRADITION

Sages, Seers and Sorcerers

Ideas of witchcraft and sorcery amongst the early Celtic peoples need to be treated carefully.

In the 15th, 16th and 17th centuries, when the great witch persecutions were prevalent across Europe and Britain, these ancient notions were taken to mean the use of supernatural or occult forces by an individual for tangible and pre-specified ends. These ideas have come down to us in a wealth of written material which not only concerns itself with the numerous witch-trials, which characterised the medieval/early modern period, but also details much of the learned and philosophical debate on the subject during this time. As such, it has served to colour our own viewpoint on the matter.

Celtic Mythology

A primary distinction must be made here. Many of the witchcraft-notions handed down do not concern themselves with formally recognised religious practices. Medieval, and early-modern, witchcraft concerned itself with material outcomes. It did not claim to provide a conduit or channel through which the gods could make their will known; it was not a form of 'spirit possession'. It was, rather, the harnessing of supernatural forces to the benefit of the practitioner which was paramount.

Texts concerning the accusations and trials of witches make this quite clear. There are references in these documents, to a body of knowledge – spells, curses, incantations etc. that could be passed on from one generation to the next - which forms the basis of a sorcerous tradition. Some of this so-called arcane knowledge has survived in the form of ancient grimoires, or spell-books, which can still be inspected today.

Other accounts of the lives of certain individuals who, reputedly, practised such traditions give us an insight into the lore and materials upon which they drew. Further information about the society of the period allows us to place such practices within a specific frame of reference.

The ancient Celts, however, have bequeathed us no such corpus of written material. There are no extant magical texts of Celtic sorcerers nor, with the possible highly dubious exception of Merlin, do we have references to individual magicians whom we can place within their true historical context.

Druid priest and priestess

H.S. del.

Aquatinted by R. Have

A Drotte  and a Fola.

*Druid ceremony,
Cornwall*

Since their culture was a primarily oral one, the Celts themselves left us few records
of their thoughts and practices either sorcerous or mundane. Written records of their
society and religion come from observers from different cultures and it is only these
views that give us a glimpse of the Celtic supernatural world.

It is a world that seems to have been dominated by a particular class of men: priests
and sorcerers. Their influence within their society seemed far wider than the confines
of religion. It was through these men that a hidden tradition seems to have been
passed and their role in Celtic society appears to have been a pivotal one. Although
references are made to certain individuals among them, they are known collectively

as druids. Druids, who although through the centuries have been a magnet for myth and legend – being described, for example, as pagan witch-men – are actual figures. We need, therefore, to look at them from a different perspective.

The Classical Druids

The druids of the ancient Celtic world are vague figures whose mystique cast a shadow that we are still attempting to penetrate. Frequently regarded as holy-men, it seems likely that their social role was much more encompassing. Symbols of mystery, even in their own time, it was originally thought that their name, Druid, came from

an ancient Greek word, *drus,* meaning 'oak', thus making the druids men of the oak tree. The Classical Roman writers, Pliny the Elder and Strabo make this connection, citing strong links between the Celtic holy-men and their sacred tree. Recently, however, such a derivation has been called into question. The eminent Irish folklorist, Dr. Daithí Ó hÓgáin, points out in an Irish context:

> '…The favourite tree of the Druids, however, was clearly the rowan and it was on the wattles of this tree that Irish practitioners slept in order to have prophetic visions. The hazel tree was also important, as is evidenced by the Druidic name Mac Cuill, Son of the Hazel, and also by the lore concerning nine hazel trees at the source of the River Boyne, the nuts of which had a nucleus of wisdom.'
>
> (Ó hÓgáin: *An Encyclopaedia Of The Irish Folk Tradition*, 1990)

Scholars now tend to believe that the word Druid meant wisdom. Nora Chadwick, though, in her book *The Druids* (1966), puts forward the interesting idea that it may have been no more than a nickname, meaning something like backwoodsmen, given to them because they latterly lived in deep oak woods. Whatever the derivation of their name, today the druids remain as mysterious as ever.

What information we have about them comes from two main sources. The first is a body of written material compiled, mainly around the first century AD, by Greek and Roman authors. Classical writers such as Strabo, Tacitus, and Suetonius make reference to the druids. They all use as their source the work of a Syrian-Greek writer, named Poseidonius, who travelled extensively in Celtic lands, especially Gaul (France) during the early part of the first century.

The Druidic Tradition

Some of these writers refer to druids at some length and others mention them only in passing. The best and most coherent source, however, is Julius Caesar who, as military governor of southern Gaul, conducted a series of expeditions against the Celtic tribes between 59 – 50 BC. As his troops pressed deep into the Gallic heartland, Caesar recorded the culture and practices of the peoples whom he encountered. His book, *De Bello Gallico – The Gallic Wars*, is one of the better records of Gaulish society that we have and it also gives us some sort of picture regarding the status of the druid.

Generally, Classical writing on the druids falls into a number of distinct types. Several Graeco-Roman authors seek to portray them as the primitive and bloodthirsty shamans of a barbaric people, engaging in terrible and appalling rituals – including human sacrifice – in secluded groves and dark caves. They were sharply contrasted with the cultured and civilised people of Mediterranean countries and were depicted as little more than painted fortune-tellers, mouthing inane prophecies after consulting animal or human entrails.

Archdruid, Cornwall

Tacitus, in his *Histories*, scathingly mentions their 'chantings of vain superstitions' whilst Cicero, writing to his brother Quintinus states: 'The system of divination is not neglected even amongst the most barbaric peoples since, in fact, there are Druids in Gaul . . .'

A mother allows sacrifice of her child to the gods, believing that they will bequeath plentiful milk and corn

Other writers, such as Caesar, described them as men of great learning and intellect who held high status in the Celtic social order; they were judges and magistrates, mediators in disputes, teachers, healers and counsellors, philosophers and theologians who frequently engaged in learned debate among themselves. They were also distinct and separate from the rest of Celtic society, as befitted their important status. Caesar states:

'Throughout Gaul, there are two classes of men of some dignity and importance . . . One of the two classes is that of the Druids, the other that of the Knights. The Druids are concerned with the worship of the gods, look after public and private sacrifice and expound religious matters. A large number of young men flock to them for training and holds them in high honour.'

They have the right to judge nearly all public and private disputes and they also pass judgement and decide rewards and penalties, in criminal and murder cases and in disputes concerning legacies and boundaries.

'. . . The Druids are wont to be absent from war, nor do they pay taxes like the others ... It is said that they commit to memory immense amounts of poetry. And so some of them continue their studies for twenty years.'

He also tells us how the druids in Gaul were organised:

> 'All Druids are under one head, whom they hold in the highest respect. On his death, if any one of the rest is of outstanding merit, he succeeds to the vacant place; if several have equal claims, the Druids usually decide the election by voting, though sometimes the matter actually comes to force of arms.'

Interestingly, he also mentions certain aspects of druidic learning and philosophy.

> 'They have, also, much knowledge of the stars and their motion. They hold long discussions about heavenly bodies and their movements, the size of the universe and of the earth, the physical constitutions of the world and the powers and properties of the gods, and they instruct the young men in all these subjects.'
>
> (Caesar: *Gallic Wars IV*)

Druids, in effect, were a separate, priestly caste within Celtic society, formally excused from both taxation and military service. Caesar goes on to state that their influence was considerable, even within the political sphere, constantly acting as advisers and consultants to local kings and warlords. Their knowledge, he suggests, was considerable even to the point where they seem to have been acting as early astronomers and scientists. He further notes that druidism was not indigenous to Gaul, having been brought there from Britain. In fact, parts of Britain seemed to survive as druid strongholds after the druids had largely disappeared in many other parts of the Celtic world.

The Druidic Tradition

Following Caesar's depiction of an intelligent, democratic pagan clergy, other writers such as Strabo and Diodorus strove to describe them in a positive and sympathetic light, but even this had a note of condescension. The druids were frequently equated with the idea of the Noble Savage whose learning, though prodigious, was somehow inferior to the knowledge of Greece and Rome. A third description found in the works of Lucan and Pomponius Mela might be described as that of a bewildered tourist, viewing the druids and their customs as both exotic and utterly alien. It is highly probable that, at around the end of the first century when many of these authors were writing, the role and status of the druids as a learned and influential class were already in decline. The nature and functions of the druid may also have been changing, and within their ranks they may have been either subsumed or pushed to the periphery of Celtic culture.

The second primary body of evidence relating to the druids is a part of the myth-cycles of both Wales and Ireland. This source is a vernacular one, originally written or orally transmitted in the native tongue. During the period between the seventh and twelfth centuries, these scattered traditions were, mainly by monks, collected and moulded into great compilations. Among these works are the great Irish Myth Cycles such as the Ulster and Fenian Cycles and the general myth-cycles of early Wales, together with such works as the 12th-century *'Book of Invasions'* and *Táin Bó Cuailnge - The Cattle Raid of Cooley.*

These vernacular texts seem to bear out some of the comments by the Classical writers. For example, they allude to the power, and formal status, of the druids within Celtic society, drawing attention to their more political function of advisers to the king or chieftain. According to these sources, no person in Ireland enjoyed as much influence as Cathbhadh, the druid-adviser to Conchobhar MacNessa, King of Ulster. It was said that Cathbhadh could even formulate royal policy as he saw fit.

Such sources must also be treated with a degree of caution. Many of the accounts date from the early medieval period, long after the Celtic period, and were written by monks. The monks were by no means impartial historians; they worked to their own agenda. Part of that agenda was to fit the ancient Celtic fables into a Christian view of the world. Consequently, many of these tales were amended to parallel Biblical stories or to demonstrate a moral truth. Accounts of the druids were intended to portray them as dark, pagan priests, inevitably driven back by the power of the Holy Truth.

Celtic Mythology

Conflicting pictures of druids: decried by certain early Church Fathers; described as primitive shamans by the Classical writers and as a learned, austere caste by Caesar and others, make it difficult to define their true nature. Probably, they fell somewhere between the two. The very early Celts had been hunters and an extremely warlike people preoccupied with battle and with killing large numbers of animals. In all probability, their religious leaders reflected these concerns. It is also possible that, to ensure success in warfare, druid shamans employed human sacrifice during rituals. To ensure a good hunting season it may have been necessary for the druid to dress in animal skins and adopt animal characteristics. A recently discovered, antlered, head-dress found at Hook's Cross in Hertfordshire, gives credence to this theory.

It is thought, moreover, that many early druids may have been skilled in the use of narcotics. Such a suggestion is borne out by the amounts of cannabis found in some Celtic tombs in Germany. Such drugs would have been considered necessary to contact the spirits, but they may also have been useful for healing purposes, leading us to believe that druids may have been natural healers.

As the Celts became a more settled people, increasingly turning their attention to agriculture, so the concerns of the druids also began to alter. They began to focus on the changes in the year, the movements of clouds and of stars and predictions as to whether the harvest would be fruitful. We know from certain written accounts and from a number of sacrificial stones still existing – for example, the Crom Cruach in County Fermanagh - that some human sacrifice was still being carried out in Ireland just prior to the arrival of Saint Patrick. This type of sacrifice was, gradually, replaced by that of animals, particularly cattle.

The notion of prediction, whether of the outcome of a battle or of the harvest, gave the druid a particular status within his community. In the pre-Roman world, Celtic kings and rulers probably courted the fraternity of druids, thus granting them increasingly powerful positions. In order to protect those positions, the druids would pass on their knowledge, not in any written form but in a clandestine and secretive oral way. The template for the druid as the Man of Forbidden Lore was already being set.

The Druid's Egg

Between the middle and end of the first century, Celtic society was to experience a profound change. Large areas of the Celtic world, particularly Gaul and Britain, were under Roman occupation and exposure to Mediterranean civilisation was causing changes to the indigenous culture. Local rulers were adopting Roman forms of government, and the worship of local spirits was merging with that of Roman deities, producing gods with Latinised attributes.

The druids, their power and influence beginning to wane, responded in one of two ways. A few embraced the new culture, becoming priests of a Romano-Celtic type

THE DRUID'S EGG

The Druid's Egg was first described by Pliny during the firsst century. It was believed to have been formed from the foam that issued from the mouths of two serpents as they mated. It was considered an infallible protection against the excesses of Roman authority, particularly that of Roman law. The serpent foam formed a ball of viscous slime, which, if thrown in the air and caught by a druid, would provide protection against all manners of incantations.

Eggs were important in Celtic belief as symbols of regeneration and rebirth, directly connected to the fertility gods. Many Celtic deities were associated with, or actually carried, eggs. In Horchsheid in Germany, the fertility goddess Sirona is depicted as carrying a large bowl containing three eggs. About her arm, Sirona also wears a coiled serpent whose head reaches down to take the eggs.

Eggs, clearly grave goods, were placed in the grave of a Gaulish warrior chieftain and throughout Celtic mythology and folklore, eggs play a central role. The Irish goddess Cliodhna was believed to possess two birds, brought by her from the Otherworld, which laid crimson-coloured eggs. If mortals ate them, either by accident or design, they would assume the bird-like attributes of feathers and wings.

In later folklore, the egg seems to have become crystalline in form, as in the west of Scotland where the *glam-nan-Druidhe* – Druid's crystal – was frequently spoken of as a means of foretelling the future. In England too, there are references, in the works of medieval writers, to such a speculum used for predictions and the locating of lost or stolen articles.

As late as 1586, William Camden in his *Britannia* refers to glass amulets known as 'gemma anguine' which were usually green in colour, although 'some of them are blue and others curiously waved with red and white'. He states that they were mostly as wide as finger-rings 'but much thicker'. In Cornwall, Wales and in parts of Ireland, according to Thomas Kendrick (1926), they were known as snake stones, which was, perhaps, a reference to their alleged serpent-origins. Also called Druid's Glass, they were reputedly extremely magical. In Ulster there are still stories about persons finding these 'fairy beads' and using them as a luck charm or a protective talisman; they were believed to keep away evil fairies. Kendrick states, as does Stuart Piggot much later, that the mystical eggs that Pliny saw were no more than a natural phenomenon, probably caused by the fusion of tiny sea-ammonites along the shoreline of Britain.

It is also worth noting that several of the central figures of Gaelic folklore sported crystal-like objects that served them as the source of their extraordinary powers. In 17th-century Scotland, the Brahan Seer, Kenneth MacKenzie, was said to have used a blue stone that he held to his blind eye for divinatory purposes. The stone was said to have been thrown into Loch Ussie in Ross-shire where it remains until another seer finds it. In Ireland, the Clare wise-woman, Biddy Early, was believed to have possessed a blue bottle in which she could foresee the future or observe events far away. When she died it was taken by a priest who threw it into Kilbarron Lake but thereafter was able to light altar candles by just praying.

Both these artefacts contain echoes of the notion of the Druid's Egg, creating a tradition that stretches back to the first century.

religion and ingratiating themselves with their Roman overlords. The majority partly withdrew from Celtic society, retreating into hidden groves, remote valleys and deep caves, there to practise the old and pure Celtic traditions and to foment rebellion against the occupying Roman forces.

Although their influence had declined it had not been completely subsumed and young men still flocked to them − druids became a focus of Celtic nationalism and revolt and this was probably reflected in their teaching.

According to the Classical writers, the attitude of the Roman emperors towards the continuance of druidism in Celtic countries varied considerably. Augustus tolerated it, Tiberius opposed it whilst Claudius tried to eradicate it completely. Suetonius gleefully declares that Claudius had 'completely abolished the barbarous and inhuman religion of the druids in Gaul'. It must be remembered that Suetonius was a notorious scandalmonger, always anxious to secure his position with the emperor and this declaration may be seen as an attempt to curry favour with the Roman establishment. Whether or not druidism had been eradicated in Gaul during the reign of Claudius, Tacitus tells us that druids in Britain played an active part in the Boudiccan rebellion of AD 60–1, during Nero's reign. Around this time, the Roman military governor of Britain, Paulinus, mounted a successful expedition against the foremost British druid stronghold, the island of Anglesey, in order to limit persistent anti-Roman influence within the country. In the 'Year of the Four Emperors' (AD 69) when Rome itself was experiencing tremendous internal upheaval in the imperial succession following the death of Nero, druids were believed to have been inciting the Gaulish tribes to a mass uprising.

Celtic Mythology

There is no doubt that the Roman authorities in both Gaul and Britain worried about the nationalistic fervour directed against them by the druids. Draconian methods were enforced against anyone who displayed druidic connections. Pliny relates how, during the reign of Claudius, a chieftain of the Vocontii Gauls, was executed by the Romans because he wore a Druid's Egg about his neck. This egg-shaped talisman, particular to the druids was also known as an *anguinium*, and was supposed to help the wearer gain victory in the Roman law courts. The amulet was certainly considered magical and inimical to the lawful authorities. Pliny describes it as 'round and about as large as a smallish apple'. In his book *The Druids* (1968), Stuart Piggot suggests that the talisman could have been nothing more than fused, empty whelk-shells, which, though they were common in many parts of northwest Britain and coastal Gaul, were considered both exotic and mysterious by the Mediterranean peoples.

From the end of the first century, Classical writers seem to have placed a new, and slightly more sinister, emphasis upon druidic teachings and practices. Lucan, Tacitus and Pomponius Mela all speak of clandestine rites carried out in hidden places. We have to be wary, however, of their ominous references to 'the dark riddles of the druids' as part of the druid teaching seems to have been by way of riddles and proverbs. Much of this writing may simply reflect generalised Roman suspicion towards the druids.

The commonality of such texts does tend to suggest, however, that the druids themselves were consciously becoming more secretive in their ways. Many of their utterances now seemed to be in the form of prophecies and curses and these may still have been heeded by certain local chieftains, as Dio Chrysostom, still living in the second century, notes:

> 'The Celts appointed Druids, who were versed in the art of seers and other forms of wisdom without whom the kings were not permitted to adopt or plan any course.'

> (Dio Crysostom: *Oratorio*)

This may, of course, have given the druids a useful inroad into fomenting rebellion against the Romans in certain regions of the Celtic world.

Despite their new role of Druid as Political Agitator, individual druids, faced with Roman persecution, were forced to keep away from the mainstream of Celtic society. They retreated into remote and largely inaccessible places of the Celtic world – islands, isolated groves and caves. There they continued to practise their mostly proscribed rites and to teach their followers the old Celtic ways. This, naturally, merely added to their mystique as the protectors of a secret and forgotten learning. The way was now prepared for the druid to make his entry as the man of mystery upon the stage of the early world.

The Druidic Tradition

Survival in Ireland

One area of the British Isles that had not experienced the domination of Rome was the island of Ireland. Tacitus tells us of his father-in-law, Julius Agricola, one of the most able and influential Roman military governors of Britain. He was governor between AD 78 and 84 and had long considered an invasion of Ireland. When, however, he was invited to intervene in a local civil war in the north of the country, his campaign against the Picts and Hibernians kept him occupied until his recall to Rome by the Senate in AD 84.

There seemed to be a steady commerce between Roman Britain and Ireland and, although the latter was spared the full impact of Roman occupation, there was a minimal Roman influence in some Irish coastal areas. An example of this contact was brought to light a few years ago when a coastal fortress, bearing Roman elements, was unearthed near Dublin.

In Ireland, the druids seem to have enjoyed uninterrupted influence for a longer period than elsewhere. Vernacular texts show them acting as formal advisers and forecasters to the High Kings of Ireland right up until the arrival of Saint Patrick in the fifth century.

It was in Ireland, too, that they most fully expressed their roles as magicians and seers, as we learn from vernacular sources such as *The Fenian Cycle* and the *Lives* of the early saints. From what we have learnt of Irish druids we catch a glimpse of what the Celtic druids may have been like during their hey-day. The picture we have of the druidic system in Ireland shows a particularly learned class within Celtic society established into three main sub-divisions.

First, there were the brehons or judges. The brehon's formal powers seemed to have fulfilled a role combining elements of magistrate, mediator and social worker. 'The Druids', said Strabo, 'are considered the most just of men'. The brehons played a significant role in formulating, in AD 714, the system of law that was to govern Celtic Ireland during the reign of the High King Ollamh Fodhla. This High King may, himself, have been a druid as the name 'Ollamh' means 'Professor' or 'Great Historian', according to the *Seanchus Mór* which was the title of one of the grades of Bardic druidism.

It was from this codified rule by legislature, that other legal systems were founded in the Celtic world. Most notable of these were the Laws of Hywel Dda of Wales and the legendary Molmutine Law of Cornwall mentioned by Geoffrey of Monmouth. Later a new class of Celtic judges would arise, also called Brehons but which owed its style more to Roman law – having, for instance, to quote a *fásach*, a precedent or maxim, to justify their decisions. Gradually, the brehons began to lose their power and influence as Ireland changed under the ruthless onslaught of Christianity.

Celtic Mythology

The second class was the religious druids themselves, who officiated at all ceremonies organising both public and private sacrifice. Wielding immense influence throughout Ireland, they too were closely associated with magic and wonderworking, both for good and evil. Yet, if we look closely at the legends concerning the druids, we can detect certain similarities to the Semitic/Biblical tales of Old Testament prophets such as Samuel, Nathan and Isaiah. Some of these similarities spring from the relationship between druid and king, others from the use of divination by the druids reflecting the way that the will of Yahweh was often determined by his Hebrew prophets through divinatory means.

It is quite likely that this Biblical emphasis was added to the vernacular texts later, reflecting the Christian view of the monks who copied out the original material. Despite this religious connection, tales concerning Irish druids frequently depict them as enchanters and protectors of a dark and sorcerous knowledge passed down from former times.

The stories are littered with references to 'druid wands and staves', although we must also remember that the staff has connections with the early Semitic prophets such as Moses (see: 'Bachall' in **Legends of Saints and Holy Men**). With these marvellous artefacts, the druid could perform miracles, such as turning themselves or others into different shapes. The Irish druidic tradition spoke frequently of shape-shifting druids who were to be found all over the Irish countryside and these stories have found their way into vernacular Irish writing such as the *Táin*.

Many of the druids in Ireland were concerned with prognostication, the practice of which ensured their political influence in the country. It was extremely useful for local rulers to know the outcomes of their actions before a proposed battle or whether the harvest that year would be good or bad. In the role as seers, the druids could advise their masters or mistresses, if the ruler happened to be a queen, by interpreting signs and signals through which the spirits foretold the future. It is interesting to note that this prognostication mainly involved *interpretive* means on the part of the druid rather than the full-scale possession by the spirit, common amongst the Mediterranean and eastern oracles.

'The Druids', Dio Chrysostom stated, were 'well versed in the art of seers and prophets'. Throughout the ancient world, Irish druids had established a reputation for their forecasts. This was partly carried out through the interpretation of the druids' own dreams, a method of augury that was still carried on in the Western Isles and Highlands of Scotland early in 20th-century, according to Lewis Spence. This ritual was known as *taghairm*, an ancient word originally meaning 'echo' but which had come to mean 'divination by occult means'. The seer would wrap himself in the hide of a newly slain bull and lie down beside a waterfall to meditate or sleep- *dercad*. During his time in this 'altered state', it was believed that he would be visited by the spirits who would either show him the future or supply him with the answers to whatever other questions he posed them.

The Druidic Tradition

The Irish *Tairbhfheis* or 'bull-sleep' employed a more formal ritual and was used on great occasions and for more specific purposes. The best known method of druidic augury was that described by Diodorus Siculus which sought to divine the future from observing the flight or behaviour of birds. The entrails of chickens were frequently used to ascertain future events and, apparently, this method was so successful that chickens were adopted by certain Roman legions in order to determine strategy.

Yet another form of druidic divination was widely known as *coelbreni* or 'omen sticks'. The druids took certain hazel wands, inscribed with the sacred language ogham (a system of lines, carved on either stone or tree-bark). which they cast upon the ground and meaning was interpreted from the lie of their fall.

A third type of druid was the bard or *file* who was something of a cross between seer-poet and tribal historian. Most histories were not written but stored in the memory of individual druids who learned them off in rhyming form. In many cases, the events recounted by the bards had happened many centuries before and had been passed down, purely by word of mouth across the intervening period. Tacitus, for instance, states that in AD 69 bardic druids in Gaul were able to recount stories, four hundred years old, concerning King Brennos, of the Cisalpine Gauls who, between the years 390-87 BC had defeated the Romans and sacked Rome herself. Irish druids too, were able to recount great occurrences from history stretching back across the centuries.

Over the years, two types of Bardic druid had emerged. One was the bard himself, able to recite the genealogies of kings, recount tales of mighty battles and the lineage of the important families within the community, whose training required 20 years of study to attain efficiency. The other was a *file*, or rhymer, who simply concerned himself with the genealogies of various families. The training for this role, not as exacting as that of the bard, took twelve years.

Most of this history was committed to memory using the medium of poetry, a means that appears to have made recollection slightly easier.

As the influence of both the bards and *filidh* began to decrease, they would have become more dependent upon the largesse of regional chieftains and thus their song-poems may have contained less history and been more concerned with the magnification of individual leaders. Some of the poems of the *filidh*, however, had an almost satirical and unflattering resonance to them. These *fili*, regarded as extempory poets much in the style of the later Irish 'hedge-poets' such as *Cathal Buí* (Charles Gunn), may well have been in the pay of other chieftains or may just have considered themselves extremely 'arty' and amusing social commentators. It was partly to deal with the *filidh* who had composed a scathing poem regarding the High King of Ireland that the famous Irish Council of Drum Ceat was convened in AD 575.

As late as the 15th century, bardic schools were still being run in Ireland by families such as the Ó Cléririgh, O'Clearys and the Mulchonries of Clare.

Part of the study of poetry would have included rhyming curses, an example of which was the *glam decin* which punished anyone who refused to pay the poet; poetic methods of divination and a set of mystical incantations for the drawing-down of spirits known as the *tenmliada iombas forosnaí*. Through these, the druidic bard exercised a magical power over the community. Douglas Hyde, in his *Literary History of Ireland* (1899), says:

> 'These instances that I have mentioned occurring in the book of poets' instructions, are evidently the remains of magic incantations and terrifying magic ceremonies, taken over from the schools and times of the Druids ...'

Methods of effective cursing were therefore still being transmitted intergenerationally in Ireland during the late 19th and early 20th centuries.

Two further things need to be said, briefly, regarding Irish druids. The first is to stress their role as healers. The word 'healer' in a conventional tribal sense does not really

As the great druid revival developed, one of the primary strongholds of the tradition proved to be in Wales. The Welsh had chosen to focus on one aspect of druidism – that of the Bard as seer and poet.

From as early as the 12th century, Bardic courts had been paramount in Wales. These organisations maintained standards in poetry and set rules for the poets themselves. This was done through the medium of competitions and awards within the Bardic tradition. The culmination of the Bardic year was the assembly – *eisteddfod* – at which the rules and regulations were fixed and the standards examined. Such gatherings were declared in every Celtic country including Ireland, Scotland and Brittany, so that bards and aspiring bards could travel to Wales and participate in the great occasion. The *eisteddfod* was to be seen as an explosion of Celtic culture and tradition and as such was viewed as a political movement by some non-Celtic authorities. From the 16th century onwards, moves were made by the English to discourage such gatherings and to abolish them altogether but the effect was merely to drive them underground and they were never entirely suppressed.

In Elizabethan England, vagrants wandered the roads, the majority of whom were frequently drunk, often given to unprovoked violence and robbery and who became a drain on the finances of the parishes through which they passed. In order to escape the draconian Vagrancy Laws subsequently imposed, many claimed to be troubadours and bards, performing in hoselries all through England and Wales.

In order to distinguish the real bard from the common rascal, certain Welsh gentlemen were commissioned, by the Elizabethan authorities in Wales, to arrange an eisteddfod in Caewys, Clwyd, the purpose of which was to grant licences to traditional poets. Those who held no bardic licence, thereafter, were counted as 'vagrants and beggars'. This eisteddfod became a great cultural event in the style of the gatherings that the English had initially sought to suppress. Such eisteddfodau continued at various pubs, hostelries and other meeting places until the 18th century.

The effect of these assemblies was much more profound than the authorities had at first realised, for they provided a forum for Welsh songs and verse, and encouraged a widespread interest in Welsh and Celtic culture. It was a small step from the oral recitation of Welsh poetry to its publication and, in 1704, the poet Theophilus Evans published his great work *Gweledigaethau y Barrd Cwsc* – Visions of the Sleeping Bard – which was regarded as a masterpiece of Welsh prose poetry.

This was followed by such works as Edward Jones's *Musical and Poetical Relics of the Welsh Bards and Druids* (accurately linking in the Celtic mind the fundamental notion of the bard as a druid) in 1784 and its sequel, *The Bardic Museum of Primitive British Literature.*

Evan Evans's *Specimens of the Poetry of the Ancient Welsh Bards* (1764), included a lengthy Latin essay on the medieval poets. Evans's work elevated the Bardic tradition to new heights for its author was a cleric and one of the foremost medieval scholars. He was passionate about his Welsh nationality and frequently went by the name of Ieuan Fardd. He insisted that at the heart of Welsh poetry lay a corpus of dark lore that stretched right back to the time of the druids. Only a Celt, observed Evans, could understand its deep and traditional meanings. His writings provoked a spate of Welsh writings – some allegedly discovered druidic poetry of tremendous antiquity – both original and interpretive.

Welsh societies were formed, the most significant was the Gwyneddigion, based in London. Coupled with this was another London Welsh society the Cymmrodorion Society, founded in 1751 for the publication of ancient Welsh texts, which still exists today.

It was the Gwyneddigion which formally gave its backing to a great eisteddfod assembled at Corwen in 1789. Later that same year, the society organised another assembly, at Bala. Edward Williams, a London stonemason, was a member of the society. Originally from Glamorgan, he was passionately interested in Welsh antiquities. He began writing Welsh poetry, using the pseudonym Iolo Morganwg – Iolo of Glamorgan. Much of his work was radical and considered anti-English in tone.

There were worries within the English establishment that this new Welsh Bardic tradition might be republican in nature. Iolo preached that the Glamorgan druids were the inheritors of a tradition that stretched back to the bards. This pedigree was entirely invented – Iolo had forged the documents on which his claim was based – but it served to foster a raging Welsh-nationalist spirit, and formed the basis for the elaborate myth and ritual that surrounds the National Eisteddfod today.

The new druidic movement attracted many notables to its ranks including the writer John Cleland, who produced the erotic classic *Fanny Hill*, or the *Memoirs of a Woman of Pleasure*, which was followed by a number of other volumes in a similar vein. Cleland was a linguistic enthusiast. Encouraged by William Cooke, whose *An Enquiry into the Druidical and Patriarchal Religion* published in 1754 had been a best-seller, he published *The Way to Things by Words and to Words by Things;* being a sketch of an attempt at the retrieval of the ancient Celtic to which is added a succinct account of Sanscrit or learned tongue of the Brahmins.

The eisteddfodau continued and became much more organised and structured. Iolo Morgannwg had taken his writings a stage further and on 21 June 1792, on Primrose Hill in London, he created the *Gorsedd Beirdd Ynys Prydian* – the Assembly of Bards of Britain, claiming to imitate an ancient event. Most of this came from Iolo's fertile imagination but was attended by many bardic enthusiasts from all over Wales and England. By 1819, Iolo had persuaded the organisers of the important Carmarthen Eisteddfod to incorporate his Gorsedd into the central point of their proceedings and it has remained so ever since.

In 1858, the Llangollen Eisteddfod was such a success that a committee was formed to hold a National Eisteddfod each year, leading to the formation, in the 1880s, of a National Eisteddfod Association. The Eisteddfod Genedlaethol Frehind Cymru is now held annually in August, alternately in North and South Wales.

In its initial form, the Gorsedd has three orders. First, and most importantly, are the druids themselves clad in their white robes symbolising their contribution to the culture and poetry of Wales. Next are the blue-clad bards who have passed their final Gorsedd exams and, thirdly, the green-robed neophytes who have passed two preliminary Gorsedd exams or who have been honoured for their services to Welsh literature and culture. The Gaelic Celts, those of Ireland, Scotland and the Isle of Man, have rejected this particular tradition but maintain their own cultural festivals – *Mod nan Alba* in Scotland, *An t-Oireachtas* in Ireland and *Yn Chruinnaght* on the Isle of Man.

apply to them for, in fact, they could be considered doctors and surgeons. These healers spent time at the great druid medical schools that were beginning to spring up across the country, training the foremost doctors in Europe, including those of Rome and Greece.

These healers were so skilled that they were believed to have practised an ancient form of brain surgery, repairing fractured skulls and operating on the brain itself. This is confirmed by the so-called Ovington Skull, unearthed near Brighton in 1935, showing two holes deliberately drilled just above the brain. Several other such skulls have also been dug up in Brittany.

It is recorded that at the important Battle of Mágh Rath, Moira, in A.D. 637, a young chieftain named Cennfealad suffered a fractured skull as the result of a sword-blow. Taken to healers at the medical school at Tomregan which had been founded by druids, he had the injured part of his skull and a portion of his brain removed. On his recovery, it is said that his wits had sharpened and he became a great scholar and poet, founding the celebrated bardic school at Derryloran, County Tyrone. Apart from the schools at places like Tomregan, we also have references to the first-recorded hospital – as a specific foundation for the caring of the sick – in Europe, which was found at Armagh.

We know that druidic medical knowledge was passed down along the generations, usually within a family line, persisting well into Christian times. By the 10th century, several important Irish healing families are identified – the O'Callannans;

THE BULL-SLEEP

One of the most important divinatory processes at which the Irish druids officiated was the *tairbhfheis* or bull-sleep (although it can also mean bull-feast) which is described in several myths. The purpose and importance of this ritual was to select, by occult means, the next High King of Ireland.

Wild bulls were highly significant in Celtic mythology; their strength, aggression, and potency were to be admired and venerated. Domesticated oxen also were favourably looked upon since they symbolised agricultural wealth and demonstrated the power of a draught animal. There is much evidence to suggest that bulls, oxen and elderly cattle were frequently sacrificed to local spirits or were buried as an offering to chthonic deities.

Pliny, in his *Natural History,* recounts a festival at which mistletoe was gathered and two white bulls sacrificed to the horned or crescent-shaped moon. This may have been some sort of fertility ritual. Cattle were not only important indicators of wealth and status within the Celtic community but were also related to ritualised processes.

The most famous bull in Irish mythology is, of course, the Donn Cuailnge or Brown Bull of Cooley, held in Ulster, an animal allegedly capable of human reason. The story, of how this creature precipitated a bloody war between Ulster and Connacht, as Queen Maeve of Connacht tried to carry it off to her own country, forms the basis of the great Irish epic *Táin Bó Cuailnge* (the *Cattle Raid of Cooley*). The tale may be an allegorical way of stressing how important the bull was to the Celtic peoples of the time and it certainly played an integral role as to the choice of the future Irish High King.

For the *tairbhfheis*, a bull was sacrificed and its bloody carcass made into a foaming broth. A warrior was selected to eat the bull-meat and drink of the broth. After he had consumed as much as possible, he was permitted to lie down and sleep while four druids chanted around him, calling on the spirits to make their will manifest. While he slept, dreams would come to him in which, either explicitly or implicitly, the name of the next rightful king to rule at Tara would be revealed. When he awoke, he would recount all his dreams to the four druids who would then make their interpretations. Apparently, it was possible for them to know if the sleeper told the truth. Based on the *tairbhfheis*, the next High King of Ireland would be elected. Such an election provided a signal and mystical connection in the Celtic mind between the elevation to the kingship and the will of the spirits.

An account of the bull-sleep is given to us in the Irish story of *Da Dearga's Hostel*, part of the great Irish Myth Cycle. It is worth noting, however, that the tense in which the story is recounted is past, suggesting to some historians and folklorists that, even by the time of the vernacular account of the story, the *tairbhfheis* was probably no longer actively practised by the druids.

O'Cassidys; O'Lees; O'Hickeys, from *ichidhe* meaning 'healer'; and O'Shiels are all named as hereditary physicians. Maeldo O'Tinnri, said to be the 'best physician in Ireland if not in the world' died in AD 860, the first of a long line of Irish physicians that lasted into the 17th century. Writing in 1648, one of the leading physicians of the day, Baron Van Helmont of Vilvoorde said:

> 'These doctors obtain their medical knowledge chiefly from books, belonging to particular families, left them by their ancestors, in which are written down the symptoms of the several diseases, with the remedies annexed; which remedies are vernacular – the productions of their own country. Accordingly the Irish are better managed than the Italians, who have a physician in every village.'

(Van Helmont: *Confessio Authoris*)

In the early days at least, and probably much later, the healing process was surrounded by ceremony and ritual, probably involving incantations, which would have served to strengthen the healer's association with supernatural forces, adding to the image of

Druids offer human sacrifice to the gods

druids as magicians. In the Christian period, such behaviour was unacceptable to the clergy and such healers were considered as wizards and were actually blamed for spreading disease by the practice of their hideous arts.

One other notable fact of druidism in Ireland is the apparent preponderance of female druids there. Celtic women enjoyed a much different status in their communities from that of the women of the Mediterranean cultures. Greek women had no political rights at all and their social rights were severely limited. They could neither inherit property nor enter into a transaction which involved more than the value of a bushel of grain. The woman was the property of her father or her husband and if a man died without male issue, his daughters were counted as part of his estate.

In Rome, a woman's position was slightly better in that she could conduct business, if she had a male guardian to act for, and oversee, what she did. Only a few married women could hold property and all 'free' women, who had to be, or had been, married wore the *stola matronalis* to show their subservient status.

The position of women in Celtic society was much more relaxed. Women frequently appear as figures of real authority, Queen Boudicca, for instance, and Maeve of Connacht.

Celtic Mythology

The tales also support the notion of female warriors who went into battle. Celtic legend abounds with these figures, some of them boasting supernatural powers, setting themselves up as queens in some mystical realm beyond human cognition (see **The Otherworld**). It was a natural and logical step from these mythical, Otherworld, queens to the notion of a powerful female druid.

Under the Brehon Laws, women could act as judges and lawyers as is evidenced by Brigh, a celebrated female Brehon. They could also act as religious leaders. The existence of female druids, bandruid or *draoi-ban*, in Celtic tradition is explicit and references to them occur in ancient books and stories.

Many druidesses feature in the Irish epics; in *The Fate of the Children of Lir*, Aoife, who was Lir's second wife, uses a druidic wand to turn her stepchildren into swans. This placed her well within the spectrum of female wonder-workers, whilst the druidess Biorog aids Cian to gain access to the crystal tower of Balor of the Evil Eye.

T.D. Kendrick (1926) quotes a persistent tradition which states that, at Cluain Feart or Clonfert, a community of female druids had once existed which had the ability to raise storms, cause diseases and kill its enemies by supernatural spells and curses.

Nor was there any barrier, in early Christian times, to a druidess becoming a female saint, thus gathering a cult about her, just as earlier pagan druidesses had done. The best example of this is Saint Bridget, Brid. She was alleged to have been not only the daughter, or maybe stepdaughter, of a druid but also a *draoi-ban* in her own right. Even the name she took was that of one of the Celtic goddesses – Brigit, 'the high exalted one', who was worshipped as Brigantia in northern Britain and as Brigantu in Gaul. She also assumed the mantle of many of the goddesses' powers and abilities – particularly those concerning fertility. She was allegedly strongly associated with tree-worship and it is said that the siting of her first major convent in Kildare, *cill dáire* – the church of the oak – was no accident. Dr Ó hÓgain states that there was probably already a pagan sanctuary at Kildare and that Brigid simply took over its cult, perhaps transferring its authority from its chief druidess to her own person. Gradually, the role of the female druid would become transformed into that of the 'wise-woman' of later centuries.

As the Roman Church sternly began to denounce druidism, female druids became associated with witchcraft and dark magic. Because of their overt connections with ancient fertility goddesses, they were labelled Fairy Women, *bean-sidhe* in Irish, and it has been suggested that this is the true, human origin of the banshee – the wailing female spirit who portends death – of Irish legend.

Oak and Mistletoe

It is next to impossible to resolve, with any degree of certainty, the assertions made of a corpus of dark rituals and strange rites, featuring brutal human sacrifice, carried out by the mysterious druids in their sacred groves away from prying eyes. But we do have some accounts of druidic ceremonies, supposedly conducted in secret; many Classical writers, on the subject of the druids, mention sacrifice with allusions to human sacrifice amongst the Celts. Caesar makes it plain that human sacrifice was, in effect, 'the harshest penalty' for wrongdoers such as thieves or brigands, or for those who had opposed the druids in some way. In parts of Gaul, according to the same source, sacrifice was also extended to the seriously ill or those captured in battle. However, many of the rituals conducted by the druids remain shrouded in mystery.

The Druidic Tradition

For what is probably our most authentic Classical account we must turn once more to Pliny who claimed to have actually witnessed one of the druid ceremonies at the time of the horned, or crescent, moon. It is from his account that we first get our traditional picture of druids cutting mistletoe with a golden sickle:

> 'The Druids – for so they call their magii (sorcerers) – hold nothing more sacred than mistletoe and a tree upon which it is growing, provided it is Valonia Oak . . . Mistletoe is rare and when found is gathered with great ceremony, particularly upon the sixth day of the moon . . . They prepare a ritual sacrifice together with a banquet beneath a tree and bring up two white bulls, whose horns are bound for the first time. A priest arrayed in white vestments climbs up the tree and, with a golden sickle, cuts down the mistletoe, which is caught in a white cloak. Then finally, they kill the victims

Druids celebrate festival of Samhain, which was the beginning of the Celtic New Year

(sacrifice the bulls), praying to their gods to render gifts propitious to those upon whom they have bestowed it. They believe that mistletoe, given in a drink, will impart fertility to any animal that is barren and that it is an antidote to all poisons.'

(Pliny: *Natural History* XVI)

Clearly mistletoe was a highly significant plant to the druids and hence was used in certain of their ceremonies. It also seems to have had connections with the moon, which was also of ritualistic importance to the Celtic holy men.

Mistletoe was proclaimed, according to Pliny, as 'healing all things' provided it was gathered in an appropriate way. It is highly unlikely, however, that it was harvested

with a sickle of pure gold, a metal too soft for such a purpose; probably the sickle was of gold-plated iron. The purity of gold, coupled with the whiteness of the robes and the purity of the sacrifice, are suggestive of a highly developed religion. Pliny's account comes from Gaul and at the end of the first century AD when druidic practice was probably more structured, and already apeing Roman religious procedures. Prior to the account from Pliny we have some evidence that sacrificial practice amongst the Celts might have been more barbaric. Just outside the village of Belcoo in South Fermanagh, in the north of Ireland, stands a tall stone known as the Crom Cruach, in all probability, a site of early sacrifice. Folklore asserts that, at the turn of the Celtic year, the first-born of that year was placed on the top of the stone and decapitated by the priests. Its blood was allowed to drain into the earth, so revitalising the ground, which had become hard and sterile during the winter months. The

grooves, which carried the infant blood into the ground, are still clearly visible on the sides of the stone. Similar stones are thought to have existed in the Clogher Valley and near the town of Portrush in North Antrim.

Blood and killing may well have played a significant part in early druidic ceremony. Blood was the life force of human beings and, as such, was believed to bring warmth, vigour and vitality to everything, so it is not surprising that it played such an important role in the ceremonies of a farming and agricultural people such as the Celts.

This centrality of blood is noted by the Classical writers. Pliny makes oblique references to hideous practices, carried out in remote groves, which involved not only human blood sacrifice but also a form of cannibalism - the eating of human flesh in order to gain wisdom. Tacitus speaks of the blood-soaked idols in the groves of Anglesey, which were demolished on the orders of the Roman governor, Suetonius Paulinus. Another such grove was destroyed by Caesar's soldiers: 'barbaric gods, worshipped here, had their altars heaped with hideous offerings and every tree was sprinkled with human blood . . . Nobody dared enter this grove except the priest' (*Pharsalia III*).

There were, too, very specific forms of human sacrifice. The most spectacular, and therefore most widely-known, was said to have been The Wicker Man. This was a great cage, constructed from wicker in a gigantic human shape, stuffed with straw and grasses, and used to burn, ritually, both animals and captured enemies as offerings to the spirits. References to the ceremony of the Wicker Man are to be found in Lucan, Caesar and Strabo. None of these accounts are first hand, though, and probably derive, yet again, from Poseidonius. The human form of the Wicker Man was seized upon by many of the Romantic poets as a symbol of humanity, consumed by the flames of its own greed and cleansing passions, or else atoning for those passions through fire. The image has survived down the years to the present day in the burning of Guy Fawkes in Britain or of the Judas Man in Germany.

The Druidic Tradition

> '. . . having devised a colossus of straw and wood (the druids) throw into the colossus cattle and wild animals of all sorts and human beings, making a burnt offering of the whole thing'.
>
> (Strabo: *Geography IV*)

Discoveries made across the years only served to disclose the full horror of druidic ritual. A find in a Bohemian cave, for example, revealed, together with a number of funerary goods, the bodies of about 40 people who had been ritually sacrificed. In this case, a human skull had been fashioned into a ceremonial drinking-cup. This terrible sacrifice probably dates from the sixth century BC and is undoubtedly the work of the druids.

The abiding image of the druids is that of venerable holy men with their sickles, cutting down mistletoe from the sacred oak tree. This probably focuses on the druidic

Magistrates assist at a confrontation between villagers and an old woman accused of witchcraft

notion of death followed by rebirth, for mistletoe was closely associated with fertility and birth, a symbol of the human spirit being reborn, to the druidic mind. Some folklorists claim that the plant was closely related to storms, quoting its Swiss name, *Donnerbesen* – 'thunder broom', as evidence. So strongly was mistletoe associated with the druids and witchcraft that it was expressly banned from holy places such as a church lest the entire building should need to be reconsecrated. This proscription remains in force; the notable exception being York Minster where mistletoe may be hung during the twelve days of Christmas, on the understanding that it must never touch the ground.

We shall never know the full extent, and exact nature of, the druids' secret ceremonies and rituals but it is safe to assume that many were extremely bloodthirsty, harking back, even in the latter days of druid influence, to a more primitive and pagan time. All that was about to change with the spread of a new philosophy throughout Western Europe.

The Druidic Tradition

Christianity

Prior to the Synod of Whitby, in 664, the Celtic Christian Church, with its head-quarters on the island of Iona, flourished alongside the more formal religion of Rome.

In many ways, the Celtic church reflected elements of the former pagan tradition. Many sacred pagan sites, for instance, would be adopted as sacred shrines and holy places by the new religion. Wells, at which the druids had worshipped for centuries, became Christianised almost overnight, their waters no longer dedicated to a nature spirit but rather to a saint. Evidences of such holy wells are to be found particularly in Ireland, but exist in many other parts of the Celtic world.

High and mountainous places, which had long been the focus of non-Christian wor-ship, suddenly became sites of holy pilgrimage. Feast days, too, took on a new and

religious significance. Thus, *Lúghnasa*, which commemorated the Celtic god Lúgh and the beginning of the 'dark time' of the Celtic year, was taken over and became 'Lammas' or 'Loaf Mass', a feast of thanksgiving for the end of the harvest.

The festival of the Celtic moon-goddess, Eostre, at which the druid had raised a cake divided into four, to symbolise the four quarters of the moon, became Easter, with the notion that hot-cross buns represented the passion of Our Lord on the Cross. In local areas, regional festivals became patron saints' days or 'pattern days'.

The purpose of all this, in the eyes of the Roman Church, was to allow the old Celtic festivals and sites to remain under another guise, and there is undoubtedly some truth in that perspective. The two Churches fiercely disputed fundamentals of faith such as the ordination of women – which the Celtic Church allowed and the Roman Church did not – and the date of Easter.

The whole matter was supposedly settled in 664 when, under the terms of the Synod of Whitby, the Celtic Church more or less allowed itself to be subsumed by Roman dogma. Despite, this it did not lose all its influence on the minds of the Celtic people.

The Druidic Tradition

There are strong suggestions that, despite alleged tales of confrontations between the earliest Christian saints and the pagan druids, Celtic Christianity was relatively tolerant of druidic practices and that druids may have actually been welcomed into the church in the guise of 'saints'. The Celtic Church was much more mystical in tone than its Roman counterpart and had a strong tradition of prophecy and miracle working. These, of course, were common to druidic worship and so the two traditions may not have been as mutually exclusive as might be supposed.

We know that Saint Brigid had druid connections and this may be true of other early Celtic saints as well. Ibar was also thought to have druidic connections, although, according to Beresford-Ellis, he was considered a fraudulent prophet because he always changed his prophecies with the benefit of hindsight.

The closeness to nature of the Celtic Church held echoes of the fertility worship of the druids themselves and these traditions may have continued at a local level, long after the Synod of Whitby and perhaps even into the tenth and eleventh centuries.

The Synod had proclaimed the supremacy of rigid Roman dogma over the more flexible Celtic religious ethos and gradually, that dogma made its presence felt. Not as accommodating towards the druidic tradition as the old Celtic Church seems to have been, it looked back towards the earliest form of druidism – portrayed by the barbaric shaman wrapped in animal skins, capering in cave or forest glade – and pronounced it evil.

Nor is it by accident that the Devil was represented as a shaggy, goat-footed, tailed creature. This chimed in well with the hints and suggestions from very early Middle-

Saint Martin's cross on Iona, where the Celtic Christian church flourished

Queen Boudicca of the Iceni

As the formal influence of the British druids began to wane, they withdrew more and more from Celtic society into difficult and inaccessible places. From these isolated fortresses, they fumed, cursed and raged against the Roman authorities, doing their best to incite rebellion amongst the British tribes.

In the middle of the first Century, the best-known druid stronghold in Britain was the Island of Mona – Anglesey off the north west coast of Wales. The Romans referred to it as *Insula Druiarium* – the Isle of the Druids – and it was reputedly the principal seat of the British druids, heavily defended against the outside world.

Anglesey was, in all probability, much more than a military fortification against the tide of Roman expansion. It also contained a number of druidic shrines and sacred groves where the druids carried out ancient rites that had come down unchanged from earlier times. Several writers, including Tacitus, hint darkly at rites involving human sacrifice and the practice of prophecy utilising fresh human entrails.

For a time the druids remained secure in their island stronghold, content to fulminate against the military authorities. In AD 60-61 a serious rebellion broke out against the Roman government in Britain and if the druids of Anglesey were not directly involved, then much of their anti-Roman propaganda probably influenced its course.

King Prasutagas of the Iceni died and his widow Boudicca assumed the leadership of this Celtic tribe inhabiting south and south-east Britain. Leading both her own people and the neighbouring Trinovantes in outright rebellion, Boudicca and her army quickly destroyed three important Roman towns – Colchester, Londinium, a one-time Iceni capital, and Verulamium – St Albans.

The Roman military governor of Britain, Suetonius Paulinus, suspecting druid involvement in the uprising, responded with a two-pronged attack: one strand directed against the Iceni settlements but, significantly, the second against the druids' stronghold on Anglesey.

The following is based on Tacitus's account of the attack, recounted in his *Annals*:

'It was late evening when our forces reached the straits that lay between the Druid Isle and the coastline, and the daylight was starting to fail. The enemy had lined the shore of their island in a dense, armed mass. Among them were black-robed women with dishevelled hair like furies or wild maenads, brandishing torches. Close by stood Druids, their faces hideously painted, raising their hands to heaven and screaming dreadful curses. This weird spectacle awed the Roman soldiers into a sort of paralysis. They stood still and presented themselves as a target. But then they urged each other (and were urged by the general) not to fear a horde of fanatical women. Onward they pressed their standards and they bore down on their opponents, enveloping them in the flames of their own torches. Suetonius garrisoned the conquered island. The groves devoted to Mona's barbarous superstitions he demolished. For it was their religion to drench their altars in the blood of prisoners and consult their gods by means of human entrails'.

When he attacked Anglesey, Suetonius Paulinus must have suspected a link between the Boudiccan rebellion and the promptings of the druids. This shows that, although the pagan clerics had lost most of their recognised power and status, they had not lost all their political influence and were still a force to be reckoned with. The attack on Anglesey, bringing the island under Roman control, marked the formal crushing of the druids as a force in Britain although there are still references to individual druid schools at the end of the first century.

Romans attack druids in Anglesey, Wales

Eastern writings that the Father of Lies might have animal form, also with the Mediterranean tradition of Pan/Dionysus/Bacchus, the goat-footed god of fertility and drunkenness. Place this figure in some remote and underground cavern and the figure of the Devil presiding over Hell quickly sprang into place.

Drawings of Satan in this animalistic guise are first found around the sixth century but burst into full fruition following the ninth. Around him were gathered the 'dia-mones' – demons or spirit-beings containing echoes of the invisible forces which the ancient peoples worshipped in remote areas – and his dark worshippers, amongst whom had to be counted the druids. Thus, the pagan Celtic holy men were quickly equated with evil witch men in the developing Roman Christian mind. This persona, as the servants of darkness and inheritors of a dark and wicked knowledge, was already growing and developing within Christian philosophy.

The Wodwoses

During the medieval period, the popular depiction of the druid became mingled with that of another: the Wodwose. In feudal society, the incurably insane or eccentric person was cared for by his or her own family or community, but there was also a strictly Celtic tradition whereby some of them were driven into the forests and left to survive how they could. Many would exist on wild berries and roots, on *coiníní* – rabbits – or other small animals.

The existence of these 'wild men and women of the forests' gave rise to medieval stories of the Wodwose – an almost animalistic, but fundamentally human, creature living well away from its own kind – to which mothers would refer in order to terrify their recalcitrant children. Some of these wodwoses were simply those who did not fit into the formal way of life – the 'drop-outs' of today; others were partly or utterly insane. Many took to the roads, travelling through the dense forests separating the feudal settlements or else living in a cave or hole deep amongst the trees.

There was another element to those wandering unfortunates, which was a purely Celtic one. It was believed that these people were in constant communion with spirits that were all around. This is not so surprising as several of the insane claimed to hear disembodied voices speaking to them, or suffered hallucinations. Nowadays treatment would be offered but in early Celtic times, madmen were often considered mouthpieces of the gods. As a 14th-Century Muslim historian said: 'The mad have cast upon their tongues words from the Unseen and they tell them' (Enid Welsford: *The Fool and his Literary History* 1935).

The Islamic and pre-Islamic traditions had a long tradition of inspired madmen, known as the Kahins or Oracle-mongers. These were men who had their wits taken away by djinns - elemental spirits - and who chose to live in the valleys and deserts

The Druidic Tradition

of Arabia, uttering prophecies and begging for their food. Their 'madness' was treated as spirit-directed intoxication, in which other worlds, times and presences were revealed to them. In such a state they could predict the future or speak of things occurring far away and of which they could have no knowledge.

The wodwoses of medieval England had something of that quality about them, too. Because they chose to live in the forest and appeared to have an affinity with nature, they were also thought to have closeness with the world of spirits.

As Christianity began to grow and develop, the notion that the insane were somehow special began to creep into religious thinking and gave rise to the widespread image of the Holy Fool. Because their minds were unblemished by worldly ways, it was declared, madmen had been touched by angels and had been chosen by God to reveal His purpose for the world – hence the still-used colloquialism 'touched' to describe someone of doubtful mental ability. Consequently, no religious house could refuse them succour and had to meet their immediate needs.

In the larger monasteries, they were often allowed to rest for two or three days before being encouraged on their way. Their hair would be cut, probably for hygienic reasons but also, perhaps, to reinforce the influence of the Roman Church through the Tonsure of Peter. By cutting off the shaggy and pony-tailed manes of the woodsmen, they severed all links with the druids who also wore their hair in that way and with the Celtic Church, which had adopted the Tonsure of John.

Celtic Mythology

In addition to receiving succour at the monasteries, the wodwoses were often allowed to beg for alms at the feast-day fairs and markets, which came under the control of the Church. It is not a giant leap of imagination to see the wild-eyed woodland hermit, begging and uttering wild prophecies in the corner of a market place, as the natural successor to the forest-dwelling druid. The aura of holiness about them would lend a certain weight to their prognostications, no matter how outlandish. Many still believed themselves to be in touch with the wilder spirits of nature, a fact recognised even by the Church, since some monasteries kept imbeciles as a kind of oracle, especially to warn of changes in the weather such as storms or drought. Indeed, so close were the connections between these holy fools and the Church that some of the more eccentric may have actually become saints; we have only to think of Saint Joan and her 'voices' to recognise this possibility.

The elements of wildness and sagacity became fused in many medieval legends and romances and added a fresh layer to the druidic tradition as it was passed down through the centuries.

Wise Women, Wizards and Witches

The recipients of traditional druidic lore, concerning herbs and plants and the ways of nature, generally stayed within the communities into which they had been born

MERLIN

The figure most closely connected with druidic magical forces is the British enchanter Merlin.

His name is so closely associated with arcane arts that it has become a byword for sorcery throughout the western world. He is also closely connected with the legendary King Arthur to whom he reputedly acted as adviser and mentor.

Despite his widespread renown, Merlin's origins are somewhat obscure. Probably Welsh, he is claimed by many parts of the British Isles.

One of the *Trioedd Ynys Prydein* (Welsh Triads) tells us that Britain outside of Wales was originally known as *Glas Myrddin* ('Myrddin's Enclosure') before it was inhabited.

Historians, such as Professor John Rhys, have suggested that Myrddin may have been a local deity worshipped at Stonehenge. This ancient site – ancient even in the times when Merlin was reputed to live – had strong traditions linked to him. One of his great works of magic, it was believed, was to transport this mighty henge, in the reign of King Vortigern, from its original home in Ireland to Salisbury Plain.

Although originally a localised spirit or god, Myrddin seems to have gradually adopted human characteristics and form and it was said that, with nine attendant druids, he fled the onslaught of Christianity, taking with him to Bardsey Island – off the Lleyn Peninsula of North Wales – the 'thirteen treasures of Britain'. In his godly form, British folklorists have attempted to link Myrddin with the Hellenistic fertility god Cronos, an extremely ancient deity who was reputed to be the father of Zeus.

Much later, Myrddin became a human figure of Celtic legend adopting quasi-druidical attributes and powers, despite little evidence to suggest that he was ever a druid, and changing his name to the Latinised Merlin. At the same time, he seems to have crossed the Welsh border into Britain.

This geographical shift may have been due, in part, to Geoffrey of Monmouth's *Libellus Merline* – *Little Book of Merlin* – written around AD 1113, the first fully-developed account of him. The ideas put forward in the *Libellus* also formed the basis for Geoffrey's allegorical Latin poem, *Vitae Merlini – Life of Merlin* – written in 1150 in an attempt to compose a complex and prophetic text in the style of the Welsh Bardic school. Supposedly drawing on Welsh sources, Geoffrey describes Merlin as an incarnation of the bard Taliesin, giving the distinct impression that the two were certainly intertwined in the Welsh mind. Certain Welsh traditions attributed to the druids, did in fact, claim three incarnations for Merlin, one being Taliesin himself.

The idea of a multiple Merlin is found again in the works of the early medieval scholar, Geraldus Cambrensis – Gerald of Wales. Writing in around 1180, he drew a distinction between two different Merlins: Merlin Wyllt, a wild man of the forests, and Merlin Emrys, the venerable sage.

Merlin, the enchanter

Arthur was not the only ancient king with whom Merlin was associated. There are tentative connections with King Vortigern but there are also links with Gwenddolau, a British king who may have had druidic connections. This ruler, in AD 575, fought against his cousins Gwrgi and Peredur at the Battle of Arfderydd – literally, 'larks' nest' and associated with the ancient British port of Caerlaverock, which means 'Fort Lark'.

The forces ranged against Gwenddolau were considerably strengthened by the intervention of the powerful king of Strathclyde, Rhydderch Hael and during the course of the battle, Gwenddolau was killed. Welsh tradition asserts that Gwenddolau was Merlin's liege lord, although Geoffrey of Monmouth disputes this stating that, being his brother-in-law, Merlin would have sided with Rhydderch Hael. If Merlin did fight for Gwenddolau in the period following the British king's death, he and his brothers formed part of one of the 'six faithful companies of Britain' which continued to fight on against the Strathclyde king for another six weeks, until overwhelmed by opposing numbers.

During those weeks, all of Merlin's brothers were slain. Merlin, driven wild with grief, fled into the deep forests of Britain where he dwelt with his sister Gwenddydd. He lived on wild berries and spent much of his time uttering dire and insane prophecies concerning the future of Britain. Here was his incarnation as Merlin Wyllt, the wild man touched by the forest spirits. In this persona he had much in common with the wodwoses of medieval England and the *kahins* – oracle-mongers – of eighth century Arabia. Later, he lived as a hermit in the great Caledonian forests of Scotland before returning to Britain. Here he settled down, to incorporate the knowledge of nature that he had acquired in the forests. This was his incarnation as Merlin Emrys, venerable sage, druidical in his wisdom and intellect.

During the Renaissance he was transformed yet again into the classical enchanter, emphasising his distinctly Celtic flavour. The 13th century Auchinleck Manuscript had already linked Merlin to the British warlord Uther Pendragon, father of King Arthur, and this link was strengthened by Sir Thomas Malory's *Morte d'Arthur* which was written between 1469 and 1470.

In the late 1500s and early 1600s many writers seized on the characters of both Merlin and Arthur, turning the former soldier and wild man into a wise, all-knowing, sage and magician in the style of John Dee, William Lilley, Marcilio Ficino and Ananasius Kircher. Merlin, the consummate wizard, had arrived.

and in which they had received their handed-down wisdom. The community treated them in an ambivalent manner: they were to be feared and respected, but they also had their positive uses.

Much of the rural Celtic world was without formalised medicine and that which was available was expensive and usually beyond the means of the simple peasant on the land. Wise women and rural 'doctors', therefore, usually served the scattered Celtic communities, using the lore of herbal medicine to treat day-to-day sicknesses.

Such people usually fulfilled other social roles as well; as vets, for example, treating sick animals as well as humans; finding, by supernatural means, property that had been mislaid, and foretelling the future – warning and advising the country people of what was to come. In this respect, they carried on the role of the druid in the early community.

In Scotland, they were known as *spae* folk or seers, in England and Wales as cunning folk or witches. In Ireland they were fairy doctors and in Cornwall and the West Country, conjurers and conjure women.

The Druidic Tradition

The assumption of the role of doctor, vet and social worker was a central necessity in rural life but was also dangerous, since its actual practice was usually at odds with the formalised Rule of the Church. Many of these rural practitioners were, like the medieval wodwoses before them, rather eccentric and malcontent with organised society in general, often choosing to live away from, or on the very edges of, villages and towns. They often shunned the rigorous authority of the local clergyman, refusing to receive the Sacraments, so that a confrontation between the two perspectives seemed inevitable.

The local wise woman or fairy doctor could be accorded the respect usually reserved for the cleric; a state of affairs hardly popular with the Church – and the Church struck back. It had already declared upholders of ancient druidic tradition to be followers of the Devil and now the local healers, seers and general wonderworkers were to be included within this satanic corps. The clergy queried the source of their knowledge and powers, though it was a rhetorical question as the Church had already supplied the answer: from evil spirits; from the fairies; from the foul ghosts of those long departed. In his classic work, *La Sorcière*, the French historian Jules Michelet has shown how the local healers and miracle-workers of rural France – through the subtle prompting of the clergy – were gradually transformed, in the popular imagination, into witches and night-hags.

By their activities and manners, a number of rural 'magicians' did themselves little good. Many were women, albeit women who refused to accept their conventional and traditional place in society; many were living in extremes of poverty. Using their reputation as a way of making a modest income, they actively encouraged rumours

STONEHENGE

Summer solstice at Stonehenge.

It is frequently claimed that druids were skilled in astronomical matters possessing great knowledge, now lost or forgotten, regarding the movements of stars and planets. From this comes the belief that the megalithic construction of Salisbury Plain's Stonehenge, is evidence of an ancient observatory.

It has even been suggested in some quarters that the druids were the inheritors of extra-terrestrial knowledge and that Stonehenge was some form of prehistoric, interplanetary signalling station.

'Stonehenge', wrote Henry Wansey in 1796, 'stands in the best situation possible for observing the heavenly bodies, as there is an horizon nearly three miles distant on all sides. But till we know the methods by which the ancient Druids calculated eclipses with so much accuracy, as Caesar mentions, we cannot explain the theoretical use of Stonehenge'.

However much we might wish to, we cannot claim Stonehenge, or many other such ancient megaliths, as the constructions of either druids or Celts. The period of construction is thought to have started around the second millennium BC – safely outside the era of British Celts and their druids.

People such as Miranda Green have stated that Stonehenge is the work of a people earlier than the Celts – a proto-Celtic people whose identity and origins are unknown. Stonehenge and other such megalithic constructions represented a staggering feat of prehistoric engineering and the reason for them can only be guessed at.

Although the druids did not build Stonehenge there is little doubt that, finding it already in place, they used it for their own purposes. The Celts, being an agricultural people, were concerned with the cycles of all things, with the construction of calendars and how the movements and alignment of the earth affected weather. Strabo, Diodorus Siculus, Cicero, Caesar, Tacitus and Pliny all extol Celtic knowledge with regard to astronomy. Pomponius Mela refers to the high regard in which the druids were held for

their 'speculation by the stars'. We know from Caesar that the druids knew the size and shape of the world and that they were able to explain the relation of tides to the moon.

It is quite probable that Stonehenge was used as an early form of calendar. Not only Stonehenge but also Callinish, Carnac and other such sites display alignments of the sun, moon and certain stars enabling the druids to advise on planting and harvesting of crops and other crop-related matters attuned to the various seasons of the year. The arrival of Christianity and the introduction of the Church calendar saw the abandonment of these pagan structures, leaving the ruins to puzzle subsequent generations as to their exact purpose.

In 1710, William Stukely visited a megalithic circular grouping known as the Rollright Stones near Chipping Norton and declared them 'a heathen temple of our Ancestors, perhaps in the Druids' time'. Stukley's fieldwork on ancient sites was impeccable but his reasoning as to their origins was certainly suspect and he developed what could only be called 'Druid mania' which attributed practically every ancient site and standing stone to the Celtic holy men. In 1723, he produced the highly questionable *History of the Temples of the Ancient Celts*, changing the title of the work in 1733 to the even more erroneous: *The History of the Religion and Temples of the Druids*. He mistakenly identified Stonehenge as the primary temple of the druids in Britain, publishing in 1740, *Stonehenge: A Temple Restored* together with another volume on Avebury in 1743. On the strength of these books, he gave a number of lectures, including one to the Society of Antiquities in London, detailing supposed connections between Stonehenge and other megalithic sites and the druids.

The books and lectures caught the mood of the time with the notion of a 'learned savage priesthood' and full of hints of forbidden knowledge and the occult and soon Stonehenge had become the focus of the great interest that remains to this day.

about themselves – often by strange or eccentric behaviour. They would charge a modest amount, usually taking payment in kind rather than in money, for simple healing, for the curing of a beast or for finding lost articles but this laid them open to charges of witchcraft and sorcery in the eyes of the authorities. Many of these local wise people carried some sort of artefact about them, drawing upon it as the source of their unnatural powers. During the 17th century there lived, in the west of Scotland a famous prophet. Coinneach Odhar Fiosaiche (Sombre Kenneth of the Prophecies or Kenneth MacKenzie, was also known as the Brahan Seer because he worked on the Brahan Estate of the MacKenzies) where he uttered most of his prophecies. He owned a queer blue stone which, when raised to his cam or blind eye, would show him the future.

Eventually Kenneth's generally recalcitrant and obnoxious attitude, coupled with scathing wit used with particular effect against his employers, led to accusations of witchcraft and ultimately to his burning, seated on a tar-barrel, at Chanonry Point on the Moray Firth. The famed blue stone, however was never found.

Similarly, the Irish 'hedge-witch', Biddy Early, from County Clare, had a blue bottle which she was said to have either won in a game of cards with a fairy man, or received from the ghost of one of her husbands, Tom Flannery of Carrowroe. After her death, a priest was said to have hurled the bottle into Kilbarron Lake where it is supposed to lie to this day.

The Druidic Tradition

Such artefacts, of course, were a link between the individual and the world of the supernatural. They were, declared the clergy, a focus for dark and evil forces, those elementals which had inhabited the countryside since primal times, and which continued to exert an influence upon the gullible and weak-willed who were not protected by the ceremonies and powers of the Church. These healers could be the servants only of the Devil, using their amulets for dark and sinister purposes. This dogma blossomed during the explosions of witch-persecution in France, England and Scotland where it was openly encouraged by the Protestant clergy.

Many of these persecutions were caught up within the differing perceptions of religion which characterised the times, but they also formally represented the end of a darker and more superstitious period which stretched back to the Celtic era and to the druids. It is interesting to note that in Ireland, witch-persecutions were not as common as they were elsewhere. Fairy doctors continued to flourish in remote areas up to and within living memory, as they did in some parts of Cornwall. Beneath the veneer of so-called civilisation and modernity there lay, still, a darker core of superstition and lore that would not go away.

The Druids Today

With the onset of the 1960s and the proclaimed mystical Age of Aquarius, a widespread interest in druidism was rekindled. During the hippy era, druids were credited as the prototypes of many of the New Age ideals and beliefs. They were even seen as the forerunners of a type of new Christianity!

A Toronto-based Christian astrologer, Alexander Blair-Ewart, saw the Celts as a spiritually advanced race and the druids as the embodiment of a harmonious conscience at one with nature and with mankind. Therefore, he stated, they were the best equipped to take Christianity into the New Age. His declaration was to stir other Christian writers such as Shirley Toulson. Her monographs *The Celtic Alternative: A Study of the Christianity We Have Lost* and *The Celtic Year* (the latter published in 1993), retraced the links between Celtic pagan belief and the early Celtic Christian church, hinting that some of the druids might be feasibly equated with certain Christian saints. The tradition was linked with Chinese and Buddhist philosopies to form curious hybrids, including Tantric Buddhism and the worship of nature spirits such as the tulpa and torma. It also was linked with the Japanese philosophy of Shinto – both state and shrine aspects.

In fact druidism was swept along in a general interest in ancient religions, inspired by all sorts of books concerning ancient wisdoms, lost civilisations and even pre-historic extraterrestrial visitations, Erich Von Daniken's *Chariots of the Gods* being an excellent example. The druids' use of narcotics added a dimension in keeping with the times and so much of the interest simply generated a mish-mash of philosophies and practices that had little to do with classical druidism.

Some of the overall interest was channelled into witchcraft – or Wicca as it came to be known. The Wiccans saw themselves as inheriting the natural, druidic, lore which was to be used in positive and beneficial ways, continuing the tradition of the local wise women and fairy doctors. The appearance of 'witches' such as Sybyl Leek, ontelevision only added to the impetus of this new philosophy. Books on Wicca started to appear everywhere. Many were simply jumbled collections of hocus-pocus masquerading as witchcraft, druidism or the wisdom of the ancients. Most looked back to the earliest times of the Celts and to a mother goddess symbolising the oneness between man and nature.Eventually this new philosophy formed itself into the Neo-Pagan Movement that still exists today. The Neo-Pagans are primarily a religious group, tracing distinct links between the past and the present, while some have become involved in political issues encompassing the Green Party and animal rights. A newspaper-journal produced by the Neo-Pagans, *The Wiccan*, has recently changed its name to *Pagan Dawn* in order to incorporate a wider spectrum of ideas and philosophies from all quarters. With the advent of the new millennium, interest in Neo-Paganism and ancient faiths seems to be increasing.

The Bardic strand of druidism is still maintained in Wales within The National Eisteddfod, which can be justly described as an annual cultural fair of poetry and music. It takes place over eight days, at the beginning of August each year, at venues alternating between north and south of the country, and has to be proclaimed by the

Gorsedd y Beirdd – the Gorsedd or Assembly of Bards – a year and a day in advance. Here, poets are crowned – but only if the quality of their work is deemed worthy – and medals for the best prose in Welsh are distributed. Eisteddfodau, whether community-, school-, or society-based, national or international, are a valuable link between Wales's past and present, at which culture and literature are accorded great status. However, it has to be stressed that the Eisteddfod is, nowadays, a cultural event and not a religious one and has only the most tenuous of links with the ancient druids.

From time to time, self-proclaimed druids descend upon certain historical sites to enact ceremonies which, they maintain, have been handed down from the dim and distant past. The most famous of these druids is Arthur Uther Pendragon whose court appearances for 'upholding his druidic beliefs' and trying illegally to access Stonehenge have frequently appeared in the press. Although the Criminal Justice Act now prohibits Stonehenge to all but a handful of fee-paying druids, the influence of those ancient men of lore echoes down even into modern times.

The Druidic Tradition

LEGENDS OF SAINTS AND HOLY MEN

Miracles, Monasticism and Magic

Myths and stories with a religious slant, especially concerning Christianity, have always been a strong feature of Celtic folklore. This may be because, after aeons of paganism, the Celts accepted the Christian faith with both alacrity and enthusiasm.

The early days of Christianity in the Celtic west remain murky and insubstantial. The earliest Christians wrote very little and it is to the eighth, ninth and tenth centuries and even the medieval period that we must turn for written accounts. Some are suspect however – from a historical viewpoint – reflecting as they do the ideas of the brethren and abbots of the monasteries within which they were compiled. Many of the stories which concerned the lives of the saints or holy-men undoubtedly incorporated old pagan folktales into their overall structure. Taken from local oral tradition, they would be altered to comply with Christian dogma. Only in this form have they come down to us.

Celtic Mythology

It seems, too, that the early Church held an ambivalent view of the preceding pagan tradition. It condemned most of the ancient worship and transformed many of the venerated spirits and gods into demons and evil powers while at the same time adapting certain of their attributes to fit into Christian teaching. A common example of this was the tradition of the holy wells. Formerly a place of worship of local water-spirits, its dedication and powers would be transferred to a local Christian saint. The matter was further complicated by the fact that there were two Christian churches, one based in Rome and one based in the Celtic West, its headquarters on the Hebridean island of Iona. Each followed, for a time, its own specific agenda.

It is to the distinctiveness and nature of the Celtic Church that we now turn our attention.

The Celtic Church

In AD 380 Christianity became the established religion of the Roman Empire. The Church became what has been described as 'the gilded crutch of absolutism'. Now backed by the formal sanctions of Rome, it began to formulate absolutist dogma and

*Mithras, pagan deity,
worshipped in Rome
and usurped by
Christianity*

teachings rigorously codified. Christianity had replaced the worship of Mithras as the official religion of the Roman army and it quickly spread throughout the legions, even those stationed as far away as Gaul and Britain.

In addition, there had been a dispersion of the faith westwards, well in advance of the legions. This form of Christianity, less dogmatic, less formalised and geared more towards local needs and issues, was already tentatively established in the western lands. Early Christian churches, founded by those fleeing from persecution, undoubtedly absorbed much local pagan tradition and this adaptability enabled these rather insular churches to survive beyond the sphere of Rome.

THE MEANING OF 'SAINT'

Nowadays, there is a strong tendency, both inside and outside Church circles, to think of saints as particularly holy people. The Catholic Church now goes to great lengths to select those who have been proposed for sainthood. This has not always been the case and was certainly not so in the early days of the Celtic Christian religion.

The word 'saint' then referred to any Christian missionary and to any preacher who could draw a following about him or herself. Any person who claimed to have heard voices, had supernatural gifts or the power of prophecy might also be termed a saint and many who assumed the mantle of sainthood would be considered unworthy today. A consequent rise in cults of personalities greatly alarmed the Roman Church and led to the scrupulous and methodical selection procedure for saints existing today.

Many legends show the early saints in a rather unsavoury light. A popular joke current of the medieval Roman Church concerned Saint Kevin of Wexford. The saint boasted that each night he retired to his lonely cell cave near Glendalough, County Wicklow, in the company of two young, local girls. Such was the piety of the holy-man that he was able to resist their undoubted charms throughout the night, preferring to concentrate upon his holy meditations. This was taken as a sign of his fortitude and was considered a nightly test of his sanctity. Saint Kevin prayed loudly that this test should be removed

Saint Anthony of Egypt

from him but each evening he was compelled by God to take the girls up to his cell. Saint Brendan, who doubted both his motives and his sanctity, attempted the same test and later admitted that he was kept up all night by 'the promptings of the flesh' and could not get a wink of sleep! He proclaimed Kevin one of the most pious men within the Church and worthy of the title saint because of his holy fortitude.

Other saints experienced ecstatic visions. Cuthbert of Northumbria, while tending a flock of sheep on a hillside, saw Saint Aidan being carried into Heaven. Aidan, claimed Cuthbert, had named him as his successor – disputed, of course by other saints who claimed conflicting visions of Aidan. This was quite a common scenario and the Roman Church genuinely feared a clash of cults as devotees struggled to promote the righteousness and authority of their favoured saint.

Historians, such as Peter Beresford-Ellis, have suggested that Saint Brigid of Kildare lived at her foundation for a time with a lover, named Derlaughdacha, who became abbess of the Kildare foundation after Brigid's death (See: P. Bereford-Ellis, *Celtic Women*, 1995)

In the saint's defence, however, Derlaughdacha means daughter of Lúgh and her feast-day is 1 February, so Derlaughdacha may just be an alternative name for Brigid herself.

It has been suggested by a number of historians that the Celts, insulated from Roman influence by ever-increasing Saxon activity had to evolve their own distinctive type of Christianity but the evidence does not really support this theory. What records we have show that, during the fifth, sixth and seventh centuries, there was frequent contact between the two strands of Christianity. Celtic representatives attended, and made significant contribution to, many of the grand church councils convened to formulate early Christian dogma and policy and sent reports of their own councils to the Pope.

From the mid-fifth century onwards, there appears to have been an increase in missionary work into former pagan lands and both the early Roman and Celtic Churches converted and baptised in a haphazard way, often using pagan ritual. Many of the earliest missionaries were formerly pagan, or of pagan tradition, and may even have held important positions within their old religion.

Our chief source for this period is a set of documents known as *Vitae Sanctorum – Lives of the Saints*. Applied to all missionaries, the word 'saint' does not necessarily imply any sort of holiness or virtue and was also used to denote those who exhibited unexplained powers of whatever religious source. We must also remember that the 'Lives' were written by monks many centuries after their subject was dead, and were amended and reworked across the ages until the late Middle Ages. The earliest 'Life' that is available to us was written within half a century of its subject's demise and concerns the sixth - century Samson of Dol, a Gaulish Celtic saint. This is the exception rather than the rule, for most of the 'Lives' were not written until the 10th or 11th centuries. It is not even certain whether several of the so-called saints ever existed or whether they were just symbolic human representations of local deities and Celtic spirits.

Celtic Mythology

The theology of the Celtic Christian church was, in essence, closer to that of the present Eastern Orthodox faith than to that of Rome and any similarities were vastly outweighed by the fundamental differences.

The Papacy, while recognised by the Celtic Church as the head of Christianity provided a bone of contention between the Roman and Celtic worlds. The Roman Church traced the papal lineage from Peter, the Rock on which Jesus founded His church. The Celtic Church traced the lineage from John, 'the disciple whom Jesus loved' and into whose care the Virgin had been given. This accorded well with traditions of ancient mother-goddess worship and was regarded by the Roman authorities as 'a bastion of barbarity'. The Roman church extolled the virtues of celibacy for its clergy and often forbade them to marry; the Celtic Church did not. In the Celtic world monasteries were mixed, under the authority of a local abbot whereas under Roman dogma, they were strictly segregated and under the direct authority of a bishop appointed by Rome. Women preached and held office in the Celtic Church but were not allowed to do so under Roman orthodoxy.

The Celtic Church also favoured a greater monastic tradition than did its Roman counterpart. With its emphasis on mysticism and supernatural experience, it argued that the best place for such doctrines to be realised was within the monastery cloister. Rather than delegate power to bishops like the Roman Church, Celtic theology granted power to individual abbots who ran their foundations more or less as they saw fit. While a basic framework existed, dogma tended to be much more lax and open to individual interpretation than that of Rome.

The greatest contention between the two Churches was the date of Easter. The crucifixion and resurrection of Jesus was the cornerstone of the Christian faith and it was important that its date should be fixed in the Christian calendar but neither Church could agree on when this date was.

The rules governing the Christian calendar had been determined, in AD 325, by the Council of Nicaea, which reckoned important dates from the birth-date of Christ. Later amendments agreed by Roman Councils – at the specific behest of the reigning Pope – were considered by the Celtic Church to render the original meaningless.

It therefore immediately reverted to previous computations agreed in AD 314 by the Council of Arles. This, significantly, allowed the incorporation of ancient, Celtic pagan feast-days, recognised by Arles but not by Nicaea, within the religious period. Prominent among the festivals was that of the moon-goddess Eostre who gave the festival its name: Easter. The Roman church claimed that this was proof that the Celtic church had wanted all along, to return to paganism, and refused to consider the Celts' position. Furthermore, Celtic computations allowed Easter to fall on the same day as the Jewish Passover. This flew in the face of the Council of Nicaea, which had expressly forbidden any Christian festival from falling on a Jewish holy day and Rome told the Celts to fall into line. After much arguing and the trying out of different computations, a compromise was reached and Easter became a moveable feast, dependent on the Lunar Calendar and the phases of the moon.

Legends of Saints and Holy Men

The differences in the fundamental natures of the two Churches were much greater. While the Roman Church concentrated on dogma and teaching, the Celtic church placed great emphasis on mysticism, miracles and supernatural experience. This accommodated the old 'wonder religions' of the early Celts, remnants of which still lingered on in the Celtic world, but it also undermined the authority of Roman orthodoxy. If local preachers were allowed to experience their own visions and to expound their own gospels based on those experiences, there could be little cohesion of belief. The debate concerning the nature of religious experience continued between the two Churches.

This difference manifested itself even in the hairstyles of the respective monks. The now-familiar, pudding-bowl tonsure of the medieval monks was known as the

Tonsure of Peter. Celtic monks, on the other hand, shaved a line from ear to ear, allowing a ponytail to hang down their backs. This was known as the Tonsure of John and closely resembled the hairstyle worn by the druids. Thus provoked, the Roman Church quickly condemned this tonsure referring to Celtic monks as barbaric and as druids in disguise. This latter insult may have contained a grain of truth because many of the preachers and monks of the Celtic church were probably more sympathetic to druidic doctrines than were their Roman equivalents.

Celtic Mythology

Saint Brigid

This fierce and growing dispute between Churches could not be allowed to continue and the matter was formally resolved at the Synod of Whitby in AD 664 with the Celtic Church officially giving way to Roman orthodoxy. The authority of the Insular Church had been declining in any case – too fragmented and individualistic to maintain any sort of religious cohesion, its scattered network of abbots and preacher could not compete with the rigid hierarchy of bishops within the Roman Church.

But the Celtic church gave way only grudgingly. Abbot Colman, the Bishop of Lindisfarne, refused to accept Roman authority and, as his monastery was taken over by Roman teachings, he set sail for Inishboffin – the Island of the White Cow or Heifer – near the coast of County Mayo in Ireland. Here, he established a colony that maintained the Celtic perspective. Many other abbots did likewise; some trying in vain to bring order and discipline to the remnants of the Celtic church. Many more paid lip service to the Roman ideals while retaining the Celtic spirit in their hearts. In the West, Celtic doctrines may have lasted well into the late medieval period, colouring the folktales and legends of the early churchmen that are still told today.

The Early Saints

Because of its emphasis on mysticism and the miraculous, the word saint must be considered carefully. Nowadays, it specifically refers to an exceptionally holy and virtuous person. Where saints are associated with miracles, rigorous committees scrupulously assess both claims and candidates. This was not the case in the Celtic church. Anyone who did missionary work, who claimed to have experienced visions or heard voices or who was an eccentric or unusual person able to gather a following about him, was usually described as a saint. Many people whom we would today regard as mentally deficient were venerated in both the early Roman and Celtic Churches. We know that Saint Columcille planned to steal a copy of a book owned by one of his best friends.

Mental instability or undesirable behaviour was not a bar to sainthood. Saints proliferated in the early Celtic Christian world. The majority of these were localised figures – charismatic individuals, fiery preachers, ascetic anchorites and those claiming miraculous powers or even, like Peter of Morino, direct contact with God. Peter of Morino was a mad hermit who became Pope Celestine V by claiming that he had a letter from God telling him to become Pope. The cardinals believed him without seeing the letter – Peter claimed that only he could see it – and made him Pope. He renounced the papacy after his eventual successor, Boniface VIII, visited him at night pretending to be the Holy Ghost and instructed him to resign.

Legends of Saints and Holy Men

One of the favourite miracles of the early saints involved the power of prophecy. This was undoubtedly a hangover from the time of the druids, who often acted as oracles for local kings (see **The Druidic Tradition**). The difference between the prophecies issued by druids and those given by saints was that the latter received divine inspiration and the druids did not. The saints, therefore, were infallible. This did not mean that their prophecies always came true but, like the druids before them, the early saints could initially issue prophecies so vague that they were open to any form of interpretation or subsequent events. For example, the Irish saint Ibar prophesied that the Virgin Mary would appear to his congregation in their church on a certain day. At the appointed time, everyone gathered in the church to await the heavenly visitation. Just when Ibar had said the vision would appear, the doors of the church were opened and a young druidess wandered in. Thinking quickly, Ibar stated that this was the Virgin in human form and promptly hailed her as 'Mary of the Gael'. There may have been a certain veracity in his prophecy for, according to legend, the druidess was converted to Christianity and went on to become Saint Brigid.

Many saints also claimed to hear voices, which they attributed to God or His angels or deceased saints. One has only to think of Saint Joan, during the medieval period, to recognise the potency in the common mind of such 'visitations'. Joan made many rash pronouncements about visitations by phantoms and saints and about hearing voices.

From out of the mysticism and miracles of the Celtic Church came many saints who were re-vamped gods and druids. The most famous of these 'god-saints' is probably Saint Brigit – Brigid or Brighid. Usually described as a former druidess and the daughter of a druid, she may well have been the humanised representation of an ancient Celtic fertility goddess – possibly one aspect of the ancient Celtic Triple-Goddess (see **Spirits of Earth and Air**). Her name comes from the vernacular Celtic word 'brig' meaning 'exalted' and a goddess Brig, with two shadowy sister-deities, appears to have been venerated in the Irish province of Leinster. Similar mysterious deities, with much the same name, appear in other parts of the Celtic world. Brig was associated with the planting of crops and with fertility in both humans and animals. Women in childbirth prayed and offered to her. Within the goddess's power were the gifts of poetry and of prophecy and her feast day was celebrated on 1 February, the Celtic festival of Imbolc, which marked the beginning of spring. Brig appears in many forms throughout western Europe and one of her most important incarnations may have been that of the British goddess Brigantia whose principal shrine was at the river to which she gave her name, the Brent in Middlesex. She was also patron goddess of the Brigantes tribe who lived there.

> 'With the arrival of Christianity, Brigit underwent a remarkable transition from goddess to the premier female saint of Ireland, although she retained the same feast day. *The Life of Brigit*, her Latin biography was written around AD 650.'
>
> (John McInnes (ed): 'Heroes of the Dawn – Celtic Myth', *Time/Life*, 1998)

Legends of Saints and Holy Men

The former pagan Celtic goddess Brig, now found herself elevated to a prominent place in the developing Christian religion and was firmly identified as a mortal.

Brig/Brigid was probably not the only early saint with roots in pagan spirit worship. Probably most of the early saints of the Celtic church were accorded powers more suited to the previous pagan deities. Many were given powers over nature, which were later translated into a holy authority over dark and barbaric forces in the form of beasts.

The most common form of myth about very early saints extols their power over dragons and serpents, and these holy-men were usually credited with defeating or slaying such creature which, more than any, epitomised evil. After all, it was the serpent that tempted Eve in the Garden of Eden.

The Irish holy man Patrick was the saint who, according to legend, drove every snake out of Ireland. Even if this myth were true, Saint Patrick was not the only early religious figure to possess such powers.

Several regional saints made similar claims. Saint Cado of Brittany, is credited with expelling serpents in Gaul; Saint Clement expelled a ferocious serpent from Metz.

Saint Clement

The citizens of Paris were freed, by Saint Romain, from the horrors of the monstrous dragon Gargouille (from which the word 'gargoyle' is derived) while Saint Marcel is lauded for driving snakes from the same city. Columcille is said to have driven a monster from the River Ness while Saint Ninian is believed to have cleared parts of Scotland of 'many venomous reptiles'.

In Malta, Doue de Gazon expelled great numbers of snakes and in 1342, the tombstone of the Grand Master of the island bore the legend *Draconis Extinctor* – Killer of Serpents – a title previously adopted by a number of Celtic saints. There is also Saint George, a Middle-Eastern saint, latterly adopted by England, who reputedly slew a massive snake known as a dragon.

Celtic Mythology

Even in Ireland, Saint Patrick is not the only holy man to have had power over snakes. In Glendalough Cathedral, County Wicklow, a stone tablet commemorates the defeating of a terrible water-serpent by Saint Kevin of Wexford and his dog Lupus. Saint Enda is said to have driven snakes from the islands around the Irish coast while Columcille is supposed to have rid Tory Island, off Donegal, of all manners of vermin including rats and snakes. This myth is also associated with ancient heroes such as Murrough, the son of Brian Boru, who was certainly not considered a saint.

Medieval copyists would add fragments of Old Testament legend to stories of the saints, ascribing to them powers previously held by Hebrew prophets. The most common miracle was the finding of water in barren places. Here the copyists took Moses as their example. When wandering in the wilderness with the Children of Israel, the prophet had used his staff to strike a rock to bring forth water. In vernacular folklore, many local saints had emulated this feat and these tales were quickly passed into the canons of Church lore.

For an agricultural people such as the Celts, water was a precious commodity and featured heavily in their tales and legends. Finding or releasing water was usually cen-

tral to such tales so it is not surprising that such events, probably the former province of the druids, became miracles to be attributed to Celtic holy-men.

Many saints are credited with making water suddenly appear from the ground, and the wells thus created usually still bear the saints' names. Saint Gall is said to have caused water to flow from a stone by stamping his foot; Saint Barri was reputed to have created a well by smiting the ground with the end of his crozier, the celebrated *Gear Barri*. Both Saint Patrick and Saint Ninian caused wells to appear so that they

Miracle of Saint Clement at Chersona, 11–12th century, detail

could baptise several bishops. Wells were attributed to Saint Mungo, Saint Ronan, Saint MacCuagh and hundreds of others. The waters of many of these were supposed to possess miraculous powers - such as healing - by virtue of the saintliness of the holy-man who had created them.

Some of the Celtic holy men even emulated the miracles of Christ. The Breton saint Winwaloe, is reputed to have walked on water. He had founded his chief monastery on the island of Thopepigia in what is now Brest Harbour, but had received a summons from God to take his message to the mainland. The island community had no boat but, undeterred, Winwaloe took the hand of a disciple and stepped boldly onto the surface of the sea. There are two different folk-

Celtic Mythology

Saint Gall

loristic versions of what happened next. One says that the sea drew back, as in the Biblical account of Moses and the Red Sea, allowing the saint and his followers to pass dryshod to the coastline; another account maintains that Winwaloe and his disciples crossed the surface of the ocean to the mainland. (For a further account of Winwaloe, see **page 69**).

Other Celtic saints – such as Saint Aidan of Northumbria – are strongly associated with healing, and even with metamorphosis or shape-shifting, in order to fulfil holy directives. Strong natural elements within many tales reflect the link between the Church and Nature in the Celtic mind. Saint Aidan is alleged to have turned himself into a deer to draw hunters away from a real animal. Saint Ronan is said to have had a house built for him by birds. The Irish Saint Kevin, it was said, allowed a bird to build its nest in the cup of his hand while he stood praising God in the waters of the lower Lough at Glendalough, County Wicklow. He is said to have remained there, unmoving, until the bird's eggs hatched.

SAINT WINWALOE (GUENOLE)

Saint Winwalloe

A study of the life of Saint Winwaloe demonstrates the extremely close links that must have existed between ancient Cornwall and Brittany. Winwaloe is known by various names, most commonly the French Guenole.

Born a Breton, Winwaloe was of Cornish extraction, his family having fled to Brittany to avoid a Saxon invasion from the British midlands. He was born near Saint Brieuc, the third son of his mother Gwen and his father Fracan, who gave his name to the parish of Winwaloe's birth – Ploufragan. Fracan had made a holy vow that should he and his wife have a third son, he would immediately be dedicated to the service of God. Despite this solemn vow, Winwaloe was 15 when he entered the monastery of Saint Budoc on the island of Lavret – part of the Ile de Brehat – along with his two brothers who were soon to decide that Holy Orders were not for them. Winwaloe's friend and tutor, Saint Budoc, confirmed him in the way of holiness and saintliness and, at the appointed time, Winwaloe set out with 11 followers to found a religious establishment for himself. They settled on the island of Thibidy where they subsisted on roots and whatever barley they could grow. At length, the infertility of the soil and the harsh winds that blew across the island forced them to seek a more suitable location for a religious foundation. Winwaloe is said to have experienced visions of angels ascending and descending to and from Heaven on the opposite bank of the River Aulne and it was there that he decided to found his new holy house. The site was to become the great monastery of Landevennec. Another legend states that life on Thibidy was so holy and pure that there was no death and that the monks lived to such a great age that they wished for release. To accommodate them, a local king named Gradlon offered them land nearby. They moved there and founded the monastery of Trevenec.

Within the confines of his holy house, Winwaloe maintained an extremely austere Rule. Wine was forbidden, except at Mass, and the monks ate only wild herbs and roots boiled in vinegar and drank only water. For their beds, the brothers used either flat stones or the barks of trees with stone pillows. Each brother had manual work each day in order to support the monastery but the majority of a monk's time was spent in religious contemplation.

The strict regime of Winwaloe's monastery continued until 818, when the Rule of Saint Benedict was introduced under the specific decree of Louis the Pious, the son of Charlemagne. However, the atmosphere of great holiness and sanctity still prevailed and both monastery and founder acquired a reputation for mysticism.

Clement, a monk at the abbey of Landevennec, wrote an account of Winwaloe's life in 860. Its title was *The Golden Story of Saint Winwaloe* and it concentrated on the saint's mystical aspects and his reputation for performing miracles. His feast day, on which he died, is 3 March but he is also remembered on 28 April which marks the foundation of the church in which his body was enshrined. At some stage, his remains were taken to the monastery at Montreuil-sur-Mer near Boulogne to escape the ravages of Viking pirates who were attacking France at the time.

Although Winwaloe is often considered a Breton saint, his roots were firmly in Cornwall. He is said to have returned there on several occasions to visit his parents and, while in Britain, he founded several churches and religious enclosures. The most significant was at Landewednack on the Lizard Peninsula – the prefix 'lan' meaning enclosure. Another was at Gunwalloe and is known as The Church of the Storms. This was founded virtually on the beach and was at the mercy of the elements and of the sea, hence the picturesque name. Legend says that Winwaloe performed a number of miracles in the area; that he drove away raiders from that particular stretch of coastline by the power of his prayers and that he lived in a small cell at the foot of nearby Castle Hill. Both these tales are, of course, unsubstantiated.

But it is with the sea that Saint Winwaloe is most closely associated. In some legends, he was said to be the Abbot of sea-doomed Lyonesse, or the Cornish Ker-Ys, which sank beneath the sea between Cornwall and Brittany. He was said to have escaped this cataclysm and returned to land where he founded over one hundred churches and retreats to thank God for his deliverance. He is considered the patron saint of seafolk in areas of Brittany.

In some parts of the Celtic world, 'to curse' and 'to wither' are the same word and several saints were credited with the power to curse or blast trees that had displeased them – like Christ cursing the fig tree in the Biblical story. Other saints, cursed rivers, causing them to dry up or to change direction.

The saintly figures gathered large numbers of followers around them who perpetuated and exaggerated their exploits, sometimes by incorporating fragments of earlier pagan traditions into the tales. Faced with the growing cultism, that was rapidly becoming a feature of the Celtic Church, the Roman tradition tried desperately, with varying degrees of success, to apply some form of orthodoxy in both belief and worship. But such stories continued to be told and were eventually written down by the monkish scholars of the middle ages.

Celtic Mythology

Saint Aidan

Saint George

Saint George, patron saint of England, is often erroneously assumed a Celtic saint. Probably his position as the foremost English saint, claiming a lineage that stretched back into pre-Saxon Britain and his close association with great snakes or dragons is the reason. George, however, owes nothing to the Celtic tradition.

Little is known about him except that he was probably an early Christian bishop, martyred at Lydia in Palestine in the third or fourth century and may have been a Roman soldier. The cult that grew up around his name was an incredibly ancient one – he was called *meglomaryros* or the 'great martyr' – in the East and is referred to in the *Martyrology of Saint Jerome*. The story of his defeating the dragon is a medieval fiction found in the 13th-century *Golden Legend*, written by Jacobus de Voraigne and later translated and printed in England by Caxton.

Saint David

Arising in the seventh century, the cult of George (which may have contained elements of older, pagan warrior cults – see **In Search of Ancient Heroes**) appears to have been fragmented and the great saint of England was Edward the Confessor, the pious Saxon king who had reigned before the Norman conquest. George's popularity increased immeasurably during the Crusades. The famous victory over the Saracens at Antioch was attributed to a vision of the saint on the eve of battle that greatly heartened the English. So much did his popularity increase, that Edward III named George the patron of his newly founded Order of the Garter around 1344. From then on, the saint became a symbol of nationalist pride in England his name used as a rallying cry by King Henry V at Agincourt as, immortalised by Shakespeare. George was also adopted as the patron saint of Portugal but with no assumption of a Celtic background.

The link between another patron saint and his country is also dubious. Saint Andrew never set foot in Scotland, nor was he a Celt. His claim to Scottish national sainthood rests on a legend concerning the Celtic saint, Rule, to whom Saint Andrew had appeared in a vision. Andrew had been reputedly buried in Patras in the Holy Land and he instructed Saint Rule to take his remains, from there, to Fife in Scotland and build a church to be the home of the relics. This site was the original church of Saint Andrews. There is probably no truth to the legend since Andrew's remains were almost certainly taken to Constantinople, stolen at its overthrow during the Crusades in 1204 and removed to Amalfi in Italy.

The cults of both Andrew and George that grew in countries far away from the lands in which they had lived shows how readily local tradition became attached to recognised holy names and how rapidly they became associated with localised Celtic

Legends of Saints and Holy Men

King Edward the Confessor and Queen Emma his mother from the Encomium, 100

mythology. Had Scotland wished to adopt a native saint as its patron, it need have looked no further than Saint Ninian.

Saint Ninian and Dewi Sant

Although not widely known outside Scotland, Saint Ninian embodies much of the Celtic tradition handed down within the Insular Church. Detailed references to him

Prevoius Pages: Saint
George protects princess from
the dragon from Lombard
school, Italy, c.1470

are given in Bede but there is much doubt as to their authenticity. According to Bede, Ninian was a British Celt who studied in Rome and was sent as an 'apostle to the Southern Picts of Scotland' in the middle of the fourth century. His centre of evangelism was said to be *Candida Casa* – the White House, now generally believed to be Whithorn in Galloway – from which he sent missionaries into Scotland and Ireland. The venerable *Book of Ballymote*, compiled around AD 1390 from older sources, names Caranoc, the Abbot of Candida Casa, as the first recorded Christian in Ireland.

Legend states that Ninian's foundation – maybe just a church, maybe an important monastery – was built by masons from Saint Martin's monastery in Tours, centre of early Christian western monasticism. Inscribed stones and a dedication to Saint Martin, which is mentioned by Bede, would seem to confirm this. In other stories, the chapel at Whithorn housed an important relic belonging to Saint Martin possessing both magical and curative properties. It was a common ploy for many monastic sites to encourage legends of powerful relics on their premises and then to charge pilgrims to see them.

Bede's account of Ninian is slightly at variance with the official 'Life' of the saint, written by his famous biographer Saint Ailred in the 12th century. According to this account, Ninian was the son of a Christianised, Scottish king, thus a Celt. He was born on the Solway Firth around AD 360 and following study in Rome, he returned to northern Britain instructed by the Pope to Christianise the Britons. Instead, he travelled further north, founded the religious centre at Whithorn, and started to baptise the Picts.

*Legends of Saints
and Holy Men*

Ailred's 'Life' appears to draw more on Celtic folkloristic sources and influences than does that of Bede. He places great emphasis on the miracles performed by Ninian, especially the curing of a Pictish chieftain's blindness and the creation of holy wells in order to baptise converts. There has been great debate over the extent of Ninian's evangelism. Some restrict him to the area around Whithorn, others expand his mission into Northern Britain – certainly his followers had a mission on the Isle of Man.

Within this tradition is another more nationalist saint – Dewi Sant or Saint David – of Wales. David's ministry also stretches back into the foundations of the Celtic church. Most of what we know about this shadowy figure is what comes from a formal 'Life' written about 1090 by Rhygyvarch, the eldest son of Julian, Bishop of Saint David's. However, he was more concerned with vindicating his father's claim of episcopal independence from Norman Canterbury than in presenting an accurate history of the saint.

Celtic Mythology

According to the 'Life', Dewi was the son of a Cardiganshire chieftain and born around AD 520. His mother is traditionally Saint Non, a former druidess who converted to Christianity. The young Dewi is reputed to have spent the first ten years of his life being educated in Christian teaching at Hen Vynyw, spending a further ten years studying with a learned scribe, Paulinus, whose sight he had miraculously restored. Much of his study was spent learning the Scriptures 'in a remote place', possibly Llanddeusant on Anglesey.

Following this holy education, Dewi embarked on a series of missionary exploits, founding about twelve known churches and monasteries including, reputedly, Glastonbury and Menevia – later Saint David's. In an attempt to bring discipline to the Celtic monastic orders, he made the Rule of these houses exceptionally strict. It was based on a Rule favoured in the ascetic monasteries of the Middle East and Egypt. This regime was centred about intense study and excruciating manual work; its monks subsisting, in the main, on raw vegetables and water, emphasising their piety and frugality.

Dewi earned the nickname *Aquaticus* – Waterman – from the strict abstinence that he forced on his communities. Soon tales of his holiness coupled with an almost mystical element, were being circulated throughout Cymru – Wales – and Britain, prompting Saint Gildas to assert that Dewi's rule was more ascetic than Christian. His fame for learning was so widespread that he was summoned to speak at the Synod of Brefy in AD 550. He spoke so eloquently and with such passion and conviction that he was immediately and unanimously elected archbishop with authority over the whole of Wales. This is the tale, it is thought, that was invented much later by Julian the Bishop in order to give his See even greater influence and status. Similar fictitious stories have Dewi making pilgrimage to Jerusalem and slaying the last of the fearsome flesh-eating Welsh giants.

Saint Patrick

The cult grew up around the name of Dewi — now anglicised to David — following his death at his monastery at Menevia in AD 589 and was formally approved by Pope Callistus II in 1120. Dewi's relics were brought to the cathedral in Saint David's in 1131 and its rebuilding, in 1275, was largely financed by offerings received at his shrine there. The Welsh gradually adopted him as their patron saint — there being no question that he was the country's principal holy man. His monks ventured throughout the Celtic world, and principally Ireland, to spread the Christian message extending his influence far beyond Wales.

Legends of Saints and Holy Men

Most stories surrounding Saint David appear to be much later additions, probably penned in the early medieval period, perhaps in an attempt to stir Welsh nationalism against Norman English incursions into the country. It might be that Dewi Sant had even more of an influence across the Irish Sea and on the identity and mythology of a much more problematical, but nonetheless fascinating, saint.

Saint Patrick

Of all the national saints in the Celtic world, perhaps none is more controversial than Saint Patrick. On the surface his story seems quite straightforward. His Tri-partite Life and his *Confessio* and several important letters, allegedly written by the saint himself, are valuable historical documents and appear to give us a great deal of information about Patrick:

> 'I Patrick . . . had as my father Calpornius, son of the late Potitus, a priest who belonged to the town of Bannaviem Taberniae:

he had a small estate nearby . . .'
(A.B.E. Hood (ed): *Saint Patrick: his writings and Muirchú's Life* 1978)

His miracles and adventures are exceptionally well known. He drove out snakes and serpents from Ireland; he was carried away by Irish pirates and forced to herd sheep on Slemish Mountain in north Antrim; he created many holy wells; he left his footprint enshrined for posterity in rock etc. And yet, historians and folklorists have argued for many years as to who Saint Patrick was and where he came from.

SAINT MICHAEL

Mont Saint Michel, Brittany

Visions of angels, bearing messages from God, played a significant role in the lives of the early Celtic saints and such visions might have reflected the tradition of pagan communication between the mystical Otherworld and the mundane.

The chief archangel, Michael, was greatly beloved of the Celtic peoples, perhaps because of his warrior attributes and, although not a human being, he rapidly gained saintly status within the Celtic Church. Many pagan associations with Michael seem to indicate that he may have a longer spiritual pedigree than the Christian canons would suggest. Many of his churches are on former pagan sites in high, almost inaccessible places - Mont Saint Michel in France; Saint Michael's Mount in Cornwall; Saint Michael's tower on the top of Glastonbury Tor and Skellig Michael off the Kerry coastline.

In Hebrew, the name *Mi-Ka-el* means 'Who is as God' perhaps denoting a powerful Semitic spirit which somehow appealed to the Celtic mind. He was assigned as commander of the heavenly host and as a divine messenger, carrying the most important messages between God and man. He was the protector of the faithful, was assigned to those who had suffered injustice, and he held the keys to the Underworld over which he had control.

The Celts believed that Michael would be the one to assess the souls of the dead before they entered the Afterlife. In addition, he was the saint of high places and, as the angel who

had pleaded that the fairies not be consigned to the Underworld, he is their patron saint. But, it as the slayer of the Dragon on the Final Day that he is best known in Christian circles. In this, he is equated with his earthly counterpart, Saint George.

From earliest times, the cult of Michael was widespread throughout the Celtic world. The Venerable Bede mentions an oratory near Hexham, in Britain, which was dedicated to him. A number of medieval writers noted that Cornwall is placed under the protection and authority of Michael or San Myghal.

He reputedly appeared on the western promontory of the Mount, on 8 May, 495. In the guise of a common fisherman, sitting upon the chair now referred to as the Cedar Myghal – Michael's Chair – he proceeded to heal all the sick that were brought to him. Helston still commemorates this with its Flora Day in honour of its town-patron. A similar apparition is said to have taken place on Mont Saint Michel one hundred years later.

References to Michael are to be found in the Dead Sea Scrolls where he is described as a 'Prince of Light'. This has prompted mythologists to compare him with the Celtic god Lúgh who was embodied in the rising sun – the connection, it is argued, which made Michael so special to the ancient Celts.

Saint Michael on a 13th-century altarpiece displayed in the Museum of San Casciano Cathedral, Italy

The location of Bannaviem Taberniae is not known but locations suggested include: Old Kilpatrick; near Dumbarton; and, as suggested in 1998, the West Country, making Patrick a Cornishman. Strong tradition suggests that he was a Welshman but other origins include the East of England.

Even the place where he was captured as a boy by Irish pirates is unknown. Tradition says that it was on the slopes of Slemish Mountain in County Antrim where he herded pigs or sheep. Other accounts favour the popular 'lonely place' so common in early Celtic folklore. This of course is of no help at all in pinning down a location in Ireland. Traditions and legends all differ. In the north of Ireland, it is believed that he landed in Strangford Lough to begin his mission to Christianise Ireland, but it is also claimed that he arrived in Wexford. Although most traditions say that he came alone, some provide him with at least two helpers.

If, as was claimed, Patrick managed to travel all over Ireland during the fifth century, just this task was little short of miraculous. The country at that time was thickly forested, boggy and mountainous and travel was incredibly difficult. The whole story – including the identity of Patrick himself – is complex and confusing. In order to find any answers it is necessary to look deep below the surface of the 'Patrick legend' where one conclusion becomes increasingly evident: the saint that we know as Patrick was not one man, but a compilation of at least three separate men. New evidence suggests that three main missionaries/bishops, Palladius, Sucat and Ibar, took the title Patricius – Patrick. The title was strongly identified with the Christian religion in Ireland.

Legends of Saints and Holy Men

It is possible to say with some degree of confidence that he was not the first Christian in Ireland. Missionaries had been arriving from Christian settlements in Romanised Britain, Wales and Scotland for many years before Patrick allegedly set foot on Irish soil. *The Book of Ballymote* records that Caranoc, Abbot of the foundation at Whithorn in Galloway was the first Christian in Ireland. According to the ancient historian, Prosper of Aquitaine, around AD 430 a British Celt named Congar, or Docco, was working as a missionary in Ireland. He wrote to Pope Celestine I (AD 422-32) saying that the Irish were now ready for a formalised mission and for the appointment of a bishop. The establishment of a bishop's authority, as quickly as possible, was urgent because the Church was in the grip of a serious heresy being carried all over the Celtic world.

This heresy had its roots in the teachings of Pelagius, undoubtedly the most influential British Christian of the time, whose words were greatly respected even in Rome. He was born around AD 354, possibly in Ireland and one of his foremost detractors, Saint Jerome, mocks him as being 'stuffed with Irish porridge'. Pelagius went to Rome in AD 380 and was dismayed at the laxity of both religion and morals among the Christians there. This laxity, he argued, was rooted in the doctrines of the greatly respected early Church Father, Saint Augustine of Hippo, whose doctrines became

part of Church dogma. All was preordained by God in the full knowledge of what was to happen, said Augustine. So, why should any man strive towards salvation? Those who were to be saved had been identified at the foundation of the world and those not chosen had no chance of salvation anyway.

Pelagius taught that salvation, while certainly being a gift from God, was the responsibility of each individual who should seek to attain it, regardless of what Saint Augustine and the Church said. He argued that Augustine's teaching made the Church's entire teaching on morals wholly untenable because if the theory of predestination was true, there was nothing to restrain Christians from sin. This was a direct challenge to the teachings and authority of the Church. Followers of Augustine clamoured to have Pelagius declared a heretic. They pointed out that his theology was based on the pagan Celtic notions of individual responsibility towards spirits of nature and condemned the teachings as a crude attempt to re-establish druidism and druid law in the Celtic west. In Ireland, where druid influence still lingered, the Pelagian doctrine was being widely taught and it was asserted that these missionaries allowed the retention of pagan festivals and were even adopting druid laws and ways themselves. The appointment of a Roman bishop, it was argued, would stamp the authority of the Church on this situation.

Ireland had been the first country outside the Roman Empire to have been Christianised and Celestine took the problem of creeping heresy seriously. He referred the matter to the great 'nursery of missionaries' at Auxerre and to its Abbot, the influential Saint Germanus. The person appointed by Germanus as 'the first bishop to the Irish believing in Christ' was an experienced missionary. A Gaulish Celt, Palladius had served as a deacon at Auxerre for a number of years and bore the Latin title *Patricius* – 'well-born'. Palladius's journey to Ireland was long and he was not in the best of health and there is much debate, among historians, about his subsequent mission. Professor Thomas O'Rahilly argues that Palladius never reached Ireland but succumbed to plague in Britain, dying there around AD 431.

Legends of Saints and Holy Men

Professor James Carney believes that Palladius arrived in Ireland and preached there for several years, aided by three other missionaries – Secondinius, Auxillius and Iserninius. He also proposes that Secondinius founded the great religious centre at Armagh and became its first bishop when this previously important pagan site later became the seat of the Irish Primacy. Iserninius was already in Ireland long before Palladius's arrival, since he had been imprisoned by Ende Censelah, a petty king of Leinster, and was only released with 'the coming of the Patricus' and the conversion to Christianity of one of the king's grandsons. If Palladius did preach in Ireland, then the period of his ministry did not last long. Ireland, too, was gripped by plague and it is possible that he died in its throes in the early 440s, and with his mission only partly completed.

A successor was quickly found by Saint Germanus and dispatched to Ireland. This was a British Celt named Sucat, reputedly born into a Christian community at Alcluyd –

SAINT PATRICK AND THE DRUIDS

Although probably not a single individual, the Patricius, the first Christian bishop of the Irish – probably Palladius succeeded by Sucat and then Secondinius – certainly had to deal with the existing pagan religion. The Druids enjoyed an important status in Ireland long after their influence had diminished in other parts of the Celtic world, acting as advisers and soothsayers to kings including the High King of Ireland. It was said that some of the High Kings would not make a decision concerning matters of state or warfare without first consulting their druids.

Druids, who enjoyed their greatest influence directly prior to Patrick's arrival, were said to be the followers of Crom Cruach. This was a fertility god whose cult had been established by an ancient king named Tiernmas or Tighearnmhas who could have ruled as early as 1000 BC. Whatever the cult's history, during the middle of the fifth century, the priests of Crom Cruach seem to have enjoyed the confidence of many of the local rulers as well as that of the High King, Laoghaire.

Saint Patrick defeats the druids at Tara.

In his seventh century account of Patrick's life, the biographer Muirchú states that Laoghaire was both 'a great king' and 'a fierce pagan'. The son of another famous king, Niall of the Nine Hostages, he was greatly feared and respected throughout the length and breadth of Ireland. As king he had been warned, by the druids, of a certain prophecy that stated that a 'messenger from another religion' would one day arrive in Ireland. That person was Patrick.

According to Christian legend, the saint arrived at a particularly auspicious time. It was 30 April, the Feast of Bealtane, when the local kings kindled great, hilltop bonfires in honour of the proto-Celtic god Bel or Baal. No one was allowed to light a fire before the High King had kindled his own on the Hill of Tara. Patrick, in defiance of the king's orders and pagan tradition, kindled his Paschal fire on the upper slopes of Slane, stating that he had lit a fire 'which would never go out' in Ireland. Angered by this open act of defiance, Laoghaire ordered his soldiers to arrest the saint and bring him to Tara.

This was done but, while at the king's court, Patrick performed miracles that astounded the king and in a contest of power between Patrick and the pagan druids, the saint easily triumphed. Laoghaire was so overcome that he converted to Christianity, together with the majority of his household.

Another seventh century biographer of Patrick, the monk Tíreachán, gives a different but perhaps more historically accurate account of the meeting between saint and king. He states that Laoghaire did not convert to Christianity, because the ghost of his father Niall would not allow it. However, two daughters of Laoghaire were impressed by Patrick and wished to convert. Although the druids tried to dissuade them, they approached the saint while he was resting at a well near Cruachain – Rathcroghan, County Roscommon – and asked to be instructed in the Faith. The saint willingly complied and baptised them both at the well. The girls then persistently demanded to see the face of the Risen Christ and, although Patrick counselled against it, finally their request was granted whereupon both girls were immediately struck dead since no person can look upon the face of God and live.

These tales are probably no more than monkish inventions used to illustrate the triumph of early Irish Christianity over the native paganism. The contest between Patrick and Laoghaire's druids contains echoes of various Old Testament stories of similar contests between the early prophets and pagan priests. There was a further series of Celtic additions to the tale in medieval times. One, dating from the 11th century, tells of how the Ulster champion, Cú Chulainn, appeared to Laoghaire and exhorted him to accept the new faith. Across the years, such tradition has been absorbed into the realms of folklore and is sometimes treated as actual, historical fact. Muirchú's *Life of Patrick*, although being the best known and the one accepted by the Church, is suspected of being not altogether trustworthy. Many of these biographies contain exaggerations and invented, or altered, stories designed to make the subject more saintly or wonderful. Tíreachán's account is thought to be more historically accurate.

Dumbarton, who also bore the title 'Patricius'. This missionary would appear to have been the Patrick of the *Tripartite Life* and the one who wrote the *Confessio*. His own father was a Christian deacon with the Latinised name Calpornius and, early in life, he seems to have been taken prisoner by Irish raiders who carried him back with them to their own country. There he was forced to herd either sheep or swine in 'a lonely place' before escaping to Gaul where he joined the important Christian settlement at Lerins, becoming a church deacon himself. From Lerins, he travelled to Auxerre to study under Saint Germanus. The date of Sucat's dispatch to Ireland is hotly disputed – Carney suggests AD 456, while O'Rahilly argues for AD 461. Reportedly landing in Lough Cuan – Strangford Lough – in the north, via his home in the kingdom of Strathclyde, he was accompanied by at least one follower, Seginis. Sucat was the most effective of the missionaries and appears to have been an extremely able bishop. Thanks to his early captivity, he was relatively familiar with Ireland. He spoke the language, knew the ways of the people and the network of mission-stations set up by Palladius and his predecessors. Whether or not he travelled the entire country as claimed is unknown but it is highly unlikely. His followers – ordained by himself as bishops – went about in his name, taking for themselves the title 'Patricius'. Soon Irish monks were travelling back into Europe, and further, as missionaries themselves.

Patrick's third incarnation is a much more shadowy figure. Ibar, also predating Sucat and maybe Palladius, was not a bishop, but was in charge of a Christian mission-station in County Louth in AD 460. He is generally assumed to be a Briton who was the pupil of an even earlier missionary called Mocteus, who must have come to Ireland directly from Rome. Mocteus, accompanied by three Munstermen, consecrated as Roman bishops, had set up his station around AD 440.

Legends of Saints and Holy Men

Like both Palladius and Sucat, Ibar seems to have been a very capable missionary leader with references to him in the *Book of Ballymote* and the *Book of Leinster*. Very little is known about him except that he was one of the earliest missionaries in the country and that he too styled himself Patricius, in Roman fashion. This was a title widely used by early Church Fathers in Ireland. When Saint Enda, Bishop of Killeany (AD 530), reportedly went to Rome with his companions, Aibe and Puteus, all three were baptised by Pope John II as 'Patrici of the Irish'. Saint Fintan of Clonnard may also have assumed the title, as did Erlatheus, Bishop of Armagh, at the end of the fifth century. Patrick, therefore, would seem to be a Roman title that evolved into a personal name adopted as nomenclature by the early Irish bishops. If Patrick was a religious composite of several men, it makes us wonder about the origin of the legend that has the saint driving snakes and serpents from Ireland. Other holy-men are reported to have carried out similar cleansings which, as Bonwick has suggested, probably banished not snakes, but the adherents of a serpent faith that was known to be common among the ancient Celts, particularly those on the Continent.

'The serpent was certainly the token or symbol of an ancient race celebrated for wisdom, giving rise to the naming of the learned after dragons or serpents. The Druid of the Welsh Triads exclaims "I am a serpent".'
(James Bonwick: *Irish Druids and Old Irish Religion* 1894)

Bonwick continues:

> ' . . .Ireland never had any snakes. Solinus was informed that the island had neither snakes nor bees and that the dust from that country would drive them off from any other land. But the same authority avers that no snakes could be found on the Kentish Isle of Thanet, nor in Crete. Moryson in 1617 went further in declaring "Ireland had neither singing nightingall, nor chattering pye, nor undermining moule".'
>
> (Bonwick: ibid)

According to this same tradition, a race of ancient Egyptian serpent-worshippers led by Nuil, husband of the daughter of Pharaoh, arrived in Ireland and continued their worship in the new country. The followers of this tradition quote both 'serpent stones' and the 'druid's egg', created from the froth of two mating serpents (see **The Druidic Tradition**) as evidence. While this may have relatively little basis in fact, there is at least some evidence of serpent worship among the ancient Celts - a tradition that seemed to have been particularly strong in Ireland and that was later subsumed into Irish Christian iconography.

Celtic Mythology

> 'Is it not a singular circumstance that, in Ireland where no living serpent exists, such numerous legends of serpents should abound and that figures of serpents should be so profusely used to ornament Irish sculptures? There is scarcely a cross or a handsome piece of ornamental work, which has not got its serpent or dragon.'
>
> (M. Keane: *Towers and Temples of Ancient Ireland,* 1880)

Evidence that the serpent was highly venerated among Celtic tribes was especially obvious within the Roman Empire because the Romans also venerated snake-deities: as household protectors. Both Roman and Celtic belief fused to form spirits of tremendous power and influence whose image decorated many Romano-Celtic structures. In the developing ancient world, the snake often became the embodiment of fertility, of healing and of the underworld. The Cult of the Three Mothers in the Rhineland was associated with snakes - in some cult depictions, the snake is shown as being wrapped around a tree, the symbol of life and development, as if protecting it. In southern Gaul, similar depictions show the serpent curling protectively around an oak tree. The Celtic healing goddess Damona had a snake as one of her attribues. Although outside the sphere of Romano-Celtic influence, snakes loom large, too, in Irish legend and folklore but seem to have adopted a much more negative aspect than in Romano-Celtic worship. The Ulster hero, Conall Cearnach, overcame a ferocious and poisonous giant reptile which guarded a great treasure in the ancient fort that he was attacking; Meiche, the son of the Irish war goddess Morrigan was believed to have two intertwined snakes as a heart.

The snake was anathema to the early Christians who viewed it as the symbol of ultimate evil – it was the serpent who had tempted Eve in the Garden of Eden. The

'The Temptation of Saint Anthony'
by Hieronymus Bosch

expanding new religion drove the snake cults before it and Ireland may well have become a refuge. When Christianity eventually reached Irish shores in the fifth century, the early missionaries made the expulsion of the pagan snake cults a priority. Their iconography would have been incorporated into early Irish Christian art in an attempt to placate them, providing a basis for the most famous legend concerning Saint Patrick.

The Culdees and the Sacred Bachall

By the beginning of the eighth century, Celtic monasticism was beginning to break down. There was no real, cohesive monastic order. Individual abbots would interpret their house's Rule very much as they wished and, consequently, observance had become very lax. From earliest times, attempts had been made to impose austerity and holiness on the religious houses. Dewi Sant's success seemed to be the exception and was even criticised for attending too much to the ascetic qualities of religious worship.

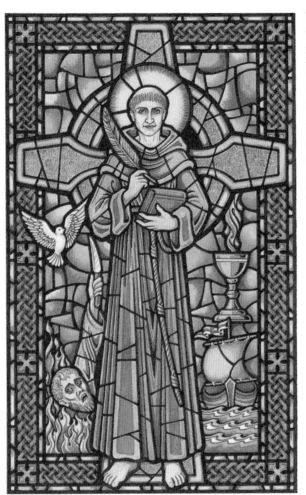

Saint Columcille

Celtic Mythology

By the end of the seventh century, Celtic monasticism had become almost degenerate and needed a charismatic figure to restore a sacred framework in which devotions could take place. The need for cohesion became even more urgent as Celtic monks came into contact with regimented Orders of the Roman Church such as the Augustinians and Benedictines, which competed in terms of holiness and sanctity.

A Celtic movement for reform gradually emerged following the Synod of Whitby led by the forbidding figure of Mael Ruain, Abbot of Tamlachta – Tallaght – in Ireland. His Order founded in AD 769, known as the *Céile Dé* – Servants or Companions of God – followed an austere and rigid Rule. Mael Ruain was an obsessive ascetic and imposed severe restrictions on those who chose to follow him. Each

Community was required to spend a year on bread and water following the death of one of their members as, it was believed, the soul of the departed could then be released more readily to Heaven. Self-flagellation, using knotted cords, was practised although such scourging was extremely rare in other Celtic monasteries of the time. No Culdee, as they were known, might leave his holy house except in extreme circumstances, nor was he allowed to ask visitors to the monastery about the outside world.

In contrast to the rest of Celtic monasticism, the Culdees took a jaundiced view of women and, while not excluding them from formal worship, refused them the Sacraments of the Church during their 'unclean time'. The Rule of the *Céile Dé* is quite specific: 'During the monthly disease which is upon the virgins of the Church ...they shall not go to hand then, because they are unclean during that time' ('Going to hand' meant receiving the Sacraments and the priest's blessing following Confession).

For those who failed in the slightest way to meet the demands of Culdee monastic life, there were lengthy and demanding penances. Strangely enough, Mael Ruaine's Rule attracted many: those who were disillusioned with the monasteries of the Celtic church. After the foundation of Tallaght, houses at Finglas on the other side of the Liffey, and Terryglas, on the banks of the Shannon, were set up. The Rule moved north where, in 1183, Culdees were driven out of Down Cathedral by the Norman Knight, John de Courcy; branding them heretics he immediately replaced them with his favoured Benedictines. A community was set up in the See of Armagh and further expansion was made into the Western Isles via Rathlin Island. The isolation of the Hebrides was spiritually attractive offering the silence desired for contemplation. There was a substantial settlement at Dunkeld on the mainland of Scotland and a further settlement was founded at York. Each house, no matter where, held to the same strict Rule, yet this regime of austerity and discipline produced writing and poetry of unimaginable beauty and tenderness. Two main works that survive are *The Stowe Missal* and the *Martyrology of Oenghus* but their imagery also survives in fragments of poems such as *The Hermit's Song*. Much of it has to do with Nature and the natural world and owing to their reclusive and introspective lives, is often highly mystical in tone.

Legends of Saints and Holy Men

'I wish, O Son of the living God, O ancient and eternal King,
For a hidden little hut in the wilderness, that it may be my Dwelling.
An all-grey lithe little lark to be by its side,
A clear pool to wash away sins through the grace of the Holy Spirit.
Quite near, a beautiful wood around it on every side,
To nurse many-voiced birds, hiding it with its shelter.
...A choice land, with many gracious gifts, such as
be good for every plant'
(*The Hermit's Song*, Culdee poet unknown: ninth century)

Naturally, with their austere, withdrawn regime and their inward-looking, mystical qualities, the Culdee movement was later considered the repository of ancient wisdoms handed down from previous eras – perhaps even from the druids. While there is no evidence for this, there is equally no evidence that the movement discouraged such speculation.

Although it had initially spread across much of Celtic Britain, the movement was just too fragmented and haphazard to survive. Both its energy and enthusiasm began to wane and gradually it sank back into the mainstream of the Christian church. Most Abbeys now followed the Rules of Augustine, Benedict and, later, Saint Dominic, which gave a structure and purpose to Roman monastic life. Besides, the emphasis of Celtic Christian life was gradually swinging from the strictly monastic to the diocesan. Nevertheless, small pockets of Culdees remained in Ireland until the 16th century, the most prominent being within the Holy See of Armagh. Jeffries records that a community still existed there in the early 1500s but suggests that its numbers may have been very small. He states:

> 'It is not possible to offer an estimate of the size of the *Céile Dé* community at Armagh in the first half of the sixteenth century but William Reeves suggested that the community normally consisted of a prior and five brethren. Despite its not inconsiderable land holdings, one suspects that the *Céili Dé* community at Armagh is likely to have been small on the eve of the reformations, given that the priorship was only worth Stg. £4 in 1492'.

> (Henry A. Jeffries: *Priests and Prelates of Armagh in the Age of Reformations, 1518–1558*, Dublin, 1997)

He also states that although few in number the Culdees continued to hold large areas of land and exerted considerable influence on medieval Armagh and its environs. They invariably provided a number of Brothers to serve as Vicars Choral for the Holy See. The Master of Works for Armagh Cathedral was also usually a member of the Brotherhood and Jeffries further cites the Vicar of Ardee – Mgr. Ruairí MacGiollamuire – as one of the Culdees (Jeffries: op. cit.).

Because of their associations with ancient and largely forgotten wisdoms, the Culdees also became connected with another element of early Christian lore. This was the *bachall*, or staff of a saint or holy-man. The *bachall* occupied a central position in Celtic religious folklore. Just as the staff had been the mark of a druid, so it was the sign of an early saint or a holy-man with supernatural powers. There were those who said that the *bachall* was the actual source of those powers. In any event, the *bachall* was something held in common by the pagan and Christian worlds.

The rod or branch seems to have been part of the insignia of the pagan Celtic kings and bards - a symbol of their oneness with Nature. References to Celtic royal inau-

Celtic Mythology

SAINT COLUMCILLE (COLUMBA)

Saint Columcille was the most celebrated early saint, whose influence extended from Ireland into the heartland of Western Scotland. Columcille is a nickname, and is composed of two words borrowed from Latin: *columba* meaning 'dove' and *cella* meaning 'church'. His given name seems to have been *Criomhthann*, meaning 'fox' or 'cunning wolf'. He came from a noble line and was a descendant of one of the High Kings of Ireland, Niall of the Nine Hostages.

His birth at Gartan in County Donegal, had been predicted by Mochta – Mocteus – a disciple of Saint Patrick and took place on 7 December, 521. It was reputedly a Thursday, and that particular day became very auspicious among Celtic people for beginning a new task, in weaving something new, or setting out on a journey.

According to religious folklore, while still a young boy Columcille was visited in a dream by an angel who asked him to choose two virtues. He chose chastity and wisdom and the gift of prophecy was added on account of his wise choice. Columcille had a vocation to the priesthood and set out for the monastery of Saint Finnian at Moville on Strangford Lough in County Down. There he studied theology, philosophy and the art of copying and illuminating manuscripts. He became a deacon, an officer of the Celtic Church who mediated between priests and people. He also found time to learn bardic poetry and music from the bard Gemman. He also learned the traditional and heroic tales of Ireland and Alban – Scotland – that he loved for the rest of his life. Some of his own, illuminated, verse is preserved in manuscript form in the Bodleian Library in Oxford.

As a student, Columcille showed great intellect and scholarly promise and he continued his studies under Finnian at Clonnard then moved on to the monastery of Mobhi at Glasnevin near Dublin. Upon leaving Glasnevin, he travelled north again and in 546, at the age of twenty-five, Columcille founded his first monastery. The place he chose had been a sacred one belonging to the druids; it was an oak grove in which they had conducted their rites. Columcille renamed it Doire Cholum Cille, which later was anglicised into Derry: to become one of the most important cities in the north of Ireland. Although he was happier in Derry than anywhere, Columcille set out on a number of pilgrimages. During his journeys, he founded religious houses at Durrow, Kells and Moone and maybe as many as 40 religious centres altogether, though this may an exaggeration.

In AD 561, Columcille returned to Moville to revisit his friend Saint Finnian, though he seemed to have an ulterior motive – the celebrated manuscript known as *Saint Martin's Gospel*. This was a beautifully-illustrated text, comprising the Psalms and the Mosaic Law as well as the Four Gospels, which had been copied into Latin by Saint Jerome. Saint Ninian had brought it from Gaul and placed it in his abbey in Whithorn where it had been copied by Finnian. Columcille coveted the book.

Secretly, night after night, during the course of his stay in Moville, Columcille copied large portions of the text for his own use. He was discovered by Finnian himself who demanded that the copy be handed over for retention in the abbey at Moville. Columcille refused, demanding that the matter be taken to the court of the High King Diarmaid for his adjudica-tion. Diarmaid listened to both sides of the argument before giving his decision – "To every cow its calf, to every book its copy". The copy was to stay at Moville.

Refusing to abide by the High King's decision, Columcille returned to his own kinsmen and demanded that they take revenge on Diarmaid for his 'unjust' decision. The result was the terrible Battle of Cúl Dreimhne – Cooldrevny – in a valley in Sligo, where thousands of men on both sides were killed. Although Columcille defeated Diarmaid, opinion turned against him. The High King appealed to the Irish church leaders who held a great Synod at Teltown in County Meath to decide Columcille's fate. The sentence, initially, was excommunication for causing bloodshed and civil war but Brendan of Birr interceded on Columcille's behalf and the decision was overturned. In remorse, Columcille sought sanctuary on the island of Devenish in Lough Erne, the retreat of the holy Saint Molaise who imposed upon him the penance of lifelong exile. He bade him go and win as many souls for Christ, as had been lost in battle.

Bitterly, and vowing never to set foot on Irish soil again or to see the sun in Ireland, Columcille set sail for Alban in 563 with 12 companions. They came ashore on the island of Oronsay but Columcille found that he could still see the shores of his beloved Ireland from the highest hill so, after resting, they sailed onwards. Finally, they landed on the island of Hii – also rendered as Hu – or I-Shona, once home to an important pagan shrine dedicated to a Celtic water-god and to the Celtic god of Light.

Their landing site was afterwards known as Port na Cruaich or the Port of the Coracle. Above this bay is a pile of stones that is still known in folklore as Cairn of the Back Turned to Ireland and legend says that the saint climbed the hill to check that he could no longer see his home-land. The saint annexed the small church built by his cousin and expanded it into what was to become the centre of the Celtic Christian Church of the West. I-Shona became Iona and from his new foundation, Columcille – now known as Columba – set out to convert the Pictish kings of the Western Highlands.

Columcille wandered throughout Scotland, founding many other churches and religious houses, converting and baptising as he went. He returned to Ireland only once, to attend the famous Council of Drumceat in Derry as a guest of the bards and *filí* – two occupations that were very close to his heart. To keep his holy vow he had his eyes bound so that he could not see, and had clods of Scottish turf tied to his feet so that he would not even touch the earth of Erin with the soles of his sandals. He died on 9 June, 597, the very year that Saint Augustine arrived on the shores of Kent from Rome.

He was buried on Iona but legend has it that his body was later taken to Downpatrick to be interred with that of Patrick. His official biographer was Adhamhnán, one of his successors as Abbot of Iona who wrote the 'Life' of the saint. It contains many curious stories of Columcille's pilgrimages and miracles and has a strong emphasis on the supernatural.

guration ceremonies speak of the kings being handed the 'rod of kingship' by a person of spiritual authority – perhaps a druid and or bard – who accompanied him to the inauguration mound. In Christian times it would have been a representative from a leading monastery, although the involvement of a Christian authority seems to have been a much more recent development. Nevertheless, there seems to have been at least some firm connections between the sacred and the pagan. The second 'Life' of Saint Maedoc of Ferns states that when the King of Breifne in Ireland was inaugurated, his 'wand of kingship' would be cut from a hazel tree growing at the site of Maedoc's hermitage (see: Simms, *From Kings to Warlords,* 1987).

Part of the *bachall* legend concerned a mystical tree that existed in both the Otherworld and the mortal sphere. The *bachall* was a branch cut from this tree and contained the almost-magical powers that were associated with that Other Realm. This idea, unique in ancient Irish literature, probably has its origins in the mythology of other cultures – the Upanishads, the Kabbalah and, significantly, in Norse religion where the World Tree *Yggdrasil* is the ash tree at the centre of existence. The strong links between ancient Ireland and Scandinavia should not be forgotten, of course. The notion of a Sacred Tree also endorsed the Christian symbolism of the Cross:

Celtic Mythology

'Learned tradition tells of a wonderful tree, with its upper part in the firmament, its lower part in the earth and every melody in its midst. Another of its marvellous features was that it grew downward from above while every other tree grows upward. It grew downward from a single root with innumerable roots coming from it below. There were nine branches, every branch more beautiful than that above. There were pure white birds on the forks of the branches, listening to their many melodies throughout the ages. The tree is Jesus Christ, the acme of all God's creatures, above them by reason of his divinity, who came forth from the earth, assuming humanity from the Virgin Mary'.

(The Yellow Book of Lecan quoted from *Stair Nicodéim* (The Irish Gospel of Nicodemus) in Herbert and McNamara (eds), *The Irish Biblical Apocrypha*, Edinburgh, 1989)

Here was an attempt to equate the mythological Otherworld Tree with the Christian tradition. The branches of this marvellous tree formed the *bachalls* that the holy men carried. These were translated into 'silver branches' or 'rods' to denote kingship. The silver branches, sought after by such Celtic heroes as Bran and Cormac, symbolise the rod of kingship.

The rod, itself, appears as a silver sceptre in the hand of Conchobar MacNessa, King of Ulster, in the Irish myth *Fled Bricenn* (Bricriu's Feast in the Ulster Cycle of Irish Mythology). Conchobar used the branch not only to demonstrate his ecclesiastical and pagan authority but also to create peace among disputing nobles. This he did by striking the sceptre against the bronze head of his couch as a signal that order was to be restored. It is therefore called 'the peacemaking branch'.

In the Norse tradition yggdrasil *was the Tree of Life at the centre of existence.*

Thus, the *bachall* is the foundation of three symbols of power and authority – the bishop's crozier, the king's sceptre and, because of its supernatural powers, the magician's wand.

Folklore seems to suggest that there were only a certain number of *bachalls* and that these belonged to extremely holy men. The most important of all the Celtic *bachalls* – simply because we have an account of the saint's receiving it – was the sacred *bachall* of Saint Patrick. According to the *Tripartite Life* Sucat received the *bachall*.

'Patrick stayed three days and three nights with them and went after that to Mount Hermon in the neighbourhood of the island. There, the Lord appeared and told him to go and preach to the Gael, and gave him the staff of Jesus and said that it would be a helper to him in every danger and in every unequal conflict in which he should be.'

(*The Tripartite Life of Saint Patrick*: W. Stokes (ed), 1887)

Other folkloristic traditions state that Patrick was given his commission and handed his *bachall* at the Skerry Church in north Antrim, within sight of Slemish Mountain where he had herded pigs. Wherever he actually received it, the *bachall* had tremendous powers; it was able to bring water from the rock, in the style of Moses, and, traditionally, the Saint used it to expel the serpents from Ireland. Even after Patrick's death, it was said that his crozier was borne into battle at the head of the armies of a number of Irish kings to assure victory.

Patrick's *bachall* was not the only crozier so borne. The *bachall* of Saint Columcille was, according to the *Fragmentary Annals*, carried into battle by an army of Dalriadic Scots at Strathearn against the forces of Ivar II, Norse King of Dublin, and secured them, in AD 904, a great victory:

'Columcille's *bachall* . . . was therefore called *Cathbhuaid* – battle victory – from that time on. It was a just name because they often won the victory in battle through it, even as they did on that occasion, when they placed their faith in Columcille'.

(*The Fragmentary Annals*, J. Marsden (ed), 1994)

Sacred *bachalls* were even used by some local communities as a kind of 'lie detector' over which oaths were sworn and accusations and treaties were made. Several *bachalls* were closely linked to the Culdee Brotherhood. This seems reasonable, given the affinity of the Brotherhood with Nature and the fact that many of their communities existed close to former sacred trees and druidical groves. The Culdee ascetic and hermit Oenghus, for example, is supposed to have had his dwelling close to a yew tree.

Legend says that the *bachall* of Patrick – the *Beculam Jesu* – was given to the House of the *Céile Dé* in Armagh where it was kept away from public gaze. What befell it is not specified though it is said that it was destroyed, or carried off, by the O'Neills of the Fews when they attacked Armagh in the early sixteenth century. A number of ancient Culdee texts were also reputedly carried off at this time. There is no formal record of such a holy staff or crozier being held at Armagh so this may simply be a legend.

The early Celtic Church was convoluted, combining elements of both the pagan and Christian traditions. With its emphasis on miracles, magic and mystical spiritualism, the Celtic Church may have been closer to the druidic tradition than we realise, even today. It would be many years, some say well into the 19th century, before the two traditions joined to form a unified Christian Church within formerly Celtic lands. These lands included Ireland, Scotland, Wales, Cornwall, Isle of Man, Brittany, Gaul, Iberia, sections of Byzantium and Egypt, parts of Delphi, Galacia, possibly Tarsus and the Pu valley. It has recently been suggested that even parts of Russia, Mongolia and Scandinavia had Celts living in them.

Legends of Saints and Holy Men

GIANTS, MONSTERS AND FAIRIES

Curiosities and Supernatural Creatures in Celtic Folklore and Mythology

Insubstantial spirits, gods and partly-defined forces, all dwelling in some far-away, nebulous Otherworld were not the only type of supernatural entities feared by the Celts. There were more immediate sources of awe and mystery; beings of magical powers with which, folklore maintained, the tribes shared the land. Some of these creatures were the implacable enemies of mortal man and must be either avoided or else destroyed at all costs. A good number of these tales stretched back into the dim history of the Celtic peoples. There were stories of huge, pre-human people who had dwelt in the Celtic lands before men arrived. Other tales spoke of diminutive, immortal races that, although seldom seen, co-existed with mortals by dwelling in remote and secretive places. There were creatures, left over from a previous age, which still roamed the secluded valleys and hills of the countryside. All of these tales began to draw together into a rich tapestry of folklore and, some have argued, of folk-history. They formed an oral tradition that was later compiled by scribes and pre-served in the written word. The tradition has been handed down to us through pop-ular stories and legends that, across the generations, have been sanitised and entered into the realms of children's fiction. However, when dealing with folklore, we must remember that the stories that we tell today as bedtime fables once formed part of the nightmares of our distant ancestors. It is easy to dismiss once-frightening figures: the cannibal witch in 'Hansel and Gretel'; the monstrous ogre in 'Jack the Giant-Killer'; the wicked Rumplestiltskin and the monstrous serpent in 'Saint George and the Dragon' but all these, at one time, were a grim and horrid reality. They, as well as the gods and sacred beings demonstrated the richness and diversity of existence placing man as a lowly figure within an overarching and often hostile natural order.

For the Celts, then, something strange and monstrously terrifying awaited them in the darkness each evening or in the hidden recesses of an unknown land.

Giants

The giants who strode confidently through the earlier unrecorded epochs of Celtic mythology had, when Christianity reached the West, become little more than stunted curiosities of local folklore. Yet, in their heyday, they had been the very embodiment of the old, natural powers and elemental forces that had governed and

Celtic Mythology

shaped the landscape. When the Celts first arrived in the western lands, they found widespread evidence of the rawness of nature. Some of this consisted of great heaps of boulders, left behind as the Ice Age retreated, forming immense pseudo-constructions, often resembling the ramparts of ancient fortifications. There were gigantic rocks, far too big for any man to lift, dumped in inaccessible places by the disappearing ice, together with tons of rock and rubble that the earlier aboriginal inhabitants of the land had made into vast earthworks. All this, declared Celtic wisdom, could only be the work of a vanished race of mighty men.

The concept of giants was nothing new. Many ancient peoples, all across the world, had tales of great races comprised of formidable beings. No doubt, some of these gigantic men actually existed, but their exploits often became confused with legends of ancient gods and of supernatural entities.

The first tradition to mention giants and to equate them with already-existing supernatural lore was a set of ancient Hebraic and Egyptian texts that formed the basis for the Pentateuch (the first five books of the Old Testament). The earliest reference occurs in Genesis 6:4: 'There were giants in the earth in those days'. The Hebraic text renders the word *Nephilim* as a description of these creatures. Subsequent translation into Greek changed the word to *Gigantes* – Giants – an interpretation to which all later writers and commentators have adhered. In translation the word loses something of its supernatural force, for the original form *Nephi-lim* is plural and is taken from its three occurrences in Biblical text to mean 'those who fell', or 'those who cause others to fall'. This has always been taken to refer to their great size and strength, but other Biblical commentators have suggested that it might also refer to those fallen angels who were cast out of Heaven with Lucifer after his unsuccessful rebellion. This interpretation puts them into a mystical context and subsequent Biblical writings do not clarify the picture, alternately referring to the *Nephilim* as 'sons of God – the spawn of supernatural entities and mortal women' – and 'mighty men of renown' which suggests a mortal origin.

Giants, Monsters and Fairies

The situation is further confused when the Bible goes on to describe as giants the Anakim – the sons of Anak – who inhabited stretches of land in what is now the Gaza Strip. Here were the windy deserts of Gath from which Goliath and his brothers came with the Philistine armies to be defeated at the hands of the Israelites under King Saul.

References to other actual giants or giant races are also liberally mixed with the tradition of supernatural entities throughout the Hebraic texts. We learn of Og, King of Bahsan; the gigantic tribes hired by King Chedorlaomer of Elam in his war with rebel kings. Then there were the Raphaim or Sons of Rapha who were called Zamzummims – literally meaning 'gibberish' or 'inarticulate ones' – because of their strange sounding language. In the popular mind some of these races retained vestiges of supernatural powers and might even have been regarded by the Hebrews as manifestations of ancient and demonic gods.

Back castles in Mourne Mountains, Ireland. Celts believed these heaps of boulders to be the work of a vanished race of mighty men and women.

The Biblical tradition seems to have had some impact on early Celtic notions concerning giants. The Celts, an Indo-European people, believed that the first giants had come from either the Middle East or from Africa. The first giant-king to arrive in the West was Albion and, according to tradition, he and his people took possession of the empty lands of Europe around the second millennium BC. Later Christian mythology was to identify Albion and his race as direct descendants of Noah's evil elder son Ham. Several medieval chroniclers maintain that their lineage could be traced back

to another of Noah's sons, Japheth. The Greeks gave Albion another name: Poseidonus, tracing his ancestry back to the Hellenistic god of the sea. The Celts seemed to have adopted this notion, for many early tales concerning giants depict them as living in coastal areas or on islands and having strong oceanic connections.

Albion is one of the oldest names for parts of the British Isles, connecting them with the giant-king and his monstrous race. Greeks, writing two or three centuries before

Christ, apply the name to the larger of the two islands. The smaller island, Ireland, takes its name from the Greek *Ierne*, the meaning of which is uncertain but might have referred to a giantess. A derivation, albus, was further used by the Celts to denote high ground: cliffs and especially high hills and mountains; local etymology conferring, on a particular range of mountains, the name Alps.

The oral tradition of ancient giants was eagerly seized upon by medieval scribes such as Geoffrey of Monmouth (1100-54) who frequently used the names of 'gigantic men' without adding very much detail about them. Geoffrey was not the first to mention giants. They had already appeared in some of the great Myth Cycles written by earlier Irish and Welsh monks, dwelling in remote abbeys throughout these Celtic lands. Sixteenth-century chroniclers such as Holinshed, and poets such as Spenser, hint at a fabulous prehistoric age when giants stalked the earth. More was to be found in oral folklore, passed down from Celtic times and sometimes mixed with the stories of other cultures. Some of these tales state that the father of all the giant brood was a creature known as Dan whose gigantic descendants came from the east to settle in Ireland. This is reflected in the ancient Irish *Leabhar Gabhala - Book of Invasions* - a 12th-century compilation of ancient manuscripts, tracing the mythological history of Ireland. It names the Tuatha Dé Danann as one of the founding races of the country. The Dé Danann are also described as a race of supernatural and mystical beings from which the Irish fairies are descended. Again, giants become confused with other magical beings.

Celtic Mythology

To these early giants were attributed great and awesome miracles. Geoffrey of Monmouth gives a largely-fictionalised account of how these prehistoric superhumans carried Stonehenge from its original site 'The Dance of the Giants' in Ireland and placed it on Salisbury Plain. Throughout the rest of the Celtic world, both individual standing stones and megalithic complexes were ascribed to the prowess of giants. In European folklore, a race of gigantic creatures flourished both in the British Isles and in the western European continent between the first and second millennia BC and were responsible for all the great stones and stone structures to be found in various locations throughout the English and French countryside. The ancient writers had no other way to understand these massive monuments. Gradually, these beings died out and the final concentration of west European giants was to be found in Cornwall, where an abundance of standing stones reflects their passing.

Tradition tells that the Cornish giants survived well into the medieval period. By this time Christianity had taken a firm hold on the lands of western Europe and to the early Christian fathers, these titans represented the fading face of a monstrous paganism existing long before the foundation of the True Church. The giants were then ascribed evil and perverse ways. They ate children, they ravaged the countryside, they sexually assaulted women and they attacked men of God. Giants were lewd, unwholesome and obscene, and deserved to be removed from the face of the earth.

The developing Church also objected to the fact that several of the ancient, localised Celtic gods had been transformed through folklore into giants. It is probable that the

Norfolk giant Tom Hichathrift, who was reputed to have lived there during the reign of William I, was a popular representation of the god Hiccafrith, a deity of the Iceni, a southern Celtic people of whom at one time Boudicca was queen. Other gigantic figures, often carved into hillsides might have been objects of local worship. The gigantic Cerne Abbas figure with its enormous phallus is believed to have depicted an ancient fertility god, although certain historians have recently argued that it might have been nothing more than a scandalous 17th-century cartoon of Oliver Cromwell. The monstrous Gorm, carved on the side of the Avon Gorge, was probably the depiction of a god and used for regional worship.

Christian theology could not tolerate these monstrous pagan survivals and so the folklore and legend that surrounded them subtly altered in accordance with Church teaching. Giants were no longer the mighty personification of supernatural powers or the gods of antiquity, but nothing more than hideous and depraved creatures of yesteryear whose eradication was mankind's spiritual duty. Rather than being objects of veneration and awe, they were depicted as both stupid and brutish, easily outwitted and defeated by an expanding Christian population. The holy monks set about recording a history of the giant race much different from that which had gone before.

Mythology and legends were now full of terrible, man-eating giants and ogres, all of whom were quickly defeated and dispatched by Christian knights and kings. Geoffrey of Monmouth recounts the story of King Brute, or Brutus, the exiled Trojan prince who, in legend, ruled Britain for a time. The war Brute waged against the Cornish giants was later to be translated into the exploits of Jack the Giant Killer. According to legend the giants, and in particular the Cornish giants, held out against the steady advance of Christianity for many years. The fearsome giant king of Cornwall - Cormoran, Lord of Saint Michael's Mount – is said to have controlled, well into the sixth and seventh centuries, large areas of the Cornish countryside. In other legends, Cormoran lived much earlier and was defeated and slain by King Brute who hurled his body into the sea. Yet other legends say that his body was given to Irish pirates and was eventually buried at a remote location in the north of Ireland.

Giants, Monsters and Fairies

Other Cornish giants lived much later than this, usually in coastal areas, reflecting the giants' long connection with the sea. These giants were depicted by later monkish texts as base creatures, both in habit and temperament. They were slow and dull-witted and were easily killed by the far more skilful men.

But in some parts of the Celtic world giants retained their reputation for wisdom, sagacity and, sometimes, cunning. Tales of Irish giants, for example, merged with heroic stories of great kings and leaders, transforming these leviathans, again, into 'mighty men of renown'. They righted wrongs, acted in the best interests of a fledgling humanity and, on occasion, outwitted their more dangerous and much more stupid counterparts in other areas of the Celtic world. The Irish Fionn MacCumhaill, often portrayed as one of a heroic band of warriors known as the Fianna (see **In Search of Ancient Heroes**) is often equated with the giant Finn McCool whose exploits litter the folklore of Ireland, particularly in the north of the country.

Impressive feats of engineering and architecture were attributed to giants and Finn, for example, is credited with building the spectacular Giant's Causeway on the north Antrim coast, amply demonstrating the ancient building skills of his titanic race.

The time of the giants was passing and they were relegated to the status of storybook creatures that continued to terrorise settled communities well into the early 13th century. One story told that they were the sons and daughters of Japheth, but might have been nothing more than the invention of antiquarians. These connections might have been deliberate concoctions, by Tudor scholars such as John Bale, to harmonise tradition with the Scriptures and to display the alleged evil of former paganism. Bale traced British and Irish giants from a non-Scriptural son of Japheth named Samothes and later writers such as Holinshed were to feature a gigantic Celtic race known as Samotheans which, despite the attempts of subsequent chroniclers, have no real basis in Celtic legend or folklore. Bale had been deceived by a faked ancient history of western Europe which was probably the work of the Italian Annius of Viterbo in 1498.

As the centuries passed, it is noticeable that, even without any historical reference, the giants appeared to grow in stature physically with each tale told. Geoffrey of Monmouth's Cornish giant, Gigmagog, was transformed in later texts, into two terrifying ogres: Gog and Magog. They threatened the town of Londinium – London – and were eventually defeated by King Vortigern. They were described as being approximately twelve cubits, some 18 feet, tall. Yet, in the same story, a single, average-sized mortal warrior is able to lift this giant and carry him on his shoulders, revealing something of an inconsistency. Another Cornish giant, Bolster, was reputed to be able to stand with one foot on Saint Agnes 'Beacon and the other on Carn Brea', just over six miles away. Great age was attributed to these gigantic creatures. Some were credited with living over six times as long as any mortal man while others were believed to be practically immortal. In some parts of the Celtic world, the epithet *Old* was frequently placed in front of their names to denote this longevity, for example Old Gall and Old Denbras.

Giants, Monsters and Fairies

The tradition of giants continued longest in the more northerly parts of the western Celtic world. Places like Cumbria, the Orkneys and Shetlands had a strong Norse influence and the Vikings' mythological and folklore traditions included giants. The preponderance of great single stones and curiously shaped geographical features in the landscape only added to these myths. Among such features to be found all over the counties and islands of the north are Giants' Graves, Giants' Chairs, Giants' Caves and Giants' Footprints, many of which have associations with early Celtic monuments and tumuli nearby.

A fearsome giant named Cubby Roo, who lived on the little isle of Wyre in the Orkneys, was believed to have been responsible for building the stacks and islets which characterise the northern seas and which he used as stepping stones for going to and from the mainland. As their numbers began to dwindle, and the human pop-

Early Christian theology portrayed giants as immoral, lewd, flesh-eating ravagers.

Chun castle and Quoit, Cornwall

ulation increased, so the giants appeared to withdraw from the world. They retreated into the remote and inaccessible places of the Celtic landscape such as isolated islands or cloudy mountaintops. Seen only infrequently, the tales of their exploits began to fade slowly from human minds. Some giants such as Finn McCool accepted the Christian faith and became anchorites or hermits, living well away from the centres of population. Finn is said to have ended his days on the remote Runkerry Peninsula in north Antrim.

THE GIANT'S CHILD

Scottish giant, Benandonner, terrified people along the Antrim coast in Ireland

In Ireland, giants were generally considered extremely shrewd and cunning. The following humorous story concerning the titan Finn McCool demonstrates this, although it retains the notion that all ogres outside Ireland are slow and easily duped.

Many years ago, a great Scottish giant named Benandonner, who lived on the Island of Staffa in the Hebrides, began to ravage the Antrim coastline in Ireland. Descended from old Norsemen, Benandonner was ferocious in his manners and animal-like in appearance, inspiring terror among the people of the coast. Unable to fight the monster, they approached Finn McCool another giant, who lived near the Giant's Causeway, to drive away the Scottish giant. Finn was a placid fellow who did not like too much fuss and, while he had no option but to agree to their request, he really did not want to fight the fearsome and aggressive Benandonner. He sought to find a way out of his dilemma and soon devised a cunning and unusual plan.

He made a great show of challenging the Scottish giant to come across to Antrim. Finn declared that he was so confident of beating him that he would allow Benandonner to choose whatever day suited him best for the contest. He then went off and bought some old tarpaulins that he instructed his wife to fashion into baby clothes to fit Finn himself.

Finn's challenge was one that Benandonner could not easily resist. He travelled quickly from Staffa, over the Giant's Causeway and came, striding, up to Finn's house, carrying a large and menacing-looking club over one shoulder. On entering, he found Finn's wife baking bread and beside her, in a gigantic crib, a monstrous infant whom he took to be Finn's son.

'Where's this Finn McCool who's challenged me to battle?' he thundered in a loud and booming voice. 'For I've come to give him a thrashing this day!' Finn's wife barely looked at him.

'Finn's away cutting turf on the mountain', she told the Scottish ogre. 'But he'll be back shortly. Why don't you sit down and have a cup of tea?'

All his roaring and plundering had made Benandonner extremely tired and thirsty and he was grateful for the rest. He sat down in a corner of the kitchen while Finn's wife continued baking. The child in the cradle gurgled at him.

'That's a bonny infant', remarked Benandonner. 'Even if he has a bit o' a beard about the chin. Is he like his father at all?' He asked this in order to get some measure of Finn before he fought with him.

'Och', she answered, 'He'll not be half the man his father is. He's a weak and sickly child'. At this, the infant threw a couple of massive rocks out of the cradle. 'There! He's dropped his toys. Could you lift them for him please?' Benandonner bent down but could hardly lift the rocks because they were so heavy. At the same time, the infant clubbed him over the head with a gigantic tree trunk.

'Stop that!' commanded Finn's wife sternly. 'If your daddy was here, he'd soon take that sapling off you and break it across your back for treating our guest in such a fashion'. The infant looked suitably cowed.

'Here!' Finn's wife lifted a wheaten bannock from the fire. 'Eat this and behave yourself!' She handed the bannock still on the griddle to the child. In an instant, he had bitten through the bannock and the iron griddle, and was munching contentedly. Finn's wife sighed in exasperation.

'That's the third griddle you've destroyed this week!' she said. 'Still, there's no harm, for you'll need to be built up if you're to become anything like your father!' At this, Benandonner could stand no more. If the infant played with boulders, waved a giant tree-trunk as if it were a mere sapling, bit through an iron griddle with ease and was supposed by his mother to be weak and sickly, what must the father be like?

Hurriedly excusing himself, Benandonner fled from the house and back across the Causeway to Staffa, never to torment the people on the coast of Antrim again.

The child in the cradle had, of course, been none other than Finn McCool in disguise.

Giant's Causeway, County Antrim

The legends of giants, even localised ones, began to dwindle and take on new and less bestial aspects. Today, they form the core of several fairy stories, many of which date from Victorian times. These giants appear as monstrous oafs or flesh-eating monsters outwitted by some clever tailor, serving man or peasant. They also feature as the playthings of young human children.

This tradition does the giant race a great disservice. They are the race memory of a prehistoric time when great men probably did walk the earth. More importantly, in the mighty stature of the giant we have a dim and distorted portrayal of our own early beginnings. In the monstrous face of the titan, we find what is perhaps one of the last vestiges of our rich and varied pagan heritage.

Monsters

Monsters in Celtic folklore are of two distinct forms. The first type seems to be a race memory. Actual and fearsome creatures, great serpents, bears, wild pigs, etc., might well have existed and lingered on in the memory. These traditions formed the basis of folk stories concerning dragons, monstrous boars and shaggy, half-human beings that appear in many of the great Celtic Myth Cycles and hearthside tales alike.

Viking rune stone from Gotland, seventh century

The second was of the purely supernatural kind and might have retained some of the awe and mystery that surrounded many of the ancient Celtic gods. They were an extension of great heroic stories related by the earliest Celts. Some of the creatures that feature in these tales are instantly recognisable, gigantic horses, fearful wolves and murderous stags. Other strange and ill-defined entities, were hybrids of humans and animals. Such intermingling gave them a particularly feral aspect and rendered them incredibly dangerous. This, in turn reflected one of the characteristics contained within the Celtic perception of the supernatural: the lack of rigid boundaries between human and animal forms.

As with the giants, many of these monstrous creatures were depicted by the Church as the final remnants of a dark and pagan past which had to be conquered by the light

Finn McCool and the heroic warriors of the Fianna

Ring of Brodgar, Orkney

of Christianity. Stories were concocted or amended by early writers, in order to demonstrate the ultimate defeat of these terrible creatures by ancient, though not necessarily Christian, champions.

Vernacular lore in Ireland and Wales is filled with many curious hybrid monstrosities: three headed beings, monstrous ram-horned snakes – Saxon 'Wyrrms', giving us our word *worm*. There were woodland creatures: part human part goat; men with horns or antlers; enormous wolves and boars; gigantic feral men and so on. As humankind spread into and mastered their world, these monsters are confronted, and defeated, by its heroes. These tales are a symbol of the triumph of the human race over the natural world. The most curious of all monsters is the so-called Tarasque depicted by a strange sculpture in Noves (Bouches-du-Rhone). It appears to be a ravening wolf or lion with a dismembered human limb hanging from its jaws. Underneath the extended claws of its front paws, are two bearded, severed human heads. The sculpture is thought to date from the fourth or third centuries BC and might simply be a representation of death, claiming human lives. Folklore of the area tells a slightly different story. The Tarasque has its roots in a legend, undoubtedly Celtic in origin, concerning a fearsome monster that clambered out of the Rhone at Tarascon and ravaged throughout Provence devouring the inhabitants. In desperation, the local people approached Saint Martha, who dwelt at Les-Saintes-Maries-de-la-Mer, and asked her to rid them of the beast. She did so by making the sign of the Cross and the creature is believed to have returned to the Rhône where it is still confined by the power of the saint. Perhaps the Tarasque is just a symbol of the paganism that had once ensnared humankind but has now been banished by Christianity.

Similar in nature to the Tarasque is the Linsdorf monster from Alsace. This is another curious representation – the gigantic stone figure of a beast, perhaps a wolf, with its forepaw resting on a human head. Its jaws are empty and gaping, revealing awful pointed teeth and it has rolling eyes and a great, lolling tongue. The sculpture appears to date from a slightly later period than the Tarasque and doubts have been cast on its supposed Celtic origin; it certainly has something of Roman funerary symbolism about it. In Rome, icons of wild beasts were sometimes used to demonstrate the eventual fate of the dead suggesting, for example, that they would be devoured by Otherworld animals or demons.

Sometimes, in Romano-Celtic symbolism, gods and beasts were juxtaposed as can be seen in the imagery on some of the columns set up along the Rhine which are probably in honour of the Celtic sky-god combined with the Roman god Jupiter. The images show a mounted warrior trampling down a monstrous, rearing, vaguely anthropomorphic serpent-type being. In fact, only the legs of this entity are snakes but the whole body bears a serpentine aspect. While the columns and supporting plinths are Classical Mediterranean in origin, the iconography is purely Celtic. Nowhere in the Classical world does Jupiter appear as a horseman and the monster that he is in the process of defeating is certainly a Celtic hybrid creature.

Giants, Monsters and Fairies

Hybrids were not the only form of monster for the Celts. Familiar creatures often took on gigantic proportions, coupled with supernatural aspects and abilities. There are tales in vernacular lore of a monstrous horse. This creature appears quite frequently in both Scottish and Manx folktales. In Scotland, it is widely known as the Kelpie or Each-Uisce – water-horse, dwelling in rivers and lakes, and is regarded as either extremely ferocious or incredibly cunning and sly. It seeks either to capture or lure men to its under - water lair where it devours them. It and the remote rivers and lochs in which it is said to dwell are to be completely avoided. In Manx it is known as the Cabyll-Ushtey, a monster which in many respects parallels its Scottish counterpart except that it is said to be uniformly grey in colour and to have the power of speech.

Another beast that assumed monstrous proportions in the Celtic mind was the boar. This is easy to understand since boars were widely hunted and were considered very dangerous and exceptionally wily and were credited, in the popular mind, with wonderful and miraculous powers. Obviously, boars that got away from the hunter were able to do so only because of their supernatural powers. Boars frequently featured in Celtic legend, evil kings would take the form of a boar, reverting to human likeness only when the boar-shape had been killed. Celtic heroes were lured into the Otherworld while pursuing large boars, later revealed as fairy creatures in disguise. There were tribal totems, or protective gods, in the image of boars (see **Spirits of**

A dim-witted giant is fooled by a valiant tailor who pretends to crush a stone.

Earth and Air) and the animal might have developed its supernatural reputation from its totem persona.

In some legends animal merged with giant to create an awful hybrid of titanic proportions that usually threatened the questing hero or guarded great treasure. In the Irish mythological tale of Diarmaid and Gráinne, the hero Diarmaid, while fleeing from Gráinne's aged lover, Fionn, had to fight a one-eyed giant named Searbhán – Surly. This monster, with boar-like tusks and scaled skin, was the guardian of an enchanted tree in the forest of Dubhnos. Initially, Diarmaid had befriended the ogre but, when Gráinne asked if she could eat the fruit of the tree, Searbhán became enraged and attacked his former friend. Diarmaid was eventually compelled to kill the giant in order to escape. Biblical imagery in this tale is obvious, the tree represents the Tree of Knowledge in the Garden of Eden from which the woman wishes

SAINT AGNES AND THE GIANT

Nowhere was the stupidity and lewdness of the general giant race more clearly illustrated than in the Christian fable of the beautiful and holy Saint Agnes and the lustful Cornish ogre, Bolster. The story was frequently used to demonstrate the triumph of Christian virtue over the forces of darkness and paganism, portrayed by Bolster.

The giant dwelt at Carn Brea in Cornwall and was a greatly feared tyrant in all the villages around. Although married to an old and ugly giantess, Bolster had an eye for every pretty, young woman in the vicinity and lost no opportunity in making unwelcome advances. In his twilight years, he became infatuated with the beautiful Saint Agnes, a religious recluse who lived just six miles from his home.

The saint was as virtuous as she was beautiful and resisted all Bolster's advances,

Saint Agnes

Excited by the thought of having the beautiful saint as his own, Bolster readily agreed. Saint Agnes, however, was wily and had no intention of living with the monstrous, vulgar creature but simply wanted to be rid of him. She took him to a large cleft in the rock, just above the raging ocean and told him that if he could fill the hole with his blood, she would be his forever. In lustful anticipation, Bolster hacked at his wrist and allowed the resulting gore to fall into the hole. The stupid giant did not realise that the hole fed directly into the sea; the blood washed away as quickly as it fell and there was no way he could grant the saint's request. With most of his lifeblood shed into the rocky crevice, sorely weakened he fell to the ground before the saint, still professing his love – or rather his lust. Saint Agnes proved as unyielding as ever. At last, even Bolster's

explaining that she had chosen a holy and celibate life. Bolster would not take 'no' for an answer. He persisted in his courtship, making many lewd suggestions of a personal nature, in the vain hope that the saintly woman would succumb.

At last, when Saint Agnes could no longer tolerate his behaviour, she agreed to go and live with him if he would do but one small thing for her. As a token of his love and undying trust in her, he would have to shed a small portion of his blood.

heart stopped and the evil giant of Carn Brea fell dead at the feet of the very woman he had tried to win.

A variant of a number of stories of mortal wit against immortal stupidity, usually it is a male saint who outwits a dull-witted ogre. The saintly Christian hero was later replaced by the clever tailor or peasant, as in such well-known children's tales as 'Jack the Giant Killer' and 'The Brave Little Tailor'.

to eat. Although the story is thought to have come from much earlier sources, its developed form probably dates from around the medieval period when, largely due to Christian thinking, the ogre often became equated with the Devil.

Other gigantic but distinctly monstrous figures – usually boasting only one eye – appear in both Irish and Welsh folklore. They include Pencawr, the flesh-eating cyclops in the tale of Culhwch and Olwen and Balor of the Evil Eye who dwelt on Tory Island off the Donegal coastline. Both of these awful titans had distinctly feral natures and were eventually defeated by enterprising heroes.

On the Isle of Man, the image of the feral animal is combined with those of the giant and the dead corpse to create the Buggane. This was a fearsome creature, with eyes as big as saucers, living underground and connected with some of the ruined churches scattered across the island. The writer Sabine Baring Gould suggests that the name is of Scandinavian or Central European origin. In some East European languages, the word 'bog' is another term for 'god' and buggane might mean 'little' or 'lesser deity'. He traces the first use of the word to the Vikings' occupation of Man following the Battle of Clontarf in Ireland in 1014. This would seem to suggest that they were localised gods transformed into hideous monsters. Such transformation might have been the result of the gradual Christianisation of the Island.

Celtic Mythology

Across the generations, the legends of some monsters faded while others were incorporated into medieval literature via the great Bestiaries of the Middle Ages. Many of these creatures, while maintaining the combination of human and animal, were often so outrageous that their existence was immediately suspect, even in an age of superstition. Nevertheless, the thought of the ravening monster often disturbs even the modern mind and, from time to time, we are all slightly afraid of what might be hiding in the darkness beyond the glow of the farthest light. The idea of the monster lurking just beyond our knowing might not be all that far away.

Fairies

In folklore, fairies are usually described as an Otherworld race who inhabit the countryside along with, but usually invisible to, human beings. Fairy lore might have its basis in notions of unseen spirits residing in geological features, and of the dead lying in their burial chambers.

Fairies often formed a kind of spiritual community different in nature from that of humans'. Various names have been given to them: the Tuatha Dé Danann – the people or children of the goddess Danu – in Ireland; the Tylwyth Teg – Fair Folk – in Wales; the Pobel Vean – Little People – in Cornwall; and Duine or Daoine Sith – the Folk of the Mounds or Barrows not, as is sometimes translated, the People of Peace – in Highland Scotland. Even within these specified groupings, there were other types of fairy – for example, spriggans, 'Peghts' - Pechts, and Piskeys. These names have less to do with the Otherworld than with the aboriginal communities whose cunning was probably their only weapon against the Celtic invaders, earning them a reputation for magic and wonder-working.

All over the Celtic countryside are traces of this earlier occupation: the so-called fairy forts and raths of Ireland; the Pesky's Halls of Cornwall; the Pixies Crows of Cornish-Breton tradition, which comes from the Breton 'Krao' meaning a shed or a hovel; and the Pecht's Houses of Scotland. Probably, these were earthworks abandoned by the aborigines and taken over by the Celts. Later generations associated them with the fairies, and credited them with magical powers. There were entrances to the Otherworld; they were the places where the fairy monarchs held court or centres where the fairy-folk danced and made merry. Humans were not welcome and few strayed close after nightfall. The connection of fairies with ancient tumuli strengthened, in the popular mind, the links between the Good People and former gods and/or spirits. The sacred groves where ancient druids had performed their rites also became fairy places (see **Shrines and Sacred Sites**), probably because they were already associated with mysterious and magical beings.

Fairies would often bestow social prestige, even kingship, on those to whom they felt friendly. Legends tell how poets and musicians received both inspiration and tunes and how others received magical powers of curing and prophecy.

Giants, Monsters and Fairies

In many of the more ancient tales, fairies were not depicted as being very different in size or appearance from ordinary mortals, as the Otherworld was generally considered to be just an extension of the mortal sphere of existence (see **The Otherworld**). The idea of the tiny fairy is thought to have been an invention of the medieval Church which wished to discredit the worship of pagan gods which it viewed as the origins of fairy belief . Fairies also engaged in mundane pursuits, they attended fairs and markets, though incognito, in order to buy and sell stock and could appear at will to seek the loan of a tool from a mortal farmer or his wife. They played games such as football and hurling and, in Scotland, there are numerous references to games of shinty between rival troops of fairies. Their tastes reflected those of the human world; they danced and played music and this Fairy music, usually heard at night, was said to be exceedingly beautiful and the fairies expert musicians. They were fond of strong drink and of human food, both of which they consumed with gusto. However, a mortal who partook of food prepared by the fairies should beware as he could be trapped in fairyland for 7 to 100 years.

At some stage, fairies came to be associated closely with the dead. Several of the fairy tales in both Ireland and Scotland seem to be little more than an extension of old lore concerning the Celtic cult of the dead. For example, it was said that in the period between Hallowe'en and Christmas, fairies conducted 'phantom funerals' where they escorted those who had died within the past year to the Gates of Heaven. Having no souls, they could not enter Heaven and so they were vicious and spiteful towards the Children of Adam, for whom Christ had died. In Wales and Cornwall, the appearance of a fairy was commonly described as an apparition, similar to that of a ghost or spectre. In many stories, fairies were given charge over the dead, and suicides and the unbaptised automatically became their property.

Many legends tell of fairies frequently being outwitted by early saints. In one of the most famous tales from Ireland, the holy Saint Patrick struck a deal with the Good People that they should inhabit all the lands that the sun does not touch while mortals should have the rest. He made this deal on a cloudy, gloomy day. The fairies readily agreed to the bargain, only to find that they had been cheated. As soon as the sun came out, they were confined to the gloomy glens and shadowy hollows of the world, some even had to dwell under the earth. Their fury knew no bounds.

This hostile aspect of the fairies included their supposed propensity to fire tiny darts at humans, fine cattle or sturdy horses causing them to pine away and so belong to the fairy nation. They created all manner of mischief about the local houses – overturning milk pails, pulling burning coals from the fire and breaking crockery on the sideboard when no one was looking. Milk, food and strong drink had to be covered

BALOR OF THE EVIL EYE

Balor – or Balar – is something between a giant and a monster.

In classical Irish literature, he is described as a heartless tyrant who dwelt on an offshore island – usually Tory Island off the coast of Donegal. He is often given the sobriquet *Bailchbhéimneach*, which means 'strong-smiting', denoting his ferocious, warrior status.

Originally, the name seems to have meant 'the flashing one' and may have been rendered as *Boleros* in the ancient Celtic tongue. A number of Classical writers, Ptolemy among them, make reference to a cult in the southern part of England that may have worshipped him as a warrior god and to a promontory in Cornwall, known as Bolerion, the preserve of a deity of the same name. This place was probably Land's End, although several other sites may be considered.

In very ancient Irish mythology, Balor is closely associated with a mysterious deity known as Nét. He is described as being an 'offspring of Nét' and his name may well be another title for the Nét-deity himself. Nét seems to be closely associated with promontories and rocky outcroppings and he may have been a sea-deity. Balor is said to have met his death at a site named Cairn Uí Néit – The Cairn of Nét's Child – Mizen Head in County Cork.

Also associated with Nét is the setting sun. Many of the promontories with which the shadowy deity is connected are in the west where the sun sets and this would coincide with the image of Balor as piercing-eyed that is having eyes that shot out rays like the setting sun. This was later translated into a single eye that could shoot out something like a death-ray to destroy the hosts of his enemies. In ancient literature, this eye is often described as 'spreading poison' among his foes.

Balor usually appears in stories with the Celtic god Lúgh, the Lord of Light. Balor's daughter seems to have given birth to Lúgh's child very much against her father's wishes and

the birth was considered a great scandal. Balor, described in medieval texts as the leader of the Fomhóire, a scavenging, pirate race, is very different from the divine and mystical Tuatha Dé Danann of whom Lúgh is a part. It had been prophesied that Balor would be killed by his own grandson and the ogre wished to avoid this fate at all costs.

A confrontation occuring between Balor and his grandson – the personification of Lúgh himself – during the second Battle of Moytirra contains echoes of the Old Testament clash between David and Goliath.

It was 12th-century Christian monks, after all, who wrote down this account. Instead of the slingshot, however, Balor's grandson threw a javelin that blinded his terrible grandfather by driving out his single eye. Once deprived of his most terrifying power, Balor was easily killed and beheaded. Some versions of the tale have Lúgh then placing Balor's head over his own and using the poisonous eye himself. Other variants have the head being placed on a rock by the seashore to be pounded to pieces by the ocean. This affirms the idea that Balor, in a Nét-incarnation, might be a sea-deity who eventually returned to the deep.

Although Balor is said to have had several strongholds around the coastline of Britain and Ireland, he is most closely associated with Tory Island. From here, the rays of his evil eye were said to decimate the Donegal coastline if the people there refused to pay him tribute.

Balor has a number of counterparts across the Celtic world. His Irish story parallels the story of the Welsh titan Yspadaddan Pencawr who appears in the story of Culhwch and Olwen (see **In Search of Ancient Heroes**).

He may even be a remnant of the contact between Mediterranean and Celtic mythologies and he retains more than an echo of the Greek Cyclops, Polyphemus.

else fairies were sure to make off with it. The colour red was believed to repel them so red ribbons or pieces of cloth of a red or reddish colour were considered effective protection against their wiles. Various religious amulets and certain types of wood were also considered effective and the rowan, or mountain ash, was supposed to be an effective talisman against witches, fairies and the night-walking dead.

With Christianity, came new ideas on the origins of the fairy race. No longer were they an ancient pagan community inhabiting a nebulous Otherworld; they were fallen angels. During Lucifer's attempt to usurp God, said the Church, some angels had taken neither side. When Lucifer had been defeated and cast into hell, God had to consider the fate of these demurrers. They were not good enough to be accepted back into heaven nor wicked enough to be consigned to hell. In the end, Saint Michael interceded on their behalf and suggested that they be condemned to the world of mortals to live as a kind of 'second class citizen' which, he argued, was punishment enough. God concurred and the angels were doomed to live on earth, inferior in status to humankind, for whom His Son had died. Consequently, Saint Michael became the patron saint of fairies and the great enmity between men and fairies developed. Having once enjoyed a position vastly superior to mankind the fallen angels resented their subsequent inferiority. The tale brought much of fairy lore within the jurisdiction of the Church and provided a Christian explanation for fairy origins. It also tangentially linked them with the Devil and in many of the later tales, fairies are sometimes regarded as the servants of the Evil One. Contact with them was to be avoided at all costs and it was unwise even to answer a direct question from a fairy, as this would invariably place the mortal under fairy power.

Celtic Mythology

As the notions of an older race and fallen angels became more confused in the popular mind, children, especially unbaptised ones, were considered especially vulnerable. Fairy women it was said, found it extremely hard to give birth; they were frail creatures and their bodies were not as suited to birthing as those of their human counterparts. Their offspring, therefore, were usually small, stunted and deformed creatures that rapidly became outcasts in the rather glamorous fairy world. In order to replace these misfits, the fairies would spirit away human children to the Otherworld. Over baptised infants, they had no power, but all others could be claimed. The shrivelled, complaining fairy child was left in place of the kidnapped human baby and was known as a changeling. Few changelings ever survived into their teenage years in the mortal world. It is fair to assume that the notion of changelings served to explain sudden disease and deterioration among children in areas in which infections such as tuberculosis were rife. As a normal, healthy child began, inexplicably to fade away, becoming a whinging and complaining creature, the supernatural explanation of the changeling was invoked. In the absence of a proper medical diagnosis, when the child eventually died, this explanation often gave the grieving parents a modicum of comfort. After all, it was not their child who had expired - he or she was still alive and with the fairies. Changelings were to be greatly feared as they had magic about them that would draw the luck, namely the goodness, well being and prosperity, from a home.

It was therefore prudent to have children baptised as soon as possible. Immediate baptism was not always easy in remote rural areas so, until the priest arrived, the child would have a crucifix or holy medal placed above its crib to keep malignant fairies at bay. Another protective device was to throw some item of the mortal father's clothing, such as a coat, over the child while it slept to remind the fairies just whose child it was. Human urine was believed to have both magical and curative properties and to be an infallible defence against supernatural creatures and their attendant ills. So, another way to defend a baby against the fairy kind was to sprinkle urine around its crib.

The notion of difficult fairy births appears in stories from all over the Celtic world concerning local midwives or 'handy women'. Many stories follow exactly the same format and address very similar themes. A man whom she does not recognise calls out a local midwife at night. He takes her some distance to a house or cottage where a woman is enduring a difficult birth. The midwife assists in the delivery of a small, scrawny creature, then is returned home rewarded with some money for her trouble. Unfortunately, this later turns to acorns, leaves or horse-manure as soon as the fairy

CAER SIDHE

Within differing folklore there seems to have been a common need to know the source of the fairy-kind. The notion of Caer Sidhe – or Sidi or Shee, depending on the local variants – fulfilled that need. The name was taken to mean The City of the Fairies and the idea appears to have been a predominantly Welsh one – the historian and folklorist, Professor John Rhys, even described it as part of *Annwn*, the Welsh Otherworld.

The Emperor of all the fairies and his wife were said to dwell in Caer Sidhe. All communities of fairies, dwelling in the forts and raths that were scattered across the Celtic lands, paid homage and swore loyalty to him. In many ways, the Fairy Emperor paralleled the Celtic ruler, demanding loyalty and honour from his sub-kings and queens. There were similarities too between the fairy-city and the early Christian church. In the centre of Caer Sidhe burned a great fire that lit the entire city and consequently was never to be allowed to go out. This echoed the eternal flame that burned on many altars of the early Celtic churches, a flame that, too, must never be quenched.

The idea of Caer Sidhe appears in the work of the noted Scottish folklorist and mythologist Lewis Spence (1874–1955). Like Rhys, Spence described it as the principal city of the Celtic fairies and noted that four massive organs were supposed to play around its central fire. 'This instrument', he goes on, 'has a long association with mysteries, from those of Byzantium to the present day, as in Masonry' (See: Spence , *Celtic Britain*). Thus, the fair-city became a dark and mysterious realm, closely connected with ancient wisdom and ritual.

There also seems to be some association between Caer Sidhe and the dead. Again, taking his lead from Professor Rhys, Spence described it as being part of 'the dreary land of *Annwn*' – a description of the unchanging realm, or Otherworld, beyond

death. Again, he refers to it as 'a gloomy world of Death' into which the rays of the health-giving sun cannot penetrate. *Annwn* was frequently regarded as being far underground and certainly had connections with the dead, so it is possible to find the fairy-city populated, in part at least, with ancestral spirits.

A similarly centralised fairyland features in Irish folklore. This is Cruachmaa, a solitary hill in County Galway, under which the fairies were said to have their kingdom. The notion appears most frequently in Lady Gregory's *Visions and Beliefs in the West of Ireland*, written at the end of the last century, and was taken up by a number of the Irish writers and poets who formed her circle. It was to Cruachmaa that those whom the fairies had carried off from the Galway area were usually taken. Normally they were held in Cruachmaa for a period not exceeding seven years, when they were abruptly returned to the mortal world. The notion of being so carried off was used to explain medical conditions as lapses of memory and severe depressive or delusional mental states. Lady Gregory herself referred to the sister and the housekeeper of the priest at Kilcloud who was taken by the fairies to Cruachmaa.

Her body remained in the Parochial House but her wits, or soul, appeared to be gone. She would sit in the corner of the kitchen on a rush mat and if anyone came near her or asked how she was, would moan like an animal and cover her face with a bit of a blanket. After seven years, however, she suddenly 'came to herself', got up and went about her duties, just as she had done before.

Nowadays, we would simply ascribe her behaviour to a mental aberration but to country people in that period, her behaviour was regarded as incontrovertible evidence that she had been with the fairies in Cruachmaa.

THE BREWERY OF EGGSHELLS

Changelings were feared in many Celtic lands. They were believed to be stunted, irritable fairy-children abandoned by their parents and left in exchange for a healthy, happy mortal child. Alternatively, changelings were old, sickly, bad-tempered fairies whose nasty and spiteful ways had caused them to be driven from the Otherworld and exchanged for a human baby.

They cried and complained, and their presence in a house could drain the luck from a family. It was usually unclear whether or not the child in the crib was in fact a changeling or whether it was the baby of the family fallen into some illness. Changelings were fond of music and often very musical themselves. One of the ways in which the fairy could betray herself was if he was discovered playing a musical instrument. So great was their love of music, it was believed, that no changeling could leave an instrument alone.

Stories from the Isle of Man tell of a changeling, who lived near Peel, who was tricked into revealing himself by a cunning cobbler who was also a musician. Once exposed for what he was the changeling had to quit the house and the fairies were compelled to return the mortal infant.

The changeling could also be unmasked if he was tricked into revealing its age. Changelings were older than mortals: by admitting to great age they confirmed their supernatural origins, and therefore had to flee. This trick was not easily achieved for the changelings were clever characters, unwilling to give up the comfort of a family home for a cold and friendless life in the Otherworld.

There was once a woman living near Malin who suspected that her infant child might be a changeling. Since birth, he had been a jolly, happy baby but in recent times he had become very pinched and wizened and was continually crying in the cradle. Nothing pleased him. The woman also noticed that since this change had come about, there had been no luck in the house. A number of beasts that her husband had planned to take to the market in Donegal town became suddenly ill and died. Crops failed and bills seemed to increase to such an extent that she never had any money 'between her hands'. She blamed the strange, squalling infant in the crib for everything. She believed he was a changeling. Yet she could not be sure, he might be her own, dear child, in the grip of some illness.

A Changeling was a fairy child who replaced a human child.

She went to see Grey Ellen, a local wise-woman who lived in the Malin Glen. She explained her problem to the wise-woman who considered it thoughtfully.

'You must trick it into revealing its true age' said Grey Ellen slowly. 'But be warned. Such creatures are usually very tricky and it may guess what you are up to and you'll be stuck with it until you die'.

Grey Ellen gave her a plan and the woman went home a little more content. Later that evening, when she was in the kitchen with the infant, she stoked the fire up and placed a large pot of water above it. Soon it was boiling and hissing and the lid of the pot was rattling loudly. When the liquid was seething, the woman went out and came back with a dozen freshly laid eggs. She broke them into a crockery bowl beside the fire, the infant in the cradle watching her with a queer, sharp stare.

Lifting the bowl into which the eggs had been cracked, the woman went over to the door and threw the egg-meat out. She then came back and dropped the eggshells one by one into the boiling water. The infant watched her intently. The woman stirred the eggshells with a wooden spoon. At last, curiosity got the better of the strange child.

'What are you doing Mammy?' he asked in a creaky, old voice. A cold sweat broke on the woman's brow for she knew that her own child could not have spoken and that this was indeed a changeling.

'I'm brewing, a mhic (my son)' she replied.

For a moment there was silence, then the changeling asked: 'And what are you brewing Mammy?' it asked.

The woman swallowed hard for she had a great fear of the fairies.

'I'm brewing up eggshells, a mhic', she answered.

'Oh!' cried the imp, clapping its withered hands in glee. 'Four hundred years have I lived in the world and I've never heard anything quite so ridiculous as a brewery of eggshells!'

He realised that he had revealed his true age. The woman turned on it and said savagely:

' I know you for a changeling. Get away from here before I call the priest and give me back my own child!'

In an instant, the changeling was gone and when she looked again, it was her own dear child asleep in the cradle.

influence has departed. In some stories, the eyes of the midwife are anointed with an ointment so that she can actually see the fairy world and the house or hall to which she had been taken invariably turns out to be a rath or tumulus.

Fairy-tale depiction of two oriental travellers mocking sluggish giant in the desert

Fairies travelled, it was said, much quicker than the wind; indeed, they often travelled in the wind. The strange little windstorms or whirlwinds which sometimes affected parts of Ireland and Scotland were often referred to as fairy winds and were believed to be vehicles by which the fairy people carried off unsuspecting mortals to its own realm. In the Western Isles of Scotland, these phenomena were known as *The Sluagh* or The Host of the Air, a band of fairies who travelled from island to island in order to carry off livestock and the odd, unsuspecting person. Such winds were sometimes seen about lonely graveyards where there had been a recent burial and it was believed that the *Sluagh* carried off corpses to turn into a living-dead servant which would then prey upon the living. The belief was widespread, and a practice of smashing funeral biers following internment, to prevent corpses from being used by the fairies, was common in Munster and on the Outer Hebrides. In Ireland, the whirlwinds which beset graveyards were known as the *slua* sí or *sí gaoithe* which literally means 'a thrust of wind' although the word sí was usually taken for *sidhe*, meaning fairy. It was the Christian duty of any passer-by who saw such a wind to say: 'God Bless You'.

AWAY WITH THE FAIRIES

In many tales from Celtic folklore, there are instances of people being carried away to the fairy realm for a number of years before being returned. Time passed at a very different rate in the Otherworld from that of the mortal sphere and what seemed like a night in the fairy kingdom might have been more than a hundred years in the human world. This temporal misalignment forms the basis of many stories.

Humans were carried off to be servants or to carry out deeds that the fairies themselves could not manage. In the Western Isles, human shepherds were often carried off to fire 'fairy darts' at enemies or at livestock. Those who had been hit by a fairy bolt would soon die and, as it was widely believed that God had forbidden the fairies to cause death in the mortal world, the Good People whisked away unsuspecting mortals and made them fire the deadly darts instead.

Usually the fairy host travelled in a great windstorm known as the *Sluagh* or 'the Host of the Air' and wrought great havoc on the countryside. They were known to flatten crops with their dancing and merriment and often frightened livestock so badly, that cows would not give milk nor would hens lay on the following morning. Thus were the frequent, tiny whirlwinds in the countryside explained.

Many of those carried away were forced to work for the fairy throng. A man who was lifted by the *Sluagh* on Barra was carried off to Skye where he was forced to work as a blacksmith, shoeing fairy horses, every night for seven years. In ancient times, a number of Skye people saw him working in an abandoned forge, while even more heard the sound of his hammer across the island as dusk began to fall.

Answering a direct question from a fairy would put an individual in peril of being carried off. People were afraid to speak to them for fear of what might happen. An Irish tale, related by the great County Tyrone storyteller, folklorist and historian, George Barnett, makes this point quite well:

'My mother's people came from a place called Lavey in County Derry and there was a girl who lived quite close to them who had had a meeting with the fairies. They'd tried to take her away with them. My mother said that she was always a very sickly person after that meeting although, before it, she had been a big, strapping child. How it came about was like this.

It was her custom to go with her sister to the woods near her house every evening to bring in the cattle for milking. That evening, her sister had gone a little way ahead of her and she was coming along across the open field towards the wood. She had got about halfway across the field when a fairy stepped out from behind a tree and said:

"Would ye like a tune on the fiddle?" And he had a fiddle cocked at the base of his neck. The girl knew right well that if she answered him, she would be in his power forever, so she walked on.

She had almost reached the edge of the woods when a fairy stepped out form behind a bush and said:

"Would ye like a tune on the fife?" Although she was badly terrified and the sweat was standing in beads on her forehead, she walked on to the very edge of the woods and as she did so, a fairy stepped out from behind a big standing stone and said:

"Would ye like a tune on the bodhrán?" She then fainted. Her sister, who saw what had happened, ran back and carried her home. She lay in a brain fever for three days before she came to herself again. But she was never the same after that experience. She became strange and dreamy and kept to her bed for most of the time. It was the fairy influence on her, don't you see? My mother never really told what became of her but I think that in the end she went to America. It's as well to have nothing to do with the fairy-kind'.

The mention of the Holy Name would disperse the fairy power, cause the wind to fail and release the person or animal that they had carried away.

Solitary trees or bushes were often closely associated with fairies, particularly in Ireland. Great misfortune would befall anyone cutting them down. Similarly, those who moved cairns or standing stones did so at their own risk. Fairy vengeance could come in many forms - ill luck or physical misfortune such as a severe accident; serious illness or madness, bankruptcy and even death.

The most often quoted example comes from Ireland in the 1970s and concerns the famous car manufacturer John de Lorean. When the de Lorean manufacturing plant was built in Dunmurray, on the outskirts of Belfast, a fairy thorn tree was removed during the land clearance. Local sages prophesied that the new car-plant would enjoy no success. By the 1980s it was bankrupt and this was widely ascribed, not to bad management or fluctuations in world car markets, but to the intervention of outraged fairies. Surely, a warning for investors not to get involved with fairy trees!
Fairies were also incredibly fastidious and extremely clean in their habits. They would not tolerate sloth or dirt about a house and would invariably punish the woman or man who did not keep a clean parlour. Of course, this was a means of ensuring good housekeeping among the community. Cattle left out in the fields at night would immediately become fairy property - a warning to all farmers to attend to their tasks before dusk.

Giants, Monsters and Fairies

The notion of fairies, is more complex than the sanitised version suggested in more Victorian fairy stories. Fairies might have been the race-memory of an aboriginal community displaced by the Celts. They were intertwined with Christian mythology, which portrayed them as angels and, latterly, they served to establish orthodox values of good housekeeping and husbandry in largely isolated and rural communities. Far from being the small, friendly creatures of Walt Disney and others, they were objects of fear and awe throughout the countryside. In the notion of fairies, we see the last vestiges of the primal Celtic worship. They are, in effect, the old gods in a different guise.

THE LAND BENEATH THE WAVES

Silkies, Seafolk and Submerged Kingdoms

Celtic Mythology

If the Celts found the early landscape awe-inspiring, they found the ocean even more so. Storms and gales, while terrifying on solid ground, were even more spectacular at sea. Although not essentially a sea-faring people, like every other ancient race they began to equate the changes in the mood of the ocean – the tides, the calms, the sudden squalls – with those of sea gods or sea beings.

Sea deities do not play a significant part in early Celtic mythology but, as they became settled in coastal areas, beliefs, customs and entities connected with the ocean started to appear in Celtic folklore. Although the very early Celts were not famous sailors, they must have done some to reach the west. These journeys would have added to their lore and in later centuries, the monks who set forth into uncharted waters on voyages of evangelism and discovery added more. The annals of Saint Brendan display a wealth of fantastic and often imaginative stories regarding his early voyages and there is little doubt that other monk/explorers detailed similar experiences. For a people who did not travel far by sea, such tales must have seemed like fantastic adventures, almost akin to tales of space travel in the 1950s. To many minds, the ocean was a doorway to the Otherworld.

Some of the aquatic deities that dwelt in the ocean were no more than extensions of the spirits that dwelt in lakes and rivers (see **Spirits of Earth and Air**). These had probably grown in power and fearsome aspect to rule the movements of the ocean. Water, in the ancient world, was considered a regenerative force – healing and cleansing went hand in hand in the ancient mind – and the gods of the sea were credited with immense supernatural powers extending far beyond the mere confines of the ocean into the sky itself. The sight of storms along the horizon would have been reason to link one deity with sea and sky. We have already seen how worshippers threw offerings into lakes and rivers to placate the spirits of the waters. The same would have happened at the seacoast where the offerings were probably washed away by the outgoing tides so that no traces of them remain.

Ancient Celts were puzzled by the bodies of sea-creatures such as great squids, porpoises, even whales, which were, from time to time, washed up along their beaches.

They must have seemed like creatures from another realm, possibly the realm of the gods. Along northern coasts, was the conundrum of large seal populations that clustered around the rocks close to the shore and what their relation was to the sea out of which they came. One answer was that seals were the inhabitants of a submerged kingdom who took animal form while on land. In Celtic eyes, the sea continued to remain a realm of mystery and wonder which formed a peripheral but nonetheless significant part of their mythology and folklore.

The Celtic Sea Gods

There is a problem when considering Celtic sea and water deities, as they are not all instantly recognisable as aquatic divinities. Often their connection with the ocean is coupled with another - such as healing. Among the Classical cultures, Neptune or Poseidon is evidently monarch of the ocean but in Celtic iconography, such status may be disguised or sublimated. This makes identification difficult. Also, of course, an entity might have been a sea-deity in one location but not in another. Then there is the problem posed by gods who might not live in the sea but just have power over it which probably reflected the Celts' more land-based traditions.

The main Irish sea god whom we can confidently classify as such is Lir. He is described by the 12th-century *Book of Invasions*, as being one of the mystical Tuatha Dé Danann who were finally defeated by the Sons of Mil – Milesians. Lir's displeasure at not being chosen as leader of the Dé Danann was immense and he withdrew from worldly affairs to live alone beneath a large hill in County Armagh – Deadman's Hill – near Armagh City, the summit of which is marked by a stone cairn. To lure him back, the elected leader Bov – Bodhbh – offered one of his foster-daughters in marriage. Lir chose Aobh who bore him four children but died giving birth to twins. Lir was despondent but Bov offered him his wife's half-sister Aoife as a replacement. Lir's new wife was an accomplished witch and took a great spite against her stepchildren and, using a druid wand, turned them into swans. This was the story *Oidheadh Chlainne Lir* – the Tragic Fate of the Children of Lir – written around the 15th century and which became the Second Great Sorrow of Irish Storytelling. This is the only document concerning Lir and the story itself probably predates its written form by several hundred years. Its origins may have been in either Britain or France at the end of the Middle Ages when it was known as the Knight of the Swan, a medieval migratory legend.

The Land Beneath the Waves

The patronymic *mac Lir* is usually added to the name of a more generalised Celtic sea god, Manannán, to establish a connection with Lir. Manannán – probably originally Manandan – is reputedly a lord of the mystical Otherworld and a wonderful mariner, aided in his journeys by supernatural powers. This assertion that the Isle of Man derived its name from his is spurious. The Isle of Man, like Anglesey and the Isle of Arran, was called Mona by the Romans, the name coming from a bloody fertility god whose druidic groves were situated there. As these three islands lay to the east, like the Otherworld, the Irish believed that they were magical realms ruled over by a supernormal king named Manadan - he of Mana, the Old Irish form of Mona.

It was believed that this mystical king was the ancestor of the Conmhaicne sept which settled in Connacht having migrated from Leinster. Folklorists argue that the belief in Manannán was of Leinster origin. Thus, it was was primarily the Leinster Celts who believed in a mythological ruler who governed a fabulous island beyond the sea. In Wales, he was known as Manawyd, an artisan and crafty trickster and clearly a being of the mainland. The name probably derives from Manaw which was the Welsh name for the Isle of Man.

As a divine ruler of the fabled Otherworld and living on an island, Manannán was naturally believed to have special connections with the sea. The Irish *mac Lir* would

THE TALKING SEAL

The vast numbers of seals gathered along the bays and inlets of the Scottish and Irish shorelines left the locals in a bit of a quandary. Some sort of explanation had to be given for the almost human-like behaviour and antics of the basking visitors. The most common folk-tale was that they were fairies or merfolk in an animal disguise, with an intelligence that matched that of humans. They were given many attributes, including that of changing into almost mortal guise to lure humans to their land beneath the sea.

Often, the seal-people were considered extremely hostile towards land dwellers. In some stories, seals actively seek to drown sailors they encountered on the ocean or those venturing too close to their basking sites. This notion of a malignant seal-race was used by the Scottish and Irish seal-hunters to justify their slaughter of seals and seal-pups along the shores. This widespread and bloody killing was carried out to 'protect the coastal fish stocks' from scavenging seals.

One of the attributes given to seals was the power of speech. It was widely believed in fishing communities that seals could talk but, because they were really fairies who had existed since the foundation of the world, they used only the old Gaelic language. Because the form of Gaelic they used was no longer in use, it was difficult to understand their speech.

A tale of one such speaking seal comes from Rathlin Island and was recorded in the 1950s

Seals were fairies in disguise who charmed and tempted men into the land beneath the sea.

by the great Irish folklorist, Michael J. Murphy. He recorded it from the account of an old man named Paddy Anderson, who lived on the island, and whose grandfather, Donal, had been a famous seal-hunter: 'The old men of the Island didn't like you to meddle with the seal for fear of what might befall you. The seals are fairies, don't you see? I heard my grandfather tell a story about them certainly. He said that, like now, the seals were becoming plentiful and were going after all the fish. The Island men put out in their boats with guns to hunt them down and to put an end to them. My grandfather was out in a boat one day and he had his gun with him. While he was out, he came on an old seal, lying on a great rock just to the south of Raughery – Rathlin. Lifting the gun, he took aim to shoot it but the seal lifted its flippers, just like a man trying to wave him away. It called out to him in a human voice and said "Donal! Donal! Don't shoot me with that gun!" It spoke in a very old form of Irish but my grandfather was a native speaker and was able to follow what it said. It called him by his own name too, as if it knew who he was.

'Well, he was so astonished at this that he lowered the gun and the seal slid from the rock and was gone into the sea. He never saw it again after that. That's a true story sure enough for my grandfather told it often'.

have been added to his name to establish a formal link. It meant 'son of the sea' and was a poetical way to describe him as a ruler of the ocean. He was considered a prosperous farmer on the 'plains of the sea' with shoals of fish instead of herds of cattle and sheep. He was also described as a mighty warlord, driving his chariot across the surface of the sea, borrowing iconography from the Roman Neptune. He acquired companions and a number of artefacts. One of these was a great war-spear with which he stirred up the raging ocean as he passed. He was also reputed to have an invincible shield that no weapon could pierce, a magical knife that could cut through stone and a marvellous shirt that also protected its wearer from weaponry. The waves were considered his horses and his champion stallion was Enbhárr – 'water-foam'. Accordingly, he was also known as The Rider of the Maned Sea.

The grey man or fir laith *was feared by the Celts and later generations of seafarers. The grey man inhabited coasts, engulfing cliffs in mist and causing shipwrecks.*

Manannán himself was identified with large and stormy waves and it was said that he travelled submerged in the ocean 'for the space of nine waves' but would rise up on the tenth 'without wetting his chest or breast'. A ninth century description paints quite a different picture. Here he is described as a 'celebrated merchant' of the Isle of Man who travelled by studying the Heavens and who was able accurately to predict the weather by the motions of the stars. Here he is in a much more human guise but still with significant magical powers.

A text from the eighth century describes Manannán as the father of the hero-king Mongan – the hairy fellow – a legendary leader of an Irish sept known as *Dál nAraidhe* which inhabited south Antrim and north Down. In yet another tale from the same period, Manannán's wife Fannd seeks the love of the Ulster hero Cú Chulainn against the will of her husband. In both of these tales, Manannán is a supernatural being who can travel where he wishes in an instant and who appears and disappears at will.

It is probable that Manannán was a pre-Celtic deity very much outside the pantheon of pure Celtic belief but who was later absorbed as one of the Tuatha Dé Danann. Latterly, medieval writings show him as a friendly trickster who takes on a number of elaborate disguises in order to fool and confuse humans. Ballads and poems were composed about him from around the end of the 15th-century, and one significantly, linked him with the Isle of Man. It claimed that he was the first owner of the Island, which was described as Ellan Sheeant, and that he was able to protect his property from raiders by throwing a cloak of invisibility over it. In some legends, he was portrayed as having three legs but this emblem is not truly associated with him at all. More likely it is a variant of the swastika, an ancient symbol of good luck across the ancient world. In County Mayo, Manannán is described as a powerful magician who had his home at the castle of Mannin, in the parish of Bekan; while in Galway he was the Black Master: a teacher of sorcery and necromancy to whom young Irish wizards were sent to be educated.

Other sea gods had cults that flourished under Celtic influence. One was the goddess Nehalennia, whose followers erected two shrines on the coast of the Netherlands. She was the mysterious deity of the North Sea and little is known of her or her powers though she is believed to have protected her faithful on hazardous marine journeys. She is also thought to have been a deity of commerce and businessmen would have appealed to her for good luck in trading. Finally, on the Isle of Lewis in the Western Hebrides, the exceptionally ancient Celtic sea god Shony was venerated until the late 19th-century. There are several accounts from people still living who remember an offering being made this century to Shony, on the Island of Islay, in the Inner Hebrides. According to Martin Martin in his indispensable *Description of the Western Isles of Scotland* (published in 1716) a cup of ale was offered to the god at Hallowtide, not for a yield of fish but for enough seaweed to manure the land. On Islay a keg of beer was pushed into the water and ritually smashed open, allowing the contents to drain away so as to guarantee a plentiful catch of fish. Martin records the 17th-century Lewis ceremonial invocation (performed, interestingly, before the Church of Saint Mulvey) as:

The Land Beneath the Waves

'Shony, I give you this cup of ale, hoping that you'll be so kind as to send us plenty of seaware – 'seaweed', for enriching our ground for the ensuing year.' The cup of ale was thrown into the tide. During this ritual, a special candle was left burning on the church altar and extinguished as the worshippers returned. No description or depiction of Shony exists but he was known across the Western Isles, the coast of Scotland and on some stretches of the northern Irish shoreline. Normans entering north Antrim by coastal routes referred to him as Shellicoat, allegedly a kind of water snake, and consigned him to the freshwater lakes of the Irish interior. There is no doubt that Shony was an important sea god among the Celtic coastal tribes.

Other Sea-Beings

Many entities, held in awe by the Celts, cannot really be classified as sea gods. Although possessing supernatural powers, they tended to be feared rather than wor-

Ruins of Dunluce Castle, County Antrim

shipped and offerings made to them were designed to keep them away. Some were associated with natural phenomena such as winds or fog, the most famous being the Fir Liath – Grey Man – who haunted the coasts of Scotland, Ireland and the Western Isles. Geographical features such as 'The Grey Man's Path' near Ballycastle in north Antrim have been named after him but he was little more than a personification of the clinging grey mists that would descend suddenly upon mariners. He was a voiceless creature who took perverse delight in human misery and misfortune and he whirled his grey cloak of mist over the ocean so that sailors might perish on the rocks and shoals. Sometimes the Grey Man is described as a grim, bearded giant, glimpsed far out to sea or in the sky overhead at the end of the day – as he briefly appears in

the Bram Stoker tale 'Under the Sunset'. At other times, he is a shapeless entity, drifting lazily from sea to shore. All mariners feared his attention and took pains to avoid him. A holy medal placed in the bow of a fishing boat would protect it from being lost under the Grey Man's cloak as would sprinkling the decks with holy water and having the boat blessed. A female on board however, and particularly a red-head, would serve only to encourage him.

Up to the present, Brittany also boasted supernatural beings associated with ocean and coast. The most celebrated was Yann-An-Ord or John of the Dunes who made his habitation among the sandy dunes that mark the Breton shoreline. Whether he was a spirit, fairy or ghost is unknown for he was seldom seen although frequently heard. He had different forms in the different places in which his call was heard. Sometimes he was described as a giant with a loud, harsh, booming voice; at other times as a dwarf with a shrill, tinny call. His call is often described as clear and ringing, like a church bell, while he is not seen. At other times, he was depicted as an old man dressed in oilskins and leaning on the single oar of a rowboat, a little way out to sea. At intervals he would issue long and piercing calls that would either warn fog-bound sailors that they were venturing too close to land or else lure the curious land-ward to dash them on the rocks. So, although generally beneficent, he has an element of trickery. His cries were also cal-culated to frighten fishermen from the rocks nearby and to protect the shoals of fish that sometimes sheltered there. He wailed as the sun went down, calling home those who had wandered too far along the sands. Most of his calls were to be heard late at night: eerie and chilling in their tone, terrifying those who heard them.

The Land Beneath the Waves

The idea of Yann-An-Ord may have its roots in early Christian times. Old Armorican – Breton – saints would process along stretches of coast, where they had set up their oratories, during the hours of darkness. They would shake little bells of wrought iron and call out to warn sailors venturing too close to the shore.

While Yann-An-Ord might have been generally well-disposed towards sailors, another entity that dwelt close to the Breton shoreline was not so friendly. This was the Marie Morgan 'Morrigain', 'the daughter who sings amid the sea'. She was said to have been the evil offspring of the ruler of the sunken Breton land of Ys – also known as Ker-Ys in Cornwall. Her sole ambition was to lure sailors onto the rocks and sandbars, so that she could seize their souls as they drowned and would sing enchanting melodies to entice them. Her main hunting area was the Bay of Douarnenez, Finisterre, reputedly one of the greatest centres of learning in France. However, during the Dark Ages, the sea engulfed it after a terrible but unrecorded cataclysm. As with the Grey Man, mariners in this region often used some form of protection against the Marie Morgan, such as a crucifix or holy amulet. Again, opinions differed as to what the creature actually was. Some said that she was a kind of mermaid, others that she was a human condemned to live in the sea for all eternity, others still that she was simply a vengeful ghost who would not be released until she had collected a certain number of drowned souls. However, her evil nature and her connection with the sea were undisputed.

Celtic Mythology

Seals and Mer-Folk

The large numbers of seals that congregated on the rocks and tiny islands along the shore fascinated the early coastal Celts. Frequently glimpsed sea-creatures, such as dolphins or small whales, playing in the ocean also puzzled them but readily absorbed

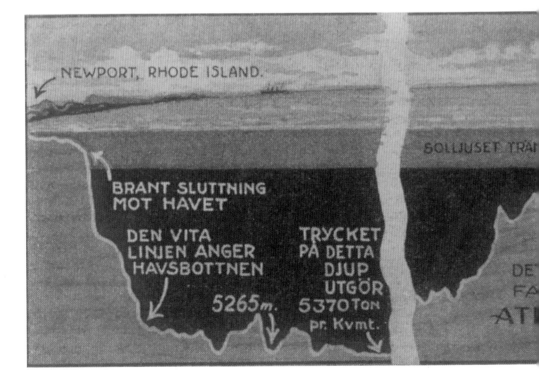

The Azores in the middle of the Atlantic are considered by some to be the site of the lost continent, Atlantis.

them into mythology – they were entities of either the Otherworld or lands far beneath the ocean and, on coming up to the shore, took the form of animals.

Initially, these creatures were counted either as the offspring, or the servants, of Manannán mac Lir, or a localised sea god, but gradually they began to develop mythologies and folklore of their own. Elaborate kingdoms far under the ocean surface were devised to describe the realms from which these beings might come. They were accorded their own natures, either beneficent or thoroughly evil, together with their own communal histories. In effect, they became a complex family of mer-folk.

The most famous is the mermaid. She features in folklore around the world, although varies in form. The most stereotyped perception is that of the upper torso of a woman combined with the long tail of a fish. This is a romanticised medieval perspective and bears little resemblance to earlier beliefs.

To the ancient Celts, mer-folk were simply humanoid extensions of the sea-gods themselves. They resembled mortals in practically every detail and, as they could usually live on land as well as in the sea, were almost indistinguishable from land-dwellers. This enabled them to travel about on the land to mate with land-dwellers who took their fancy. There was, however, an important distinction. When the mer-folk travelled through the freezing ocean currents, they wrapped themselves in seal-skin cloaks for protection, giving them the appearance of seals as they sat on rocks or on the shore. They had to discard these coverings in order to go about unobserved among mortals but could not return to the chilly ocean without them. So, if a mortal were to find one, the mer-person, usually a mermaid, would be enslaved until the garment was returned. Irish and Scottish folklore is littered with stories concerning fishermen who fall in love with a mermaid and contrive to steal her cloak so that she

The Land Beneath the Waves

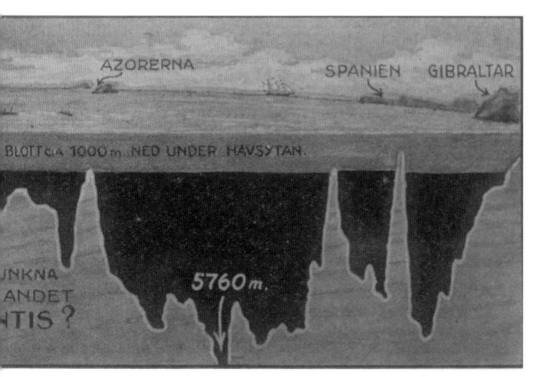

NORTH

Southern Limit of Ice Sheet

AMERICA

ATLANTEAN CONTINENT

ATLANTEAN

ATLANTEAN CONTINENT

Approximate Limit of Atlantean Continent

Bermuda

Azores

Madeira

Ca.

C. Verd

S   E   A

WEST INDIES

S   E   A

ATLANTEAN CONTINENT
During
THE ICE AGE
Direction of Ice Movement.........
Continental Shelf......................

Map indicating perceived location of Atlantis during the Ice Age.

will marry them. Many of the great clans of both countries trace their descent from the folk of the ocean. The Irish O'Flaherty and O'Sullivan families of Kerry and the MacNamaras of Co Clare, together with a number of coastal Breton families, all trace their ancestry back to ancient unions between mortals and mer-folk.

The Irish writer W.B. Yeats in his *Irish Fairy and Folk Tales* notes an interesting variant on the theme of the sealskin cloak. He mentions a red cap made of feathers that

he calls *cohullen druith* that they need for re-entering the ocean. If it is stolen, says Yeats, they are forever barred from returning to the sea. If the sealskin cloak is returned or discovered, the mermaid will invariably return to the sea, abandoning her husband and whatever mortal offspring she may have. Many folktales speak of the fickleness of mermaids and their ability to forget their lives on land as soon as they return to the swell.

A few of these sea-ancestors, it is thought, may have been humans who were swept away by floods and who somehow adapted to living in the sea. Saint Murgen, a legendary Celtic holy woman is believed to have lived in a cell just above Belfast Lough and whose final resting-place is supposed to be near Dunluce Castle on the northern Irish coast. Originally named Laban, she was the daughter of a chieftain on the Galloway coast. One day she was swept away from shore by a freak wave and subsequently caught in a fisherman's net near the present site of Carrickfergus. Taken to Calgach, a local chieftain, she revealed her true origin and later converted to Christianity. Even so, she retained much of her power over the ocean and the elements. As a saint, she was associated with healing and a spring, dedicated to her at Cave Hill, overlooking Belfast, supposedly existed up to the late 18th century. It later came to be used by members of the United Irishmen movement who were hiding up on the Hill and it subsequently became known as the 'Volunteers' Well'.

The Land Beneath the Waves

Because of its political connections it was believed to have been filled in during the early 19th century, although a number of wells in the area are known by the same name.

Seals gathered on the rocks and inlets along the coasts were believed to be mer-folk wrapped in their cloaks. Irish and Scottish fishermen often credited seals with extraordinary powers: they believed that they spoke in an ancient and long-disused

HUMAN/MER-FOLK RELATIONS

Although mer-folk were usually exceptionally hostile towards mortals, there are folk-tales that refer to bargains between the children of the sea and the children of dust. These stories usually relate to fishermen who have 'done a deal' with the sea-people to ensure large catches of fish.

One such story comes from Orkney and concerns a man long suspected of trafficking in the Black Arts. He was a fine fisherman who boasted the largest catches of anyone in the islands – and did it all without ever going to sea! Each morning at a certain time, he would go down to the rocks near his house and wait. A deep and brassy voice, like a man speaking within a bell, would sound from the direction of the ocean.

'The hour has come!' it would declaim and the magician would answer, 'The hour has come', whereupon, a large draught of fishes would be washed up onto the rocks by the wizard. He would gather them up and return home and it was widely rumoured that he had made a bargain with a sea-spirit to keep him supplied with fish for as long as he came to the rocks.

The merrow had the physical appearance of a beautiful woman. Only her webbed hands and feet indicated her origins in the sea.

One day, the magician was taken ill and had to remain in bed. At the appointed time the strange, brassy voice was heard calling: 'The hour has come!' But this time there was no reply. Three times, it called out with no response. Finally, it paused: 'The hour has come but not the man!' said the voice mournfully and fell silent. Never again did it cry out and the wizard had to catch his own fish from that day onward. Although primarily a tale told in Orkney and in parts of Ireland, it was once very popular on the Isle of Man.

Not all bargains between mortals and sea-folk involve fishing, however. A peculiar tale from County Kerry in Ireland relates how creatures from the deep buried the Cantillons of Ballyheigue. The family's usual burial ground was at Ardfert but, from earliest times, the greatest members of the household had been buried in the grounds of a ruined island chapel just off Ballyheigue Strand. The sea overwhelmed the island and the chapel sank beneath the waves. Because of an ancient agreement, made during a marriage between one of the Cantillons and a sea-maiden, some of the family continued to be buried in the submerged graveyard. Following the burial service, their bodies would be left on Ballyheigue Strand and the mourners would withdraw. Terrible beings would arise out of the sea, collect the coffin and take it beneath the waves for burial. Under the terms of the agreement, this would continue until the creatures were observed by mortals:

'When human eye our work shall spy,

And human ear our groans shall hear'.

Connor Crowe, a Clare man who had married into the Cantillon family, broke this arrangement. He refused to believe the tales of the agreement and confidently asserted that just the sea carried the bodies away. To prove his point, after the funeral of Florence Cantillon, he hid in the rocks above Ballyheigue Strand to keep watch. He was terrified of the nightmarish entities which emerged from the ocean and he cried out. The beings saw him and, recognising the agreement was over, returned to the sea and came no more.

From that time onwards, all the Irish members of the Cantillon family were buried at Ardfert.

form of Gaelic. They called them silkies, in the north of Ireland, in the Western Isles and in coastal Scotland, a Gaelic word for mer-folk that distinguished them from other ocean creatures. In the south of Ireland, they are sometimes referred to as 'merrows'.

The mer-people fell into two categories, those who were beneficent towards mortals and those who sought to do them harm. The latter were almost invariably mer-men and were horrid-looking creatures with florid complexion, thick bristles and long boar-like tusks. There were mermaids, however, described as enchantresses who used their natural beauty for diabolical purposes. Many had an enchanting voice, recalling the Sirens of Greek mythology, with which they would lure sailors to their destruction on rocks and reefs. It was widely believed across the Celtic world that mermaids laid claim to the souls of those drowned at sea, whether from shipwreck or simply from an accident while swimming. It was therefore unwise to fall asleep on the beach, except within the sound of church bells, lest one of these beings would carry away your soul with the outgoing tide.

There is a long and persistent tradition in some parts of Ireland and Scotland that mer-folk are a branch of the *Sidhe* – fairy race. It was said that when the Tuatha Dé Dannan first apportioned the lands of the West among themselves, there was not enough to go round and so some took over submerged kingdoms becoming ocean people adapted to life underwater. A certain enmity existed between those who lived under the sea and the mortals who lived on the land and thus the latter had to be very careful when venturing on or near the ocean.

The lore concerning mermaids and sea-creatures is widespread and complicated. Most of it comes from a time much later than the great mythological cycles and generally parallels stories from Roman and Greek traditions. These creatures had to come from somewhere so the sea-myths were expanded to include lost or sunken realms.

The Land Beneath the Waves

Sunken Kingdoms

Tales concerning sunken or lost kingdoms come mainly from two sources. They can be an extension of sea myths: giving mer-folk a specific home under the ocean or perhaps explaining how humans learned to live under the water following the submersion of their country. Secondly, the tales may be a memory or oral recording of a disaster in which a settlement or village slid into the sea. In all probability, there were many unrecorded geographical upheavals in prehistoric times and these stories may serve as some indication of their extent.

Almost everyone is familiar with the legend of Atlantis, the paradise continent that was said by Plato to lie 'west of the Pillars of Hercules' – Straits of Gibraltar – and that was overwhelmed by the sea during a violent seismic disturbance. Although a Mediterranean legend, it has concomitant themes in Celtic folklore.

The most famous of these was Hy Brasil – Breasal a physical embodiment of the Celtic Otherworld. Bresal was a mythical High King of the World and the island of Breasal was reputedly where he held his court every seven years. Consequently, it was visible only for a short period every seventh year. It became a Celtic version of the Atlantis myth and was depicted as a place of eternal happiness where everyone was immortal. It also had the ability to rise and submerge as its ruler saw fit, hence the

THE ZENNOR MERMAID

Creatures of the pagan past associated with elemental forces, mermaids and mer-folk were not able to enter any Christian place of worship. In many folktales, the blessings of priests or ministers or the sound of church bells were anathema to the beings from beneath the waves.

In the little church at Zennor in the south of Cornwall, there is a strange inscription, on a pew, which contains a carving of a mermaid. In her hands, she carries a comb and a mirror, twin symbols say some, of vanity and heartlessness. This peculiar adornment stems from an old Cornish legend relating to the fishing hamlet, and to one of its former inhabitants. It also concerns a mermaid who came into the holy precincts and drew one of the congregation away beneath the ocean.

The story is a simple one. Of all the young fishermen of Zennor during the middle of the last century, Matthew Trewella was certainly the most handsome and the most sought-after by all the girls of the district. He attracted the attention of a merrow. She had glimpsed him from the rocks as he hauled in his nets down by Pendour Cove and made up her mind to take him. It was widely believed that mermaids were attracted to humans because any offspring of a human/mermaid relationship would, unlike mer-folk, have a soul and eventually enter Heaven, which was forever closed to the mer-people.

During the final years of the 18th century and the beginning of the 19th, a strange lady began to attend Zennor church. She was exceptionally beautiful and drew the attention of many of the local lads but none knew who she was, or where she came from although rumours abounded that she was related to the once-powerful Arundel family. Extremely wealthy and influential, they were said to have made their money by claiming salvage from ships that had foundered on the coast – having first made sure of a disaster by employing wreckers to lure the vessels to their doom.

There was no doubt about who she had her eye fixed on – Matthew Trewella, who possessed the finest singing voice in the Zennor choir. It was also said that, although a fisherman, Matthew came from gentrified Cornish stock, related to Squire Trewella who lived some miles distant. Squire Trewella was frequently ill and, as he had never married and had no heir, Matthew was expected to inherit his estates – a great catch for any girl.

Matthew seemed to respond to the stranger's interest; he seemed as enamoured of her as any other man in Zennor. He

Mermaid carved on a pew in Zennor church, Cornwall, England.

returned her flirtatious smiles and followed her a little way whenever she left Zennor church. One evening, he made up his mind to follow her home, and perhaps even speak to her. He voiced his intention but many of the old people advised him against it. If she were an Arundel, they said, then she did not come from a very savoury family. After all, salvage could be claimed only from a wreck with no survivors…Matthew had best ignore her. Matthew ignored the advice.

The strange girl left the church the following Sunday with Matthew following her a little distance behind. She walked briskly down the road that led towards Pendour Cove and Matthew increased his step to keep pace. Whether or not he overtook her is unknown for neither of them was ever seen again. A search was made but, apart from two sets of footprints heading out to sea at Pendour, nothing was ever found. Old people claimed that the stranger was a mermaid and that she had lured poor Matthew away to her watery lair to keep as a lover. Such tales might be dismissed as old superstitions but, again, nobody was completely certain.

The tale had a surprising sequel many years later. A foreign ship, slightly damaged by a storm, had sought sanctuary in Pendour Cove. Her captain was an Englishman and knew the Cornish coast reasonably well. Knowing that Pendour was a safe anchorage, he ordered his men to drop anchor and to wait out the last of the storm. No sooner was the anchor down, than a mermaid rose out of the waves and asked the captain, in an old form of English dialect, to remove it. It was blocking the doorway of her house, she told him, and she could not return to her lover and her children within.

'Seeing that you are an Englishman', she continued, 'you may know my lover. His name was formerly Matthew Trewella from Zennor'. The captain had heard the tale and was astounded by this revelation. He sailed directly to Zennor and related the tale of his remarkable encounter. This confirmed the old people's assertion that the beautiful creature was a pagan from the ocean. They carved her likeness on the pew in Zennor church as a warning to other young men not to be taken in by her wiles and be lured away like poor Matthew Trewella.

Even now, if one walks along the edge of Pendour Cove, during the late evening hours, the plaintive sound of Matthew's voice, calling over the continual roar of the breakers, can be heard. He is still trying to free himself from the mermaid's thrall to come home again to Zennor.

infrequency of its sightings. Hy-Breasal appeared in records and on maps as an actual place and the Genoese cartographer, Daloroto, (*c.* 1325) showed it as a large landmass to the south-west of Ireland. It appeared sporadically on maps and charts right up to the late 17th century.

A story, concerning the ancient submarine Celtic kingdom of Dumnonia, featured in a collection of medieval legends known as *The Matter of Britain*. Frequently called Ermonie or Parmenia, Dumnonia stretched between the tip of Cornwall and the French coast taking in the Scilly Isles: in Cornish legend the hilltops of inundated land. It is also known as the Kingdom of Lyonesse and seems to have been submerged either during the fifth or sixth centuries or much later, in the eleventh or twelfth centuries. The land was described as having several important towns and at least 140 churches. It was traditionally held to be the home of the Cornish mer-folk and the realm to which they lured their unwilling victims.

Unlike many myths, there may be some historical evidence for this belief. The 16th century antiquarian William Camden asserted that Land's End once stretched further west and connected with the Scilly Islands. A map of Lyonesse was prepared by Agnes Strickland and published in Beccles Wilson's *Lost England* in 1901. It shows an extended coastline of about 80 miles in length stretching into the ocean beyond Saint Michael's Mount and a large forest in the area currently occupied by the Mount's bay. The promontory of Saint Michael's Mount itself is shown as part of the mainland. This agreed with the medieval chronicler, William of Worcester, who stated that the Mount was at least five or six miles from the sea and was surrounded by a very dense forest. The Cornish name for the holy hill reaffirms this: *Carreg Coedh yn Clos* means the Grey Rock in the Wood. Further documentary evidence is to be found in the Domesday Book of 1086. In the section dealing with Calvage – Cornwall – it is noted:

The Land Beneath the Waves

> 'The land of Saint Michael, Keiwal, holds the church of Saint Michael. Brismar was holding the Danish tax. The land is 8 Caracutes. There is one Caracute withe one villan and two borderii and ten acres of pasture. Value 20 shillings'.

There is no reference to this 'land of Saint Michael' being an island like the current Mount. Where islands occur in the *Domesday Book*, as the Isle of Wight and Portland, they are clearly denoted as such. What also makes this entry important is that it records the extent of this 'Saint Michael's land' as being 8 Caracutes, that is, equal to 480 acres. The present land area of the Mount is just less than 30 acres. It is reasonable to suppose that somewhere between the period of the Domesday Book and the present day, a great area of 'Saint Michael's land' was obliterated by incursions of the sea. There is further evidence from the bay at the foot of Saint Michael's Mount that an ancient forest once clung to its lower, now submerged, slopes. Scientists studying tree stumps found below the water line believe that their submersion may have been caused by sudden land subsidence rather than by gradual erosion.

At its height, Lyonesse is reputed to have equalled the fabled Atlantis in its culture and splendour. There were important Christian teaching centres and a magnificent city known simply as the City of Lions, the architecture of which rivalled anything in the Western World. Legend says that this city still lies somewhere beneath the ocean just south of Land's End and is the place where the Celtic sea god Manannán holds his court.

By far the most famous and best-studied sunken kingdom in Welsh legend is the land of *Tyno Helig* or Helig's Vale. It was said to stretch from Priestholm to Penmaenmawr on the coast of Caernarfonshire, and was ruled from Llys Helig which stood, according to tradition, near Great Orme's Head. All that remains of the site of this ancient Welsh kingdom today is the Lavan Sands, lying between the North Wales coast and the Isle of Anglesey. The Welsh word *lavan* means 'weeping': it is traditionally said that the weeping was for those who were drowned in a massive cataclysm and for the fertile lands that were lost.

In the *Cambridge County Geography for Flintshire* (1914) there is reference to an immense flood in the area:

> 'In the 5th century there was a great inundation along the whole North Wales coast and the sea once more regained a large tract of land'.

Scientists and geographers have placed the creation of the Lavan Sands at around AD 634. This tallies with local myths which tie its creation with the fortunes of a local lord or sub-king named Helig ap Glannawg, the Lord of Hereford. As well as his Hereford estates Helig also ruled a substantial part of the North Wales coastline. His castle and the accompanying town Llys Helig were supposedly situated where two important trade routes crossed. One of these led to the trading town of Conwy, which still exists today.

Legend says that Helig somehow angered the sea-folk and that the destruction of his lands had been prophesied to him by a voice calling from the ocean as he was riding along the beach one evening. In strange and unearthly tones, it reputedly warned him: '*Dial a ddew! Dial a ddew*! – Vengeance is coming! Vengeance is coming!' Recovering from the shock, the lord asked the disembodied voice 'How soon?'. The voice answered: 'In the time of thy grandchildren, great-grandchildren and their children'. Somewhat relieved Helig returned to Llys Helig and gave the prophecy no more thought. A while later, he gave a great feast at Llys Helig to which he invited his family of all five generations. The youngest, the child of his great-grandchild, was only a babe in arms. As the feast was in full swing, a servant ventured into the cellar to fetch more drink and was horrified to see water seeping into the place. He had only time to shout a warning before the walls of the palace broke open. The sea came rushing in, in a monstrous, all-consuming tide and all the revellers were swept away. Like the tales of Lyonesse, this story may well have its origins in fact. Certainly there is a record of a Welsh prince named Helig ap Glannawg. In fact, he is the father of three recorded Welsh saints: Boda, Gwynin and Brothen, all mentioned in the *Peniarth Manuscript* and the *Haford Manuscript*. The three brothers all became monks at the abbey of Bangor Fawr and some travelled across Wales founding abbeys and churches before their deaths at Bardsay Island about the middle of the sixth century.

As to Helig's town, there are accounts of the remains of an ancient roadway, stretching between Priestholm and Penmaenmawr. In 1816, Edward Pugh wrote in his *Cambria Depicta* concerning the Lavan Sands: 'It is said that at very low ebb, ruined houses are seen, and a causeway pointing from Priestholm Island to Penmaenmawr'.

Certainly many travellers report having seen what appear to be the shapes of ruins at the bottom of nearby Conwy Bay. These are, traditionally, the ruins of Helig ap Glannawg's palace. In 1864, they were visited by Charlton R. Hall of Liverpool and by a Welsh clergyman, the Rev. Richard Parry of Llandudno. Rev. Hall considered the ruins to be those of a 'grand old hall of magnificent dimensions of whose shape and properties there still remain distinguishable traces', which he took as confirmation that this was Helig's castle.

In September 1908, an archaeologist named Ashton visited the site and confirmed the existence of ancient walls as did Horace Lees in 1913. But, in 1939, the eminent archaeologist F. J. North dismissed the ruins simply as natural stones. He dismissed Ashton's careful notes that detailed the extent and dimensions of the suggested ancient fort. He also dismissed a continuous seaweed-draped stone edifice of linear construction, extremely suggestive of an ancient wall. At high tide, it was said that these ruins were inhabited by mer-folk who would lure travellers from the nearby roadway to their doom in the sea.

The Land Beneath the Waves

The legend of Helig ap Glannawg is given further credence by the nearby island of Priestholm, which has a claim to be a surviving portion of his lands. The island's Welsh name is *Ynys Seiriol* - Puffin Island. It has, however, a much more ancient name, *Ynys Lannog*, apparently after *Glannawg ap Heilig Foel*, the father of the celebrated Helig.

The name *Priestholm* is a Norse description of the island because of its monastic associations. Geraldus Cambrensis called it 'the Ecclesiastical Island' and refers to it as a hermitage. Various ascetics, wishing to cut themselves off from the outside world, probably inhabited it. There is strong evidence that Priestholm was at one time part of the Welsh mainland and that it formed part of the territory of local warlords. There are references to ancient roads and it is thought that the Romans originally constructed the causeway that runs to the island. At high tide, according to a local legend, undersea beings come ashore along this causeway, to sport on land. The ruins and the legend of a sunken land join together to form a patchwork of folklore all connected to the sea and submarine beings.

The most famous of all the Breton sunken kingdoms is the fabled land of Ys. Traditionally, Ys was submerged at the same time as Lyonesse. The connections between Brittany and Cornwall are stressed as the Cornish prefix *Ker* is often used.

The stories of the flooding of Ys, or Ker-Ys, are extremely confused, with many variations. The most common tale places the land in the Finisterre area where is it ruled by an old but very wise king named Gradlon. At the height of its influence, Ys traded with many corners of the world including China and Ethiopia. However, much of the land lay below sea-level, just as Holland does today, and the ocean was held in check by a complicated system of walls and locks. The gates on these locks could be opened only by an intricate set of keys, copies of which were held only by the Royal engineers and by the king himself.

Ys was a Christian country and Gradlon's adviser was the venerable Saint Guenole (the Cornish Winwaloe – see **Legends of Saints and Holy Men**). He had a rather flighty daughter named Dahut with whom he was besotted but whom the saint himself did not care for. Saint Guenole prophesied that Dahut would one day bring about the end of the kingdom of Ys itself and this, was to prove true.

Celtic Mythology

Dahut fell in love with a dashing figure named Cado, supposedly 'a prince of Kernow (Cornwall), and, some texts asserted, the cousin of Saint Guenole. In fact, he was a demon from the sea, anxious to bring about the destruction of Ys. Under Cado's malign influence, Dahut procured the keys to the dykes from her sleeping father and handed them to the demon. He opened the floodgates and the sea poured in, swamping both the city and surrounding lands. Aroused by Saint Guenole's shouting, Gradlon went to the window of his palace and saw his entire kingdom disappearing under the ocean. Taking a horse from the palace stables, he and the saint attempted to escape from the advancing floodwaters. Riding through the outskirts of the city, they came upon Dahut, now abandoned by Cado, and helped her up with them onto the horse.

The extra weight slowed the horse down and the rising floodwaters were overtaking the refugees. Saint Guenole advised the king to throw his feckless daughter from the horse and give her as an offering to the encroaching tide. The king reluctantly did so and Dahut was swept away to live with the demons under the ocean.

Gradlon and Guenole made solid land but the king, joining his kinsmen in Britain, soon died of a broken heart. The saint went on to found the great abbey at Landevennec. Dahut was not drowned but became a demon herself and, say many old Bretons, she lives in the deepest part of the ocean haunting the submerged ruins of Ys. She can still be seen, occasionally, sitting on a rock and combing her long hair in the manner of a mermaid. The sight of her is an evil omen, usually portending shipwreck and danger. She is the original Marie Morrigan and her story was used to explain the origin of the Morrigans, the Breton sea-people. Some Breton tales make her queen of Ys's drowned citizens who dwell, still, beneath the waves, plotting harm against the living. An old Breton poem commemorates her dark deed, her evil nature and the destruction of Ys:

> 'The sea opens its abysses and Dahut is swallowed up by the deep,
> The king's horse, now lighter, reaches the shore,
> Dahut, since then, is calling sailors to be wrecked'.

Whether or not Ys really existed in France is unknown. The story may be a medieval morality tale, demonstrating the folly of kings, the wantonness of royal courts and the power of the saints. In some versions, Saint Guenole is able to hold back the advancing tides until the king discards his daughter and escapes. Gradlon may have existed – there is a statue of him mounted on a horse at Quimper in Brittany – but he may have been a local warlord, rather than the king of Ys. Nevertheless, the story of the sunken kingdom is widely known throughout Brittany and sometimes considered historical fact. Cado is referred to in Thomas Miller's *Ancient Cornish Stories* (1817) and in a number of old stories such as Hunt's *Drolls*.

Undersea kingdoms appear to have fascinated the later Celts and they incorporated many such stories into folklore, particularly in Irish and Scottish tales. No specific kingdoms are named but are simply given a general description. The Irish poet and writer W.B. Yeats generalised the sunken areas of Ireland as *Tír Fó Thoinn*, the land beneath the waves, an all-encompassing underwater domain where merrows and silkies dwelt.

The Land Beneath the Waves

Around the Irish coasts, stories abound concerning lost and submerged cities, the spires of which can be glimpsed from clifftops when the light is right. Further along the Irish coastline there are said to be sunken churches whose bells can be heard at times, ringing out a warning to sailors to stay well clear of coastal rocks. This supernatural phenomenon is akin to the Breton *Yann-an-Ord* and probably derives from the same explanation, that of religious hermits ringing bells near rocks in order to warn away approaching shipping.

Loughs are also said to contain the remnants of sunken towns. Lough Neagh in County Antrim is said to contain a large settlement of the O'Neills, somewhere beneath its waters. There is no evidence for this assertion but it is said that the spires of the town church can be seen on a clear day when the water is low. The town was reputedly built on the site of a magic, pagan well that never went dry and over which a stone had to be placed to restrain the water and to keep it from spilling over. One careless O'Neill woman left the well uncovered and the water bubbled up and spilled over, submerging the entire settlement. This tale is a common one in many parts of Ireland and Scotland. In the Western Hebrides there are tales of small islands that have been engulfed in exactly the same manner.

Undoubtedly, in Ireland, towns did slide into the sea or were engulfed by a natural cataclysm. One such is Kilstaveen in west County Clare, which was said to lie between the Cliffs of Moher and the Ballard Cliffs. Here a famous monastery was supposedly submerged to punish its lax and profligate inhabitants. Whether the town existed is a matter of conjecture but there was seismic activity in the area that substantially altered the Clare coastline. In his Ordnance Survey letters on Clare, John O'Donovan, citing the Annals of the Four Masters as his source, dates this event to 799. The Annals state:

'AD 799. A great storm of wind, thunder and lightning happened this day before Saint Patrick's festival this year, and it killed ten and one thousand persons in the Territory of Corca-Baskin and the sea divided the island of Inis Fithae into three parts.'

In O'Donovan's opinion, this island can be none other than Mutton Island, off the Clare coastline. He cites the Annals of Clonmacnois as detailing the same event. (See: John O'Donovan & Eugene Curry: *Antiquities of the County Clare - Clare Local Studies Project*). It is unlikely, though, that in this early era, there would have been much of a monastery or township for the sea to swallow up. Local traditions aver that the bells of Kilstaveen monastery can be heard ringing out over the sea and that their sound prophecies death by drowning to all these who hear them. The legend of the 'Bells of the Drowned Town' may owe more to the imagination of Michael Comyn, a noted Clare storyteller of the last century, than to any historical fact.

SUNKEN SCOTLAND

Legends of towns and lands lost to the sea do not appear frequently in Scottish myth or folktale, probably owing to the smaller population there than in the countryside further south.

There are, however, a few tales of some notable losses. Folk legends from around Inverness-shire, speak of a terrible flood in the town of Fort George that carried away several settlements in the surrounding countryside. The devastation, it is alleged, was dreadful with many people being swept away and drowned. The Priory of Crail near Saint Andrews, undermined by the sea, collapsed in on itself and was promptly swallowed up. A large section of land between Saint Andrews Castle and the shore was also submerged with huge loss of life.

In Morayshire, the town of Old Findhorn was completely swept away by the raging sea and the bells of its church are said to be heard ringing far off the Morayshire coast. Like Kilstaveen in County Clare, Ireland, it is an evil omen to hear their sound. Old Findhorn is now supposed to be inhabited only by silkies, who take a perverse delight in announcing the forthcoming wreck of a ship by tolling the undersea bell.

Thoughtless quarrying hastened the end of some of the towns along the Kincardineshire shoreline. During the late 1700s, the town of Johnshaven was a local centre for the export of lime quarried in the surrounding area. The quarrymen did not realise that the very lime that they were digging up underpinned the stable layer of shale on which coastal towns were built. Recognition, in about 1795, came far too late as by then the shale had become extremely unstable. Several small towns and villages began to slip into the sea. And the village of Mathers, two miles south of Johnshaven, was completely engulfed in a single night. There are many stories of great loss of life at this fateful time but none have been substantiated. A new coastline was formed, up to 250 yards inland and the residents were forced to build a new village even further away from the sea.

Not only hamlets and villages were lost to the raging elements, larger towns were affected as well. During the middle and late 18th century, Arbroath suffered considerable destruction when it was overwhelmed by the sea, while on the Tay, at the turn of the century, a number of small villages were destroyed when the river burst its banks. The Buddon Ness lighthouse at the Tay Estuary was removed because of high, raging seas and, in 1879, one of Scotland's most famous railway disasters occurred when the swollen river carried off the Tay Bridge, together with a passenger train crossing it at the time.

When compared to Ireland, England and parts of Wales, Scotland seems to lack a substantive corpus of lore and legend about sunken lands and towns.

A similar town appears in Orkney-Scottish folktales about the lost town of Eynhallow that once lay on an islet between the island of Rousay and mainland Orkney where the ruins of a Benedictine monastery can be clearly seen at low tide. The folk of Eynhallow, so the old Orkney stories say, were once in constant contact, and may have mated, with the Fin People of Finfolkaheen, a twin town which lay beneath the waters of Eynhallow Sound. During each summer, the Fin Folk, half-fish and half-human, would bask on the rocks near Eynhallow village while the females of their kind would try to woo human lovers. If they were successful then they lost their piscine attributes, became fully human and could live on land. As in Ireland, a number of Orkney families trace their ancestry back to such unions. The children of a mating between humans and the Fin Folk were reputed to be exceptionally fine sailors. So close did the two communities become, it was said, the village was eventually swallowed up by the ocean and is now lost. It was also believed that, in common with a number of other Scottish settlements in the northern isles, Eynhallow became invisible to mortal eye during parts of the year. This power of invisibility was a gift granted to its people by the Fin Folk to protect the settlement from the raiders who prowled the seas in ancient times.

Further tales exist on some of the Scottish islands of fairy cattle that came out of the ocean to graze on the land. These creatures were beasts of ill omen as they had the power to lure the cattle of the island crofters, back to the sea with them. The sea-cattle could be recognised because they were much smaller than ordinary livestock, were exceptionally hairy and often had pieces of seaweed or kelp entwined in their manes. A special watch was kept for these cattle and they were driven away if they ventured too close to a grazing island herd.

The Land Beneath the Waves

In many cases, the Land-beneath-the-waves mirrored the everyday world of the Celt. It was arranged in towns, it had markets and fairs, castles and fortifications, grazing animals very like those on dry land, thick forests, high mountains and deep ravines. And yet it was, unquestionably, an alien environment inhabited by creatures that often meant harm to mortals. It was a place of immense mystery – reflecting the mystery of the endless, rolling sea itself.

THE OTHERWORLD

Glimpses of Another Reality

We cannot define the concept the Celts had of the Otherworld, we just know that they believed in it implicitly.

The 'Otherworld' could mean many things. It was a country outside the natural laws of time and space; a mystical realm home to strange and supernatural beings; a place from which the dead continue to watch the world of the living - and from which they sometimes returned. It could also be an unexplored abode of terrifying and exotic monsters, far across the ocean. It might be the halls of the gods themselves or a zone inhabited only by spirits. The term is so vague as to encompass all of these. But, for the Celts, the Otherworld was certainly very real.

Celtic Mythology

It had many names. For the Irish, it might be *Magh Meall* – 'the Honey Plain' – or *Tír na nÓg* – the 'Country of the Young' – while for the Welsh it was the land of Annwn. It was the far-away country glimpsed in the last light of day or the first glimmer of morning. Its distant mass might be seen on the horizon or beyond the furthest mountain, only to disappear if one looked too hard. It lay just beyond the borders of rationality.

The Otherworld was generally a land of contentment with continual feasting and sport. Beautiful women and handsome men, ageless and without disease or deformity enjoyed wonderful music and poetry. It was, in effect, a magical dream world, a pleasant mirror image of the harsh reality of everyday Celtic life.

It was to here that the greatest heroes and finest poets retired when their mortal life was over. While some argued that it was a harmonious and peaceful place, others suggested that it resounded with the loud clangour of continual battle as the mighty heroes of yesteryear competed with each other. The belief that such heroes enjoyed themselves only through violent conflict may have come from the Viking concept of Valhalla, the Hall of Heroes.

Even general descriptions of the Otherworld varied greatly although usually refelecting the routine, everyday world. It was a series of endless halls filled with endless feasting and drinking. It was a great battlefield across which mighty armies clashed ceaselessly. It was a breathtakingly beautiful, fertile land of lakes and forests among which poets and sages continued to dream and think profound thoughts; it was all of these.

Another school of thought portrayed the Otherworld as a dreary, barren and mist-shrouded place across which the spirits of the dead ambled ceaselessly, without purpose. This has a resemblance to the ancient Hebrew concept of *Sheol*, the original version of Hell.

From all these vague ideas, the concept of the Otherworld was fleshed out in the Celtic mind, while remaining a fluid, nebulous place existing across both spatial and temporal distances. It might be on an island in the midst of the ocean, or among the clouds above; it might co-exist with our perceived world, just out of sight and beyond mortal vision or be under the ground beneath our feet. Whatever form it took, the ancient Celts were sure that it existed.

Origins of the Otherworld Belief

Three sources for the belief in another world so close to our own might be suggested.

The first comes from the memories of the Celts themselves. Originally, they were a nomadic people, living as hunter-gatherers and travelling long distances across various terrains. Their tradition was primarily an oral one and they wrote very little about themselves. Consequently, much of the accounts of their travels was passed down between generations through song and story. While we know that the bards possessed phenomenal, and largely accurate, memories (see: **Druidic Tradition**) we are not so sure about the common warrior or farmer. Probably their memories tended to run recollections together in a muddled and haphazard way. As often happens, accounts of the places that they remembered might have altered across the years; embellishments may have been added, locations changed to fit the particular story. Gradually and almost unconsciously, real locations and sites might have assumed a legendary and mythical quality. Thus, a temporary campsite in a peaceful, sunny valley became, several centuries later, a sun-drenched, fertile land where the heroes of Celtic legend found rest and repose; a minor skirmish on a muddy plain became an unending battlefield where the warriors of old continually tested their mettle. The battles in the Otherworld, it was said, greatly outdid those in the mortal sphere in their ferocity, skill and strategy.

A second source for the belief may come from the environment itself. Celts regarded the lands that they came to and in which they settled with a mixture of awe and wonder. They viewed the great stones and tumbled features left by the Ice Age as the work of primal gods and/or giants (see **Giants, Monsters and Faries**) neither of whom had really gone away. The Celts steadfastly believed that the world of spirits was incredibly close. Natural phenomena, as for example majestic cloud formations, would require explanations. Spectacular cloud formations might resemble ships, mountains or the ramparts of mighty castles and to the Celtic mind, this may have been exactly what they were. They hinted at a strange land in the sky, beyond mortal comprehension and beyond reach. Such a place could have stirred the imagination to

The Otherworld

In 1674, according to tradition, Captain John Nesbit, a mariner from County Fermanagh in the north of Ireland, encountered the Otherworld as a large island in the sea mist between Ulster and the west coast of Scotland. He and some of his crew, mostly Scottish or of Scottish extraction, went ashore briefly and having found nothing returned to the ship, which then continued on its journey. Although the story of Nesbit's landing may have been nothing more than a tall traveller's tale, there still remain several accounts given by crew members. One is the account of Alistair MacKenzie, originally from the Western Isles, who kept a diary of his voyage with Nesbit that included the expedition to the interior of the Otherworld island. The account is fragmented, his ability to write was limited, and may owe more to imagination than to reality, but it serves to give some picture of a man's encounter with the Otherworld. The following is a short extract, adapted from MacKenzie's diary:

'When we had gone a little ways inland, Captain Nesbit suddenly held up his hand and the shore party stopped. "What can ye hear men?" our Captain asked. "Nothing Captain!" we answered him. Captain Nesbit nodded in agreement. "I think that we may be in a land of dead men."

'His words only confirmed the horror that we'd all been thinking. A wind began to rise. It blew with a growing intensity and ferocity, scattering whatever shreds of mist were left and howling about the dead trees of the plain like a demented and long-lost soul. I thought myself that I heard voices in that wind, both male and female, crying and wailing most piteously. It was a sensation that chilled us all and there was much muttering among the men that we should go back to the ship and leave this accursed place.

"We'll go on men", said Captain Nesbit. "For if this is an unexplored place, then we can claim it for the King and come back to map it. I've heard too that on these islands, there are sometimes great treasures to be found, left over from the olden times when pirates roamed such waters. I'd hate to pass any such wealth by".

'So, we followed Captain Nesbit deeper into the island. And all the while, the awful wind increased and the voices that we had thought we heard crying within it became much clearer. Some of the others began to mutter that we had come to the very borderlands of Hell and that they would go no further, even if Captain Nesbit commanded it. I myself had long decided that I would be one of them for this strange place was beginning to unnerve me, as never any place had before.

'Then, we saw in front of us the ramparts of a mighty castle built from the black stone of the island itself. They reared up in front of us, very gloomy and forbidding, and as we drew closer, none of us could see any entrance through its walls except for one low door made of stout wood and apparently sealed with a system of chains. When we drew nearer we saw that these "chains" were no more than the web of some great spider, laced with cobwebs, and this told us that the door had not been opened for a long, long time. Captain Nesbit strode up to the wall and, cupping his hands around his mouth, gave a loud "Halloo" to let those that dwelt within know that we were outside. There was no answer to his call, no head peered over the battlements and no shout answered his from within the place.

"Tis a pirate fortress, built by Scottish raiders" ventured Townsend and this was the common consensus amongst us all, even Captain Nesbit.

Nesbit strode up to the great door and struck it right hard. To our surprise it swung open at his touch with a low moaning sound, the spiders' webs breaking away as it did so. The door lay open before us but we were still afraid to enter. At last, Captain Nesbit stepped forward into the dark with a few of us following him. All about the fortress the wind rose and seemed to wail and cry all the more. The woeful cries on the wind seemed to follow us into the very castle itself. It was a large and gloomy chamber, lit only by the light of certain candles and torches placed in brackets around its stone walls. At its far end, a huge fire roared in a grand, open fireplace, although it seemed to throw out no heat for we were as cold as ever, despite its brilliance.

In the centre of this chamber was a vast oaken table upon which a series of candles had been set, and which was laid with a number of bowls containing both fruits and meats of varying kinds. Clearly, this was no pirate stronghold. The men made to move forward to fall hungrily on the food without delay for it had been many weeks since we had last seen a repast that even came near to this banquet. Nesbit waved them back, for he was a cautious man, and pointed to the far end of the hall. Among the shadows, a great stone staircase led up into another part of the castle. On the steps were several very ancient-looking men with long grey beards stretching almost to their waists, tucked into the belts of the strange, dark clothing that they wore. All of them were unarmed and yet they watched us with a terrible intensity that all of us found frightening. None of them spoke. At length, Nesbit called out to them, telling them who we were and asking the geographical location of this land in which we now found ourselves. Not a word did those old men answer. Some of the crew muttered about attacking them but, in truth, I think that we were afraid to.

Captain Nesbit asked if the food was for us and if we might eat of it but there came no answer from any of the watchers and our sense of fear and oppression grew all the stronger. Our captain turned to us and said that we should not eat anything for, most likely, it was poisoned and that we should now turn and go back to our ship.

Keeping our eyes firmly fixed upon those ancient men, we moved back again. Only then did one of them speak. None of us could tell what he said for the language seemed very old and appeared not to come easily to his lips. Lachlan MacDougall said that he thought it a very ancient form of Gaelic, no longer spoken in any part of Scotland. None of us paid any heed to his words or paused to ask him what he might mean but made our way back to the ship as fast as we could.

Soon we had set sail once more and the shores of the island had fallen away behind us. None of us dared to look back for some time but when we chanced to do so, every trace of the land seemed to have vanished away and nothing now lay behind us but the great emptiness of the rolling and infinite ocean.'

envisage trees, fields and houses among the towering cloudbanks, all suggestive of another, unknown country.

Not only cloud formations but changes in the quality of light play tricks on the eyes. The landscape that the Celts inhabited was littered with scattered rocks left in the wake of great glaciers and studded with the earthen fortifications of earlier, aboriginal peoples. In the evening, as the light began to fail, this terrain would change aspect. Shadows misled the senses, creating features that were not there at all. In the evening gloom, the tumbled stones took on the shape of a castle or fortress, a narrow valley seemed to suggest a river. When the light changed again, such things were revealed for what they were and the suggestions would be gone. To the Celtic mind, the half-glimpsed Otherworld had simply melted away. This is why most visions of the Otherworld, or the fairy world, were seen at twilight, between the lights.

 With climatic changes at the end of the great Ice Age, might have come phenomena that are no longer common. For example, mirages may have been more common in the west than they are today. Such optical illusions may well have been part of the Celtic experience – distantly-glimpsed lakes may have vanished; illusionary towns and cities may have come and gone in the wink of an eye – once again creating the myth of another country.

Evidence from relatively modern times supported this theory. On 7 July, 1878, the inhabitants of the Irish seaside town of Ballycotton, County Cork, were greatly excited by the sudden appearance out in the ocean of an island where none had existed before. Observers were able to see the new island quite plainly, its rugged coastline, deep woodlands and seemingly fertile valleys. Fishermen sailed out to investigate but, as they approached, the island suddenly winked out of existence, leaving them wondering.

The Otherworld

Similar islands have been seen off the coast of Kerry at Ballyheigue Strand, in Galway in Ballinaleame Bay and Carrigaholt in Clare. There have been reports of mysterious landmasses off Achill Island in Mayo and off the coast of Sligo at Inniscrone. (See also: Insert Box **The Island of Vanishing Men**.) These and other well-documented mirages might have formed the concept of a fairy country that came and went as it saw fit and created its own folklore.

A third explanation for the Otherworld belief may also have its roots in our own reality. We must remember that, during the time of the Celts, large tracts of the country and the seas round about lay mostly unexplored. Although the Celts were neither seamen nor explorers at least some of them made voyages of discovery, particularly during their early Christianised period. Irish and Scottish monks in particular are reputed to have sailed in flimsy craft to many parts of the world. One Irish saint – Brendan the Navigator – allegedly set foot in America, long before either the Vikings or Christopher Columbus.

*Reconstruction
of Celtic burial
in Chariot
from Somme-
Bionne, France*

Accounts of these often dangerous voyages, coupled with greatly exaggerated travellers' tales from all over the ancient world, served to create a new and fantastic landscape which coalesced into a generalised Otherworld, a place containing many exotic and diverse elements.

As the ancient world became more accurately mapped and its mysteries rationalised, these stories passed into legend and myth, but still they exerted a powerful influence on the development of the folktale within Celtic society. And, somewhere in the deepest recesses of the Celtic mind, the possibility of a distant, but utterly real, Otherworld continued to survive.

The Transmigration of Souls

Besides both natural and geographical explanations for the Otherworld, there was a religious one. The Otherworld was also the abode of the dead. Archaeological evidence has drawn attention to the richness of Iron Age tombs and the preponderance

of grave goods within them. This leads us to assume that the Celts probably believed in an Afterlife and, moreover, an Afterlife which was not all that different from the world that they knew. We have literary evidence from Caesar (*Gallic Wars*: *VI*) that seems to confirm this. In his description of the druids, he alluded to some of their lore that related directly to the movement of souls between one world and another or between one individual and another. He states:

> ' . . . the druids attach particular importance to the belief that the soul (or spirit) does not perish but passes after death from one body to another'
> (Julius Caesar: *Gallic Wars* VI)

There is a strong suggestion that the spirit passed into a body inhabiting another world. Similarly Lucan (*Pharsalia*: *I*) stated that the Celts considered death as merely an interruption in a continuous life, as the spirit passed from one form into another, or from one world to another. Other writers, such as Diodorus Siculus drew attention to similar beliefs – that the soul was immortal and, as its body deteriorated with age, it simply moved to another, usually located in another world. Celtic beliefs of the Otherworld as Afterlife even found their way into the Roman poet Virgil's *Aeneid*. The pagan creed certainly had an influence on Christian thinking and the soul-notion probably came from pagan tradition.

The Otherworld

Life in the Otherworld was not radically different from life in this world, and it was essential that those who crossed over were well equipped for the journey and for their arrival. High-ranking individuals were buried with all the trappings of their social status so that they could continue at the same social level in the Otherworld. Necessities of life were also included: enclosed in some tombs were chariots and/or carts, large amounts of food and changes of clothing. These, however, were the tombs of Celtic nobility and we have little evidence of how ordinary people approached the 'crossing over'. Before the first century BC in parts of England, formal burial was accorded to only about six per cent of the population and we have little evidence to show how the rest were treated.

The belief in rebirth was strong in the Celtic world (see **The Great Wheel of Existence**) and naturally tied in with the notion of another world. The belief also provided a comforting impression of continuity. The dead were not altogether gone, death was simply the same as passing from one room into another. From the Otherworld, those who had gone before watched and protected their descendants and took an interest in the communities that they had left. The next step in such a concept was to allow the dead to return if they wished. At special times of the year and in certain places in the countryside, said Celtic lore, the Veil between the two

THE ISLAND OF VANISHING MEN

It is possible for areas of the Otherworld to exist within our own world and vice-versa. Regions of land all across the Celtic world were believed to co-exist in this fashion, and were shunned for fear of some supernatural misfortune. In Ireland, they were known as gentle places, or 'fairy' places and associated with the Sidhe or other supernatural creatures. The belief has persisted to modern times and stories abound of those who have vanished into 'another place'.

A particularly sinister occurrence took place at the end of 1899 or the beginning of 1900. The location was not a fairy mound or a standing stone but a windswept and treeless island in the North Atlantic. Eileán Mór – Great Island – is no more than a bleak and sea-washed rock seventeen miles to the west of the Outer Hebrides. Although it is little more than eight hundred yards across, it is still the largest of seven similar islands known as the Seven Hunters or, more popularly, the Flannans.

In the seventh century, the hermit, Saint Flannan and one or two followers, inspired by the example of Monastic Fathers who settled the barren Skelligs off the Irish coast, founded a tiny monastic settlement on the rock. They remained on Eileán Mór for less than a century and it is reputed that Flannan died there having seen 'the True Face of God'. Shortly after, the settlement was inexplicably abandoned and no one knows what became of the monks.

Even in those ancient times, the place had a particularly sinister reputation and legends about it have persisted. In the 18th and 19th centuries, shepherds and turf-cutters who used the islands for pasture and fuel refused to spend the night there. Eileán Mór was widely known throughout the Hebrides as 'the other country' and was not truly considered part of this world.

It was also notorious for shipwrecks. Between 1892 and 1894, ten ships sailing to or from Clydebank foundered on the Flannans. In 1895, the Northern Lighthouse Board announced that a lighthouse was to be built on the largest of the islands. The project was supposed to take no more than two years but was beset by difficulties. Unforeseen problems in hoisting girders up a 200-foot cliff along with illnesses and injuries among the workers delayed construction and the lighthouse was not opened until December 1899. For a year, the Flannan Lighthouse served as the main beacon for shipping in the waters west of the Hebrides. Then, suddenly, just before Christmas 1900, the light failed.

Three keepers, James Ducat, Donald McArthur and Thomas Marshall, had been stationed on the island to maintain the lamp and, before radio communication, the only way to reach them was by boat. A series of fierce storms in the days leading up to Christmas made such a trip impossible. On Saint Stephen's Day 1900, the *Hesperus*, carrying Joseph Moore from the Northern Lighthouse Board finally docked at Eileán Mór. It seemed impossible that the lighthouse could have been destroyed by the storms or that all three keepers might have fallen ill at once.

The first ashore, Moore hurried up the path towards the lighthouse. No one answered his hail as he approached. Like Saint Flannan's settlement centuries before, the place lay completely abandoned.

In the main living quarters, the clock had stopped and the ashes of the fire were cold, while in the sleeping area, bunks were made and everything had been tidied away. The wicks of the lighthouse lamp had even been trimmed, ready for the night. A half-eaten meal was on the table and a chair lay overturned on the floor. Two oilskins were missing, but one set, belonging to Donald McArthur still hung in place.

Clearly, something had disturbed the keepers. Ducat and Marshall had gone out leaving McArthur to finish his meal. No one knew what had happened – perhaps McArthur was attacked as he ate or had dashed out, without his oilskins, to help his comrades.

The lighthouse log furnished no clue. Senior keeper James Ducat's last entry was made in a clear, neat hand at 9 a.m. on 15 December 1900. Three further entries were in the shaky, scrawling hand of Thomas Marshall. If anything, the entries served only to compound the mystery.

Ducat noted that, on 14 and 15 December, the lighthouse was battered by a fierce storm that showed no signs of abating. But all weather records show that these two days were especially calm with no trace of strong winds. The strong winds did not start until the afternoon of 16 December. There was no storm on 15 December 1900 – in this world.

According to writer Vincent Gaddis, not always a reliable authority, Marshall's entries said that Ducat was 'irritable', while McArthur was 'crying'. The second entry simply said 'Me, Ducat and McArthur prayed' and the third was a printed statement penned by Marshall, a strict Calvinist – 'God is over all'. This brings to mind the legend of Saint Flannan who died after glimpsing the 'True Face of God' on that lonely rock.

Mundane theories produce no evidence. The keepers might have gone out during the storms to check a winch at the jetty and have been swept away. The theory favoured by Walter Aldebert, another lighthouse keeper interested in the mystery, was that Ducat had mistakenly entered the wrong date in the log. This reasoning was dashed when the *SS Archer* reported passing south of the islands on the night of 15 December when her captain noticed that the light was already out. If they had been washed away, their bodies were never washed up in the Hebrides. Another theory suggests that the keepers went insane and rushed to their deaths but, again, not a shred of evidence exists. All were solid, sensible men.

Moore left the island after a thorough search and two days later investigators made a detailed inspection of the place. They found nothing and the mystery remains unresolved to this day. Three experienced seamen vanished on a tiny and remote island without leaving any clue as to their disappearance. Maybe they passed through a gateway between this world and another. Perhaps, on that sea-battered rock, the Otherworld is very close.

worlds was extremely thin and beings from both spheres could cross freely between them. Thus, the spirits, or reanimated corpses, of the dead were free to come back to visit briefly those whom they had left behind.

The notion of the returning dead seems to have held no terrors for the ancient Celts, certainly not to the same extent that the idea of ghosts holds for the modern mind. In some parts of the Celtic world, great feasts and banquets were held to celebrate the return of the dead to the world of the living. The most famous of these was the Irish *Féile na Marbh* – the Feast of the Dead – which was held on 31 October, Hallowe'en, when the veil between the worlds was especially thin.

At this time, the dead, usually in the form of animated corpses, would return to drink a glass of whiskey and eat a piece of bread with their descendants. Not to welcome a spirit into a house was to invite bad luck on the entire family, so the tradition said. In many cases, families simply left a glass of spirits and a piece of cake by the hearth-stone on Hallowe'en night, leaving the fire in as well, before they went to bed. It was common in some rural areas of Ireland, to scatter fine ash around the hearth so that if it was disturbed in the morning, the household would know that it had received visitors from beyond the grave during the night.

Company, especially that of their own descendants, seems to have been important to the returning dead. Souls who resided in the dreary, misty version of the Otherworld were desperate for warmth, friendship, and the company of living mortals.

The Otherworld

The traffic between the worlds worked both ways. There was a fear that those from the Otherworld could either take or coerce mortals to go with them when they returned. For example, mothers who had died in childbirth might be tempted to return in order to abduct the baby that they had left behind. Both Irish and Scottish folklore is littered with such attempts, some successful, others not. It was thought, particularly in Brittany, that dead men might return to take brides from the living world. There are numerous stories of shy or disfigured young girls, unable to find a partner, who unwittingly marry malignant corpses and are taken back 'to the cold and lonely grave'. The motif is used to great effect in a number of Breton tales and forms the basis for the Irish writer, Sheridan Le Fanu's famous story, *Schalken the Painter*. In this tale, set in the Holland of two centuries ago, Rose Velderkaust, the niece of the painter Gerard Douw and only love of his apprentice, Godfrey Schalken, is finally married to an aged suitor, Wilken Vanderhousen of Rotterdam, who it tran-spires is one of the unquiet dead. Although Schalken tries to prevent the match, he is unsuccessful and the awful corpse carries Rose away. But Schalken is granted one last glimpse into the Otherworld. Many years later in Rotterdam, before a funeral he gets chatting to the old sexton who tells him where the body is to be entombed.

Le Fanu was drawing not on any Dutch tradition but on his own Irish folklore con-cerning the living dead and the Otherworld. The glimpse into the antique Dutch apartment is strongly reminiscent of many Irish tales of glimpses into the other reality. In the tale, Schalken was able to return from the Otherworld of the dead in a single night. Others were not so lucky. Some returned from the realm beyond after a period of seven years; some did not return at all. It was believed that the realm of the dead was terribly close to this world and that the dead were continually watching for mortals whom they could lure or pull across into their own sphere. With the malignant dead so near at hand, mortals had to be continually wary. Besides being the realm of the dead, the Otherworld had other aspects in certain parts of the Celtic realm.

The Tuatha Dé Danann and the Sidhe

In 12th century Ireland, a book appeared which was to play a central role in the mythology and folklore of the country. This was the *Leabhar Gabhála – The Book of Invasions* which took its material from much older vernacular sources. Portions of the original text survive in other ancient manuscripts such as the 12th–century *Book of Leinster*. The Irish writer Micheál Ó Cléirigh (1575–1645) compiled a version in which he used several very old texts that have since been lost and it is generally this version that is referred to when speaking of the book.

Celtic Mythology

The Book of Invasions set out to detail a history of Ireland, from a period preceding the Deluge up to the reign of the High King Malachai Mór (AD 980–1002). It alluded to successive invasions of the country by strange peoples from across the sea. The first centuries BC were notable for migrations of peoples so there might be some truth in the text but much of it is highly mythologised. It was treated as history in many cases, though, and rapidly became the National Epic of Ireland.

It is the fifth of the invading groups that pertains to this section. They are referred to in the book as the *Tuatha Dé Danann* – 'The People (or Children) of the Goddess Danu'. They were said to have come from the east in a golden mist and were a race of divine beings, who inhabited Ireland immediately preceding the coming of the ancestors of the Gaels or Celts who were the sons of Mil or Milesians. They arrived in Ireland to find it already settled by the previous invaders, the *Fir Bholg* – literally 'bog men' – against whom they fought a mighty battle known as the First Battle of Magh Tuireadh.

The second battle at Moytirra, County Sligo, soon followed, this time against the Fomorians (or Fomorii – see **Giants, Monsters and Fairies**), a misshapen, monstrous and violent race who dwelt partly in the sea. They represented the evil spirits of Irish myth and were centred on Tory Island, off the Donegal coast, ruled by their gigantic, one-eyed king, Balor. In the First and Second Battles of Magh Tuireadh, the Tuatha Dé Danann were successful, their victory being attributed to their supernatural powers and to the potency of the magic talismans and sorcerous artefacts that they had brought with them.

Of all the legendary voyages of Celtic monks between the fifth and ninth centuries, no account is so widely renowned as the *Navigato Sancti Brendani Abbatis*, the journey of Saint Brendan the Navigator.

The official date for the writing of this work is given as somewhere in the 10th century; Professor James Carney has suggested that it may be a copy of a manuscript, dated about 800, which drew on even earlier sources. He claims in a reference that Brendan himself wrote the original text at some time during the sixth century. The later work became extremely popular during the medieval period, and appears in a number of Latin versions dating from that time.

Saint Brendan was born in County Kerry, Ireland in 489/90 and died 577/78. He had decided to become a monk quite early in life and had studied under two famous masters – Bishop Erc of Kerry and Saint Enda. From his earliest days, he was reputed to be a traveller and supposedly went to Iona to engage in debate with its abbot Saint Columcille.

Saint Brendan

Brendan showed great promise as a churchman, and was appointed Abbot of Llancarfan in Wales. Later he journeyed to Brittany and became tutor of the Breton saint Malo. Some Scottish legends credit him with founding a Christian colony in the desolate Orkneys, while there are other references to his preaching in the Faroe Islands. Whatever the truth of these tales, Brendan certainly appears to have been exceptionally well travelled. There is also a hint that Brendan revelled in the extent of his journeys and was exceptionally jealous of anyone who claimed to have travelled further than he.

The *Navigato* begins in the Abbey of Clonfert where the monk Barrind was regaling Brendan with stories of another monk called Mernoc, a seasoned traveller who had made a long journey into the west to discover new lands and new peoples for Christ.

Mernoc and his monks had discovered a new country far beyond the horizon and had spent 15 days there, winning many new souls for God. On hearing this, Saint Brendan was overcome with envy and vowed to equal, if not better, Mernoc's feat. He picked 14 monks to accompany him on a great expedition into the West, and they immediately set to work building a boat.

The manuscript describes, in great technical detail, construction of the vessel. Brendan allegedly kept a journal recording his voyage, describing in detail the lands that he and his followers encountered.

Accurate details are given concerning tides, currents, and navigational directions. This suggests that Brendan's voyage actually took place and modern seamen have attempted the journey in a similar craft.

It is quite possible that the saint and his monks traversed the shores of Iceland and sailed south to reach the coast of America, many centuries before Columbus. The American shore may well have seemed like the edge of the Otherworld – a place that no other mortal had ever seen. Along the way, Brendan and his followers saw many strange sights, several curious islands. They may have witnessed the birth of an island in a volcanic upheaval and visited a frozen 'sea of glass' and described icebergs and great whales in the Arctic seas.

In 1976 Tim Severin, using the technical data provided by Brendan's account, constructed a craft and attempted to voyage to America from the west of Ireland as the saint is alleged to have done. He travelled through the Hebrides and Faroes, past Iceland and on to Greenland and across the Davis Strait, eventually landing on the shores of Newfoundland on 26 June 1978. This proved that Irish monks *could* have sailed as far as the American continent, but does not prove that they *did*.

Brendan was not the only Celt to be credited with discovering America long before Columbus did. Welsh tradition holds that Madog – Madoc – son of Owain and king of Gwynedd sailed there in the mid-twelfth century. He is said to have landed in the 'Otherworld', America, about 1170. There is a persistent story, told both in Wales and America, that Madog and his followers stayed for a good number of years and married among the Mandan peoples of the Upper Missouri area. This story was highly fashionable during the Elizabethan period when all sorts of links between the Old and New Worlds were claimed, though no conclusive proof of Madog's expedition has ever been found.

In 1967, the linguist Richard Deacon, in an attempt to test the legend, made a serious comparison between the Mandan and Welsh tongues and found numerous similarities both in the pronunciation and meaning of words. Later examinations, however, showed no comparison between the cultural and social structures of the Indians and that of the medieval Welshmen. Madog's expedition still firmly belongs in the realm of mythology and folklore.

Celtic mythology contains travellers' epics that rival the Classical *Odyssey* of Homer. One of these epics is to be found in the Irish manuscript *Immram Curaig Mille Dúin* which tells of the wanderings of the chieftain Maol, or Mael, Dúin and his companions as they attempted to find the murderers of Maol Dúin's father.

On this journey, the sailors were filled with a sense of foreboding, fearful of the black, stormy sky and raging waves.

'There's some talk that we're approaching the very edge of the world,' said Murrough. 'And that, if we sail over it, we'll continue to fall throughout eternity. Most of us think that we should turn back and see if we can make the shores of Ireland once more'.

'We still haven't found my father's killer', Maol Dúin reminded the other. And I swore that I would follow him to the ends of the earth. We have come too far and faced too many hardships to turn back now. Your own brother died on the deadly Sea of Ice – would you let his sacrifice be for nothing? Think again, man!'

Suddenly, Turlough the look out said: 'I think I see land'.

Maol Dúin ran to the side of the craft. A rocky shore was emerging from the darkness where great boulders rose like fangs out of the churning ocean. 'Use the oars!' he shouted. 'I think I can see a cove!'

The men took the oars, Maol Dúin seizing one himself, and began to pull for the rapidly emerging shoreline. As the bow touched land, Maol Dúin leapt ashore. Murrough threw him a rope and he secured the craft to a large boulder on the very edge of the sea. It seemed covered in slime – a black, clinker-like substance that came away on his hand. Several of his companions joined him on the tiny beach and looked around them. They could see very little, for black fog was now rolling down across the rocks towards them, obscuring all but the faintest sunlight.

The air seemed to hold an acrid metallic tang that seared throats and lungs. Maol Dúin feared that it would prove deadly and that they could not remain for long. All the same, they had to explore – they needed water and provisions to continue on their way.

Cautiously, the warriors began to advance from the beach, heading inland. Everywhere was rock – nothing living was visible; no living creature flew or scurried from their approach. The whole island seemed to be no more than a plain of grey stone, covered in a dark and sulphurous slime, and sheathed in an throat-searing fog that blotted out most of the landscape.

'Maol Dúin!' the chieftain turned at the sound of Turlough's voice. He could hardly see his men through the choking mist but he could just make out Turlough's form directly behind him. The boy was squatting down, his hand pressed to the stone beneath their feet. 'Feel how hot the ground is becoming the further we travel inland!' Maol Dúin hunkered down and touched the rock. Turlough was right – it was steadily growing hotter.

'On the other side of that ridge,' cried Maol Dúin, pointing through the fog. 'Let's see what it is before we go!'

The entire centre of the island seemed to be a great hollow in which stood a titanic smithy. Great pieces of metal, some still semi-molten, lay scattered around a yawning chasm that seemed to plunge to the very bowels of the earth sending a column of flame into the sky. Sparks and smoke followed in its wake, clouding the air and turning it dark and dangerous to inhale.

From the sooty clouds that issued from the burning chasm, a massive figure emerged. It was at least four times the height of a normal man though human in shape. But the titanic being seemed completely hairless, its great head glinting in the firelight and, although its face seemed human it had only one eye in the centre of its forehead. The skin seemed hard and shell-like and to ripple with massive muscles. It wore a massive leather apron and in one hand carried a mighty hammer. Crossing to the anvil, the creature began to hammer the molten metal into shape.

'By all the gods', whispered Maol Dúin, fearful that the mighty being would overhear them. 'The entire island is a gigantic smithy! This must be where the giant-kind bring their metal to be forged'. He motioned back the way that they had come. 'We can go no further, or find water in such a place. We must go back to the boat'.

As they turned, a piece of the molten metal with which the smith-giant was working suddenly sheared off and went flying in their direction and Murrough shouted instinctively, pulling the ageing Dunlang out of its way. At the sound of his voice, the titanic smith looked up.

'Aha!' he exclaimed, his booming voice reverberating around the bleak rocks. 'Puny humans from far away, come to spy on my labours. They will never leave my workshop alive!' 'Run!' Maol Dúin shouted.

The men, heeding his words, rushed across the burning rocks in the direction of their boat. The ground shook below them as the giant followed. Maol Dúin and his companions had reached their craft and were sailing off before the giant approached the gravelly beach. Battling through the smoke, they made for open sea. On reaching the water's edge the giant drew from his apron pocket a piece of still-smouldering metal. With an oath, he hurled it after them but it fell short, making the ocean hiss and bubble like a cauldron as it sank out of sight, while he stood shaking his fist and shouting obscenities at the sailors.

Many Celtic tales of exploration feature a great smithy or an island surrounded by fire. Perhaps what these travellers witnessed was the creation of new lands by volcanic action – particularly common at one time in northern waters. The tale has been greatly embellished, and there seems to have been additions made from other myth cycles. The titanic, one-eyed smith is certainly suggestive of the Cyclops, Polyphemus, in the Odyssey, although it may have more Celtic connections with the one-eyed giant king of the Fomorii – Balor of the Evil Eye.

If there is a glimmer of truth in the legend of the Tuatha Dé Danann, we wonder where they came from. Some Irish historians and folklorists such as Peter Beresford-Ellis have suggested that they might have been a displaced Grecian race whose knowledge, borrowed from the Mediterranean cultures, was far superior to that of the indigenous Irish. They cite the phrase 'the East' as a traditional point of origin for these people, stating that this may be somewhere in the Mediterranean. Others have suggested that they were themselves a proto-Celtic race, pointing to the primacy of the Mother-Goddess Danu and noting her frequent confusion with Anu, a fertility goddess specific to Ireland. It is highly probable that the two goddesses were in fact one, a remnant of an earlier Celtic period. Some versions of the invasion story specifically state that the Tuatha Dé Danann had come from the Otherworld, which was the source of their mysterious powers, and that they returned there after the coming of the Celts.

There is no doubt in the ancient texts that the Tuatha were wise in magic and in druid lore. Many of their chieftains were powerful gods such as The Daghdha – the 'Good God' – who was both a warrior and a druid of frightening power. They were greatly skilled in medicine and it was under the influence of their chieftain/god Dian Céacht that Irish healers became world-renowned and much sought after by other civilizations.

By the time the Celtic ancestors arrived, the Tuatha had declined in power, having remained unchallenged for centuries, and were defeated by the incomers. Even then, they were able to bargain, mainly by stealing their milk and by causing their corn to fail. It was agreed that the two races should live side by side, although the Tuatha would have to create a special realm for themselves through their magic arts. This they did by either creating, or returning to, the Otherworld that always remained just out of sight of ordinary mortals. Traditionally, the Otherworld lay far underground and was marked by hollows, hills and mounds. It was conceived as a magical equivalent of the upper Celtic world, having its own rulers, dynasties, internal politics, loves and quarrels. In this shadowy realm, the Tuatha Dé Danann continued to live in ageless beauty and splendour and it was where they continued to practise their sorcerous arts and to exercise control over the supernatural aspects of life.

The Otherworld

It was, in later years, quite easy to confuse one magical race with another. The race with which the legends of the Tuatha Dé Danann merged was the Sidhe. The name comes from the ancient Irish word *Sidh* meaning a 'fairy mound or hillock', not to be confused with *Síth*, which means 'peace'. The concept of the Sidhe was a natural progression from the idea of the Tuatha Dé Danann as a spiritual, semi-divine race living beneath the ancient earthworks and hills that littered the land. These were the burial mounds of the long-vanished Neolithic, aboriginal inhabitants of the country, but to the Celts they were sites of awe and mystery: the entrances to the underground kingdom of the Sidhe. This kingdom soon became equated with the Otherworld as the two concepts merged, and mounds and raths in rural areas were considered places where the two worlds touched and where it might be possible to cross from one to the other. These locations were soon absorbed into rural folklore and sometimes into the great myths as well. The goddess of death and war, the Morrigan, emerges from her sidhe to bring about the end of the hero Cú Chulainn, for example.

Another word connected to the myth is 'fairy'. Some argue that the word comes from two ancient Irish words *fa*, or *fiah*, and *rí* meaning 'spirit race' which would naturally refer to the Tuatha Dé Danann, but its etymology remains unclear. There is no doubt that the fairies were associated with the Tuatha and with spirits in general (see **Spirits of Earth and Air**) and that the hills and raths were regarded as 'fairy places'. Country people tended to avoid them for fear of being dragged away into the Otherworld or 'fairyland' as it came to be known. In keeping with the idea of an Otherworld 'race', Irish fairies were imagined as being similar to humans, except that they might be somewhat paler in complexion and dressed in styles that were long out of fashion in the mortal world. The idea that they were small was not widespread until a much later date.

Traditionally, Saint Patrick was responsible for creating the underground Otherworld. Realising that the Sidhe and mortals would have to live side by side, the wily saint promised the Sidhe that they could have all the lands that the sunlight did not touch

THE PHANTOM ISLAND

Stories and beliefs concerning other worlds and phantom lands certainly owe much to the mirage phenomenon.

During the early to mid 19th century a number of mirages were common around the Irish coastline. One of the most famous appeared off the north Derry shore near the town of Portstewart on 12 July 1866. Its notoriety stems from the fact that it was the subject of much learned discussion and attention from several local newspapers across the north of Ireland. One of the main academics who discussed it at length was the Rev. Professor Witherow, then a senior lecturer at Magee College in Derry and correspondent of the *Derry Standard*. He describes the occurrence as 'an optical illusion, arising from unequal light refraction'.

It was a local paper, *The Coleraine Chronicle* (21 July 1866) that gave the clearest and most descriptive account of the phenomenon and so clearly demonstrated how a mirage could sometimes be transformed into a vision of another world in the general mind:

'At eleven o'clock this forenoon, the grandest optical illusion that we ever witnessed appeared on the coast of Ennishowen between Greencastle and the Lighthouse, at the north-eastern point of the peninsula. When our attention was first drawn to it, the place where the Lighthouse stands was, as seen from Portstewart, occupied by a magnificent castle of gigantic proportions, with two towers in the wings. In a few moments it was a villa of much humbler dimensions, surrounded by a lawn elegantly laid out, and carriageways and footpaths clearly visible. Then, in a few moments, another castle of still grander proportions, with three towers, appeared distinctly visible along the coast at Greencastle, encircled, as it seemed, by a dense forest. Magilligan Strand, seen from this point at ordinary times, is little better than a golden thread, hemming in the dark blue waters but, on this day, one end of it, next to Donegal seemed to rise up and stand as a perpendicular cliff – a grand precipice, enclosing the sea on that side like a mighty wall. In a few minutes, all had changed. The precipice at Magilligan faded away. The grand castle at the mouth of the Foyle had disappeared. Then the whole shore from Greencastle down to the Lighthouse seemed a continuous plantation, showing many openings, villas, stately mansions and, in one instance, a great square church tower, that was distinctly visible for upwards of thirty minutes. For two hours, up until one o'clock, the mirage continued, and was seen and admired by great numbers in this town. Shortly after one o'clock it had entirely vanished. We observed that, during the time it continued, there seemed a thin hazy stripe of atmosphere, accurately defined, along the margin of the water. Above this, the Ennishowen hills presented the same appearance as they do every day; on this side of it, the water glancing in the sunlight, presented the same appearance as it usually does. But through the thin, hazy atmosphere appeared the strange landscape, ever varying in its forms, which we have described. Cliffs and cottages, forests, castles, churches, all successively appeared and vanished; and at last the vapour set down on the peninsula for the afternoon, all minor objects became lost to view and nothing appeared by the long dark barrier of the Donegal mountains standing up between us and the west.

Few who witnessed this beautiful illusion for two hours this forenoon are ever likely to forget that they have enjoyed a privilege that is of no common kind and which, for many years at the seacoast, they might never have again.'

as their own and that mortals would take the rest. The deal had been agreed before the Sidhe realised that this meant that they would have to live underground and in the remote and gloomy valleys, bogs and hollows that nobody else wanted. Consequently, enmity arose between the fairy-kind and the mortals as the Sidhe reluctantly retreated into the lightless world.

The fusion of different beliefs concerning the Otherworld created a world both pleasant and frightening. Usually regarded as a world of peace, it was also a place of imprisonment for mortals – one where time flowed strangely.

Tír na nÓg

The notion of a sorcerous race living in peaceful contentment in a parallel world so close to our own aroused the curiosity of the Celtic mind about the nature of these people: their life span and the incidence of sickness and disease among them. If the people of the Otherworld were to be equated with the ancient gods and spirits, then it was quite probable that they were immortal and that death and disease never touched them. Their reputation as great and magical healers would also preclude this, as would the unending peace and bliss of their overall existence.

It was generally held that the inhabitants of the Otherworld were immortal. From their vantage point, far beyond mortal sight, they watched the passage of years in the human world with a mixture of amusement and superiority. As they were untouched by illness or decay, they remained ever young and ever beautiful. Many descriptions of fairies comment upon their great beauty, unblemished skin and stately bearing. Out of this concept arose the idea of Tír na nÓg – the Land of Youth or the Land of Forever Young – yet another description of the Otherworld. It was a land of contentment and ease where only favoured mortals might visit. This idea created questions about how the people of Tír na nÓg noted the passing of time in their world. In the mortal sphere, the passing of days, months and years was marked by the ageing process but in the land of Ever Young, there was no such measurement of time.

The Otherworld

The Otherworld was virtually timeless; if time passed it did so at a much slower rate than in the mortal world. There was no ageing, nor death, nor disease and with only feasting and bliss, there was really little to register the passing of the centuries. Anyone who entered the Otherworld, had to abide by these rules and generally ceased to age. But the ageing process would resume immediately they set foot in the mortal world once more, and sometimes it would do so at an accelerated rate. Thus people who had been away for a long period of time – though only for a few days by the standards of the Otherworld – returned home only to die from extreme old age (see **Oisín's Return from the Underworld**).

The idea of an immortal, blissful Otherworld soon became incorporated in Christian philosophy. The idea of Heaven – a bright and peaceful place – had been current in many myth cycles across the ancient world and was quickly assimilated into the

OISÍN'S RETURN FROM THE OTHERWORLD

Oisín ages and withers as soon as his feet touch land.

Oisín was the son of the great war-leader Fionn MacCumhaill. The tale of his abduction into the Otherworld, or *Tír na nÓg* – The Land of Youth – is part of the Fenian, or Fionn, Cycle of Irish Mythology. Bewitched by Niav of the Golden Hair, a daughter of the king of the Otherworld, he found that once he entered the Land of Youth he could not escape and was forced to marry her. Longing to return to his own country, he began to pine, much to the distress of his wife. Grudgingly, she allowed him to return to the mortal world, for a day, on the understanding that he should not set foot either on his own land or on the earth of Ireland.

Niav gave him an enchanted horse on which he could visit his old haunts and estates. The speed of the horse seemed to increase as it galloped through the countryside. It was moving so swiftly that Oisín saw only glimpses of the landscape around him. He noticed a subtle change to the landscape. Where there had been wild and untamed moorland and bog, the haunt of wild animals and birds, there were now bordered and cultivated fields, in which cattle grazed and crops had been planted. Where there had been desolate stretches of waste and rock, there were now clusters of small cottages that sent their smoke curling lazily into the air, and tended gardens, where men worked raising small crops of potatoes. Even the roads seemed somehow changed: where there had been no more than grassy tracks, leading off into the forests or mountains, they now seemed well paved and better laid-out with stones and proper borders. The countryside seemed to have undergone changes that would have taken decades to complete.

Oisín came upon several men who were trying to move a large rock which lay in the middle of the road. An old man sat on a rock by the roadside, watching and directing four younger men as they pushed and strained to remove the obstacle. They had no success and, as he looked at them, Oisín realised that they were smaller and less muscular than the men with whom he had fought in the great days of the Fianna.

The men all looked up as he pulled his horse up alongside them. 'Is this the road to Royal Tara?' asked Oisín. The young men eyed him warily.

'It is the road to Tara sure enough', one of them replied. 'But I've never heard it called Royal Tara before'. He spoke in an insolent fashion and in a harsh and unfamiliar accent that Oisín didn't like.

'You know that it is the seat of the High King of Ireland and of his warrior', he snapped.

'Is he a madman?' he heard one of them ask his companion.

'There has been no High King at Tara for countless years!' He spoke in the same strange accent as the first speaker and there was a general murmur of consent among the men gathered by the roadside. Suddenly afraid, Oisín felt for his sword and said:

'Have a care whom you would call mad! For I am Oisín, son of the mighty warrior Fionn MacCumhaill, hero of the Fianna'. At his words, the men broke into scathing laughter.

'Now I know that you're mad' he taunted. 'Oisín is only a figure of myth, an old legend who was supposed to have vanished into the Otherworld over three hundred years ago. Songs about him are all but forgotten and it is even said that he never existed at all. You can't be him!'

'No!' the voice came from the old man seated on the roadside rock. 'Oisín is no myth. He was a man who lived almost four hundred years ago and who was lured away by some enchantress into the world of the Sidhe. It was widely prophesied in my great-grandfather's time that he would, one day, return and that no one would know him. Tell me great warrior, are you that hero?'

Oisín's mind reeled from what he had been told. And yet, such a thing would explain the changes that he'd seen as he hurtled through the Irish countryside on his way here.

'You lie, old man,' Oisín spat. 'How can nearly four hundred years have passed, when I know that I've spent only a few days in the Otherworld?'

'But time in the Otherworld passes differently from that in the mortal world,' he said slowly. 'A day there may count for a hundred years in this. But you haven't answered my question sir. Are you indeed the Oisín of whom heroic ballads are still sung?'

Oisín struggled to reply. 'I … I am!' he stuttered. 'And I'll prove it to you. I'll move this rock that you seem to find difficult. Only a true warrior of the Fianna could move it without dismounting'.

Leaning down from the saddle of the horse, he took a grip on the stone and began to move it. The young men watched in astonishment. Slowly, and with some difficulty, the stone was eased to the side of the roadway. Strangely, Oisín found the rock heavier than he had imagined it would be – perhaps his famed warrior-strength had diminished a little in the Otherworld. As he leant forward to get a grip on the sides of the stone, the strap that secured his saddle snapped. At the same time, the snorting steed moved forward a little and Oisín found himself tumbling to the ground. Instinctively, he thrust out a foot to save himself, touching the ground only for an instant. The moment the sole of his boot touched the earth of the human world, Oisín felt a tremor run through his entire body, and remembered what Niav had said: 'Do not set your foot on the ground Oisín or you will be lost, both to this world and your own'.

The others stared at him in wonder, as Oisín, son of Fionn MacCumhaill and mighty hero of the Fianna aged before their eyes. In a moment, he had become an old man with shaggy hair and a white beard, fearfully bowed over and marked with all the signs of a long and careworn life. Even then the change was not complete, and as they watched, the ancient creature crumbled into a fine, grey dust that began to blow away in the wind.

Christian tradition as the religion continued to advance. The Celts took to it with an extraordinary enthusiasm since the idea of the Christian Heaven confirmed their notion of a blissful Otherworld. Thus, the idea of Heaven as a reward for a good and saintly life was widespread throughout the Celtic West (see **Legends of Saints and Holy Men**).

Gradually, the idea of the Land of Youth or the Place of Great Repose became incorporated into the journeys of exploration that were undertaken, particularly by monks, across the West. Rather than being a land just out of view, Tír na nÓg became an island or a lost continent far out to sea. In Christian tradition, it became the Isles of the Blest, visited only by saints or exceptionally holy persons. It was here that the King of the World held his court.

Both monks and ancient heroes would set out to find these Isles and the stories of their wanderings form part of mythological travellers' tales such as *The Voyage of Bran*. Like the Otherworld, the Isles of the Blest were said to lie just beyond the horizon and just out of sight of ordinary mariners. Such fabulous lands took the name of Hy-Brasil or the Island O'Breasail – a kind of Celtic Atlantis – and it was thought that at least some sailors might be able to find it. When sailors landed in South America, they thought that they had reached O'Breasail – the Otherworld. Now it is called Brazil. A new and even more mysterious form of the Otherworld had been established.

The Otherworld

Annwn

Just as the Irish had Tír na nÓg , so the Welsh had Annwn and here we may be nearer to the original idea of the Otherworld. It is better documented than its Irish counterpart and features strongly in the First Branch of the Welsh Classic *The Mabinogi*, a collection of ancient Welsh texts dating from around the 14th century. Annwn was an underground realm ruled by a king called Arawn. Traditions concerning him vary – sometimes he is a good, wise and courageous ruler, sometimes he is the embodiment of the Demon King himself. In his demonic form, he compels Pwyll, King of Dyfed and one of the earliest heroes in Welsh mythology, to exchange places and appearance with him for a year. During Pwyll's time in the underworld he successfully took on Arawn's great rival, Hafgan. Arawn is overjoyed and bestowed upon the mortal ruler a shower of gifts including a pig, then considered an Otherworld animal. Afterwards, Pwyll was known as the Head of Arawn, which increased his status among his own people. Perhaps to satisfy the Christian tradition, it was specifically pointed out that during his sojourn in Annwn, Pwyll refused to sleep with Arawn's beautiful wife and was able to resist her undoubted charms.

In many respects, the kingdom of Annwn was familiar. The political structure was the same as in the mortal world: the king's rule was absolute but he was aided by the advice of his druids. There were nobles there and they indulged in great feasting and drinking. So similar are the two worlds that Pwyll slips easily into his assumed role as Arawn.

THE GREEN CHILDREN

Scattered throughout Celtic folklore are stories of mysterious, supernatural beings that crossed from the Otherworld into our own. Usually they took the guise of fairies or gods but sometimes appeared as people not unlike ourselves.

One of the most famous tales dates from the 12th century and concerns two green children – a boy and a girl – who appeared in England during the civil war between King Stephen and the Empress Matilda, daughter of Henry I. They appeared in Suffolk, close to the village of Saint Mary's-by-the-Wolf-Pits near Bury, on the lands of a Norman knight, Sir Richard de Calne. Alarmed local peasants captured the children and took them as curiosities to Sir Richard's stronghold. He made many enquiries about their origins and learned that they had appeared to crawl from a hole in the ground left when a tree had been uprooted during a recent storm. No one could understand their language and they refused to eat the meat that the peasants offered to them.

Sign depicting green children who appeared in 12th century Suffolk, England

their crops. The people of Saint Martin's Land did not eat meat, but subsisted on a diet of grasses and pulses.

There was no formal religion but some people followed an old Celtic religion of pre-Christian times. The countryside around her village was dotted with old raths and standing stones.

She and her brother had come to England when they followed one of their father's strayed ewes. They wandered into a mountainside cavern and followed the sound of bells to what she called 'the upper world'. She would like to go back home but could not find the hole out of which she and her brother had emerged as floods had closed it soon after their arrival.

Father Anthony recorded other details from her about the Otherworld but he found them so shocking that he hid the transcript, declaring that 'Christian eyes would never look upon what was writ therein'. The book is said to be hidden in the vicinity of Bury Saint Edmunds.

Shortly after her revelations, the girl left the charge of Sir Richard de Colne to marry one of his squires and moved to Lenna, near King's Lynn. From time to time, she would return to Saint Mary's-by-the-Wolf-Pits as if to look for her way back home. One day she vanished and was believed to have returned to Saint Martin's Land.

Sir Richard, uncertain what to do about the children, adopted them and placed them under the care and tutelage of his personal Confessor, either Father Anthony or Father John. The boy never adapted to his new surroundings but became morose and withdrawn, refusing the education offered by the good Confessor. Both children were baptised. The boy died shortly after his baptism. The girl seemed to enjoy her new surroundings and took to both education and religion with gusto. Under the guidance of Sir Richard and his Confessor, she began to speak some English mixed with Norman French. She was eventually able to give an account of where she and her brother had come from.

Their country was underground and was known as Saint Martin's Land – a long-forgotten Celtic Otherworld. Everything about it was green - the sky, the earth, the animals, the people. In many respects, Saint Martin's Land was very like medieval England. The people lived by farming and dwelt in small, tightly knit villages along the banks of rapid rivers, each governed by its own headman. There was no distinction between day and night there, for the sun never shone. Nor were there seasons, although there seemed to be extremely heavy rains at certain times. So heavy were these downpours that the people had to move their dwellings for fear of flooding. Most of the time there was a light, misty drizzle, just enough to nourish

The legend may owe more to the imagination of medieval writers than to an actual, historical event. Most of the story comes from Roger of Coggeshall who was famous for his tall tales. Using Roger's original text in his *History of England*, other writers took up the story, altering and embellishing it.

The most interesting and plausible explanation is put forward by the Fortean writer Mike Dash in his recent book *Borderlands* (1997). In the mid-12th century when the story is set, England went through a 19-year Civil War and he suggests that the mystery may be nothing more than the tale of two malnourished waifs from the Suffolk village of Fornham-Saint-Martin's who were caught up in the general conflict. They reached Saint-Mary's-by-the-Wolf-Pits after walking through passageways winding through the Neolithic flint mines that run under Thetford Forest. Their greenness was a disease known as green chlorosis, caused by severe malnutrition, while their unintelligible language was merely a thick and unfamiliar local accent.

Annwn features in a number of early Welsh tales and poems. In one legendary story, the daughter of the king of Annwn had to wash at a place known as the Ford of the Barking until she had a son by a Christian. She was finally seduced by Urien Rheged, who had received Christian baptism, and whose twins she bore. Poem 30 in *The Book of Taliesin the Bard*: The 'Spoils of Arawn' recounts a hero-quest into the Otherworld by Arthur of Britain and his men to steal a miraculous diamond-studded cauldron, the property of the chieftain of Annwn. The cauldron, which was created, not by a smith, but by the breath of nine virgins refused to boil any food for a coward. The expedition to the Otherworld was disastrous and Arthur lost most of his warriors – out of three shiploads of men, only seven soldiers survived.

Annwn was a place of great contentment, learning and ease, a 'place of the Blest', and so it passed into rural folklore. But, as fundamentalist religion spread through Wales in the 18th and 19th centuries, the mythical realm became the embodiment of Hell from which great and monstrous devil-dogs rushed across the night sky.

These awful creatures, known as the Hounds of Annwn, played a significant part in Welsh folklore. Sometimes they were completely black and about the size of a sheep; at other times they were slightly smaller and had flecks of white and grey in their coats. They dripped fire and sparks from their mouths and eyes and were chained but guided by a sinister, horned, black figure, the Devil himself. The Hounds of Annwn may have their origins in earlier Celtic belief. This nightly procession was intent on carrying away souls and recently buried corpses to the dim Otherworld. According to folklore, it was as well to keep doors and windows locked and barred as the Hounds passed by lest someone in the house might be carried off into the Realm Beyond.

The Otherworld

The picture of the Otherworld, then, was confusing and contradictory. There was the blissful Afterlife for bards and warriors; a gloomy domain where malignant spirits of the departed seethed and plotted against humankind; a hidden land of fairies who constantly threatened Humankind; it might even be Hell itself. All these ideas flowed together to form a mythical country where the recognised laws of time and space did not apply. The Otherworld could be a vast continent; or no more than a tiny island. Time could pass at a normal rate and distances could be as they were in the mortal world or they might be altogether different.

There was no limit to the expanse or temporality of the Otherworld. It was, in effect, the land of Celtic imagination and the land of longing and desire. Each time we pick up a fairy-story like 'Jack and the Beanstalk', or read a tale of fantasy, we enter that strange country that was so real to our ancestors.

Spirits Of Earth And Air

The Supernatural Forces of Celtic Belief

Celtic Mythology

When considering the deities of the ancient Celtic world, we are faced with something of a dilemma. The fragmentary nature of its society and religion precluded a cohesive, structured and unified pantheon of deities such as the mythologies of Rome and Greece. Celtic religion was more a complex configuration of tribal and localised cults rather than a national faith. Where a semblance of unified structure existed, it usually reflected a fusion of Celtic and Hellenic or Romanised gods. There are elements of Scandinavian mythologies in later Celtic legends from increased contact with the various cultures of the ancient world. The Romans believed that all nations and cultures worshipped the same gods that they did but with different names and attributes. Thus it is not surprising that many of the gods of the conquered Celtic peoples had their names changed into Latin equivalents – Apollo, Jupiter, Minerva, etc. – and that their attributes were altered to fit the specific Roman god after whom they were named.

When Caesar listed the most popular Gaulish deities in his *Gallic Wars*, he naturally amended their names. It is believed that Mercury refers to Lugus, a god of light, whose cult centre Lugunum – Fort of Lugus – became the capital of Roman Gaul and whose feast day, 1 August, became the festival of Augustus. A British healing goddess, Sulis, became identified with the Roman goddess Minerva, becoming the composite Sulis Minerva worshipped primarily at the healing spa of Bath, later an important Roman city. Of course, Romans and Celts might have had a common Indo-European origin, which would have formed the basis of shared myth-patterns and common attributes for their gods. This made the process of Romano-Celtic amalgamation relatively easy. But these composited gods and goddesses make any study of pure Celtic religion doubly difficult.

The earliest form of worship among the Celts was probably an animistic religion, common in many ancient peoples, including the Semites – forerunners of the Hebrews. This saw the workings of vaguely specified spirits and forces reflected in nature generally. Deities dwelt in rocks and trees, in standing stones and in rivers and wells, and their influence could extend beyond the physical confines of these locations. A well spirit, or tree spirit, might create fierce windstorms or cause the crops to fail if not placated.

This type of worship is reflected in the ancient religions of both Scotland and Ireland, perhaps because of the spectacular landscapes of these places. In addition, many of the Celtic clans venerated tribal protective or hunting spirits, often embodied in the form of wild animals - deer, bulls, horses etc. These deities guaranteed sufficient animals to hunt, and imbued warriors with strength to defend their settlements against attack. These protective spirits tended to be associated with strong and wild animals - boars, bulls and horses, all widely regarded as symbols of strength and virility. The Celts made little distinction between the gods and the animals that represented them and many of the gods took on animal characteristics.

Lastly, some of the spirits were strongly associated with fertility. As the Celts settled Western Europe the notion of fertility became paramount in their religion. It was essential that the crops continued to grow from year to year, and that the cattle and sheep continued to produce young. It was also essential that the tribes themselves continued to grow and expand. The Celts had not fully abandoned their warlike nature, and their tribal history is filled with stories of cattle raids or attacks on other communities. It was essential that a healthy population of young men to act as warriors existed to defend against such raids (see **Ancient Heroes**). Offerings were frequently made to local spirits to ensure fruitfulness throughout the coming years.

GODS AND GODDESSES

While many characters in medieval Celtic literature, (the earliest form of mythological literature available to us), have at least some vestiges of the power accorded to the Mediterranean deities, few of them can truly be said to be 'divine' in the accepted sense. Most of the available literature was written, not by worshippers or those soaked in Celtic tradition, but by monkish clerics who had quite specific notions as to what constituted 'divine status'. It is reasonable to suppose that much of the lore passed down has been altered or debunked in some way, so as not to detract from the sovereign status of God Himself, or to conform to Christian perspective. The limited powers and flawed characters of the Celtic deities and god characters are not being placed against any formalised religion as we understand it. Popular among Celts was the cult of the Hero, or Great Person, and stories from several cults have found their way into the general stream of Celtic mythology.

Over time, these heroes were either imbued with godly attributes or became confused or merged with legendary Otherworld beings. This turned the Great Person into a quasi-divine entity in his or her own right.

Like the later Christian saints, the early Celtic warriors gathered cults about themselves, enjoying adulation noted far removed from outright worship. The amorphous character that emerged out of all this is difficult to categorise. Those who came to write about such figures undoubtedly added lore of their own and might have enlarged them even further. It might be true to say that the Celts never accorded their hero-gods wholly divine status in the style of the Romans and Greeks. There was always some part of them connected to the mortal world.

A good example was the Scots/Irish god Fionn Mac-Cumhaill - Finn MacCool - as he later came to be known. Originally the personification of wisdom, his cult merged his persona of earthly seer with that of an actual hero and this was how he was recorded throughout medieval Irish literature. He was described as one of the most important warriors of the Fianna - a band of heroic knights - from time to time, accorded unearthly powers.

In Celtic mythology, the concept of fertility was deemed female, since it was women who bore the children. Some folklorists argue that the original all-encompassing deity of the Celts was female, perhaps the Great Mother, although this is purely speculation.

One of the oldest Celtic goddesses known is Danu, whose cult - the Children of Danu (Tuatha Dé Danann) - invaded Ireland several millennia ago, according to the 12th-century *Book of Invasions*. The name Danu was well known all over early Europe and is most probably primitive Celtic, if not Indo-European in origin. The goddess of fertility and agriculture, she was adopted by the Celts as they settled down and became a farming people, rather than a warrior force. Other, local, female farming deities were also known to the early Celts – Bóinn, Banna and Brigid – and it is no coincidence that many of the rivers which irrigated the lands had female names and female aspects.

Fertility worship highlighted the passing seasons for the Celts, and they began to consider their year in terms of festivals associated with growing and harvesting of crops, and the raising of livestock (see **The Great Wheel of Existence**). All the while brooding spirits watched over them, weighing their every move and judging their every action. Caesar, commenting on the inhabitants of Gaul, states that they were 'an extremely religious people'. For the ancient Celt, then, spirits and gods were everywhere.

The Landscape

In many Celtic countries, the landscape is spectacular. It can be mysterious and threatening and must have affected the early Celtic settlers. The lands of the West were shaped by the Ice Age. Great boulders and heaps of stones, moved by mighty glaciers and ignominiously dumped by the departing ice, lay everywhere. Many of these great megaliths must have been suggestive of either giants (see **Giants, Monsters and Faries**) or superhuman/supernatural entities. The earthworks and stone circles of aboriginal races were treated with wonder, as the habitations of strange and unearthly beings. They rapidly became the objects of worship and a focus for localised religion. The distinction between giants and gods became blurred. In Ireland, Scotland, Wales and Cornwall, are great earthworks, enclosures or stones known locally as giants' graves, reputed to boast supernatural powers well beyond the province of any gigantic man.

Spirits of Earth and Air

Stones were important to the ancient Celts. They were used for building, as boundary and as memorial markers and it is not surprising that they became the habitation of mysterious spirits and that strange powers were ascribed to them. In Brittany, a persistent tradition told that the druids used these stones to focus Otherworld powers, in order to create storms and diseases in our own world.

Many large stones, particularly great, singles stones, were the object of druidical worship, and associated with the fertility sects. The configurations of the stones also puzzled the Celts. They were arranged in a number of ways. There were Inger stones jutting out of the earth like a warning finger and stone circles. There were rocking stones: a flat stone resting on the top of another either a natural phenomenon or the work of prehistoric engineers, dolmens and cromlechs. These latter were known as Fos-Leac in Ireland, traditionally the burial-site of a local chieftain or hero and, later, of a saint. They consisted of two upright stones surmounted by a capstone.

Many stones had special powers that formed the beliefs of the local communities. In Brittany, it was believed that an infertile woman who sat astride the capstone of a dolmen would conceive within the year. While in Ireland, a couple who kissed a Kissing Stone at the same time would find their love would last forever. (For these and other such beliefs see Bonwick: *Irish Druids and Old Irish Religions*, 1894.)

It was John Aubrey, in the 17th century, who first linked the standing stones with druidical temples, although there appears to be little evidence for such a connection. Professor Joseph Anderson has observed in his *Scotland in Pagan Times*:

' ... in the end of the seventeenth century, there was no tradition among the people connecting these places with the druids. They were simply regarded as places of pagan worship.'

Even if the Celtic holy men did not raise the standing stones and stone circles, they used them within their religion. Some of the single standing stones had the shape of an extended phallus and conformed to the overall Celtic preoccupation with fertility religions. The medieval writer Jocelyn of Furness refers to many of these as 'druid stones' which had pagan and fertility associations.

Such stones could also be used for human sacrifice. On the north Antrim coast, on the northerly tip of Ireland near the town of Portrush, a lone stone rears up in the middle of a field overlooking the sea. It is known locally as the Clogh Ór and lends its name to the land around. There is little doubt it was used, like the Crom Cruach in County Fermanagh (see **The Druidic Tradition**), for infant sacrifice which was thought to restore health and vigour to the ground and to secure the harvest for another year. It was a sacrifice to the spirit that dwelt in the stone. The stone was venerated as a living embodiment of the god. In many areas, there were a variety of Cloch Ór – Golden Stones – that might have been used for similar purposes and which were said to contain spirits.

It was believed that, in order to take away its heathen power, a stone in County Tyrone was placed within the precincts of Clogher Cathedral, which then reputedly took its name from the stone.

In 1699, an old man was arraigned before the Kirk Session in Elgin, Morayshire charged with idolatry. He had apparently set up a large standing stone near his house and raised his cap to it (See: Evan Hadingham, *Circles and Standing Stones*, New York, 1976). He was not alone. The 18th-century writer Thomas Pennant, while

Celtic human sacrifice was offered to this stone figure on Boa Island, Ireland.

GOIBHNIU

Saint Albán

Goibhniu or the Gobán Saor is the ancient Celtic god of smithcraft, sometimes also portrayed as an architect. The word 'saor' added to his name denotes an 'artificer' or 'artisan' endowing Goibhniu with wider functions than those of smith-god or metalworker. It seems that the Irish Goibhniu and his Welsh counterparts Gofannon and Gwydion were regarded as expert craftsmen and designers and much sought after, both by gods and mortals, for the excellence of their work. In Celtic Christian mythology, the Gobán Saor is credited with the design and construction of many early churches. Taking the analogy further it might be that, in some parts of the Celtic world, Goibhniu was loosely equated with God as the Master Builder of the Firmament and the Designer of Creation. He appears as such in a ninth-century poem where he is described as Gobán.

Although primarily a builder, Goibhniu was credited with power over natural forces. By throwing his axe and creating a line in the sand, he ensured that the incoming tide advanced no further than Tráigh Thuirbhe – Turvey Strand near Lusk in County Dublin. In some versions of the tale, Goibhnui is identified as one of the sons of the chieftain Tuirbhe who gave his name to the Strand. Later adaptations relate Tuirbhe to Lúgh, the Celtic god of light, giving Goibhniu his divine pedigree in the overall Celtic pantheon.

Since the advent of Christianity, Gobán became an accepted personal name and was even adopted by several saints - perhaps to show a connection with early medieval architecture or to denote their prowess as artisans. It is also used to show the superiority of the church.

In the *Life of Saint Albán*, we learn that a distinguished wight named Gobán lived near where the saint had his cell and that he frequently did work for a neighbouring monastery. The price he charged the monks for his services was too high and they cursed him, leaving him blind. Albán restored the wight's sight and Gobán became one of his most devoted followers, building a church dedicated to him that contained wondrous carvings not seen anywhere else in the world.

Gobán also appears in a tale concerning another holy man, Saint Molaing. The saint, says the legend, had a wonderful oratory constructed for him from timber by a workman called Gobán Saor. As payment, Gobán's wife demanded that the oratory should be filled with grain that would then be given to Gobán. The wily saint agreed, provided the wight could invert the oratory so that it might be filled. He stipulated that if it were damaged in any way through this manoeuvre, Gobán would receive no payment at all. In doing so, Saint Molaing thought he would trick Gobán out of the entire payment. The workman was so skilful that no damage was done to the oratory, and the saint had to pay him.

The notion of the holy or godly workman seemed to have begun in Ireland in the south Leinster area, probably associated with a local pagan artisan-cult. It rapidly spread to other parts of Ireland, perhaps owing something to the spread of Christianity. In the 10th century Gobán was described as 'the greatest smith/builder that ever lived' and a number of ancient monasteries, churches and round towers were ascribed to his handiwork. By then, the tension between the pagan gods and the Christian ideal seemed to have disappeared – several of the former deities were accepted into the Church as holy figures.

One curious tale about Gobán survives. It was said that his fame as an architect/builder reached as far as south Munster where a number of monks hired him, although he was a pagan, to build a new tower for their abbey. Gobán built the tower for them but the monks refused to pay him the rate that they had agreed, offering him a far lower wage. He refused to renegotiate the contract and while he was working at the top of the tower, the monks removed all his ladders, leaving him stranded. They would put the ladders back, they said, only if Gobán would agree to their terms. The wily builder began to drop the stones of the tower itself to the ground, one on top of the other, saying that this was as easy a way as any to come down. The monks, seeing their beautiful tower literally vanishing before their eyes, were forced to relent and pay Gobán his full wages.

The story is particularly curious because it demonstrates the triumphant guile of the pagan over the officers of the Church.

travelling in Scotland, noted that many country people left offerings or gave some sign of veneration as they passed certain stones, reputedly the 'resting places' of ancient gods. On Dartmoor, veneration was shown in past times to a stone known locally as the Bowerman's Nose which stands on Hayne Down near Manaton (See: Ruth E. Saint. Leger-Gordon, *The Witchcraft and Folklore of Dartmoor*, 1994). The word 'Bowerman' almost certainly comes from the ancient, Brythonic Celtic *vawr-maen* meaning, 'great stone', and, although not raised by the druids, was probably venerated by them. Tales of both Dartmoor and Bodmin Moor concerned stones that moved and came down to nearby water to drink during the hours of darkness. In the Celtic mind, this gave them a 'life-like' quality that agreed with the notion of animated spirits.

Trees also formed an important part of Celtic worship and many sacred groves were religious sites. The ancient perception of trees in such places may have given them a particularly sacred significance. Trees were associated with storms and lightning, perhaps because storms would centre around isolated trees. Those struck by lightning would bear growths and this is why mistletoe is known as *Donnerbesonn* – thunder-broom in Switzerland. Trees were also pillars that stretched from earth to sky, into the realm of the gods/spirits. From earliest times men looked on trees as a bridge between the two realms. It is even speculated that early men placed their dead on an upturned tree so that birds could peck their flesh and that they could be hastened on their way into the Afterlife/Otherworld. (For the Christian symbolism of the upturned tree see **Legends of Saints and Holy Men**). Solitary trees in particular often resembled grand columns stretching to the sky. Powell (*The Celts*, 1958) postulates that for the Celts, lone trees represented a cosmic pillar on which the spirits could travel to visit their worshippers below. He goes on to speculate that the Jupiter-columns of Classical temple architecture would originally have been wooden, and perhaps there would have been a sacred, live tree growing within the temple precincts. Certainly, Celtic tree worship combined well with the perceptions of many other ancient faiths. The oak was sacred to the Roman gods Jupiter and Mars, and sometimes to Woden, the supreme Norse god. At some point, the Celts started to worship trees in their own right. There are a number of sites, particularly in Ireland, that suggest trees were worshipped there. *Magh-Bhile* – Moville, in County Donegal – means the Plain of the worship of the old tree, Derry, is derived from the name *Doire* or *Dair* meaning oak-tree; Kildare from *Cill-Dara*, the 'church', or 'cell, of the oak'.

Spirits of Earth and Air

Superstitions were attached to these trees, in particular the lone trees that provided a bridge between the spirit and mortal worlds, and great harm could befall anyone who meddled with them. There were beneficial effects to be had from the leaves of certain trees and the druids, in their capacity as healers, would have used them to good effect, acquiring their Celtic nickname, *Dairaoi* – dwellers in the oaks.

Magical properties attached themselves to the quicken-tree – also known as quick-beam, rowan or mountain-ash – that supposedly had the power to banish all evil spirits, including phantoms of the dead, witches and the 'fairy kind and minor devils'. It was no coincidence that the great Celtic sage Merlin reputedly transformed himself into an oak-tree when nearing the end of his days and while mourning the loss of his consort Vivian, or Morgan Le Fay in some tales. The oak later became the symbol of the island of Britain itself.

The Bible mentions the Tree of Knowledge in the Garden of Eden and others were common in the mythologies of many ancient peoples, including the Celts. The merging, by Christian writers, in the tale of Adam and Eve of the twin symbols of paganism, the tree and the serpent, is highly significant.

In parts of France, the identification of trees with a local god was very common. In the French Pyrenees, locals worshipped the god 'Fagus' – the name means 'beech-tree' – and made offerings of food, weapons and sometimes human life to groves of beeches.

Even today in parts of the Celtic world, most notably in Ireland, Scotland and England, trees are regarded with a mixture of awe and superstition. And there are people who will refuse to cut down or tamper with a lone tree for fear of angering 'the fairies' or 'the old gods'. It seems that the roots of tree superstition go deep.

Celtic Mythology

Rivers and wells were also venerated by ancient societies. Both the pre-Celts and Celts viewed rivers and streams as a focus for their ritual practices. From as early as the middle to late Bronze Age – about the middle of the second millennium BC – European tribes cast items into them as offerings to the supernatural forces that dwelt there. Most of these items were pieces of ornamental metalwork – including valuable golden amulets and torcs – but some were swords and axes, offerings, perhaps, for vic-

DÁIRE

If the Daghdha was regarded as ancestor and provider, then Dáire is his counterpart in many of the ancient genealogies. The name often thought to be an alternative title for the Daghdha in very ancient Irish lore.

Throughout Celtic legend, Dáire appears in many incarnations – Dáire Barrach, Dáire mac Sidhe Bhoilg, Dáire Doimhtheach – associated with different Celtic heroes and families. In a manuscript concerning Saint Patrick, he is described as the equivalent to the Daghdha because he is said to own a magic cauldron of rebirth (see **The Great Wheel of Existence**). He is also represented as a great and fearless warrior who led expeditions into other parts of the world.

His son, Cú Roí, could be yet another name for Dáire himself. Cú Roí is sometimes equated with a figure known as Dáire Sírchréachtach, who appears to have been a mighty warrior with a number of foreign conquests under his belt.

Elsewhere in Irish lore, Dáire was the owner of a magical bull, Donn Cuailnge, famed for its ferocity. It seemed to have assumed many of the supernatural aspects of its master – for example, it could travel on the wind and had the strength of ten men. It was famed for its sexual prowess and was greatly revered among the early Celts. The bull itself became the chief object of

the great cattle raid, (*Táin Bó Cuailnge),* in the Ulster Cycle of tales. In these stories, it was the property of the ancient kings of Ulster, although it has been suggested that it was a gift from the god Dáire and that it rightfully belonged to him. Dáire might also be an incarnation of Lúgh, the Celtic god of light, who became confused with several Celtic deities within the fragmented nature of Celtic religion. As well as being equated with the Daghdha, Dáire is also closely associated with the poorly defined figure of *Donn.* The name was probably derived from Dubh meaning black and he was the shadowy lord of the land of the dead or a lord of one of the realms of the Otherworld. His sons are three redheaded men (red being a fatal colour) who slayed the Irish king Conaire with the words 'We are the sons of Donn, king of the dead, at the red tower of the dead'. They are further quoted as saying 'We ride the horses of Donn – although we are alive, we are dead'.

Again, the notion of Celtic triplism emerges in the character of Dáire. He is Dáire, Daghdha and Donn all at once. He combines the aspects of fertility and plenty with warrior skill, death and bloodshed – the red tower. As warrior, he linked the world of the supernatural with the world of human strength and courage.

tory in battle. Body-armour and shields such as the Battersea Shield and the Waterloo Helmet have been recovered from the River Thames. In Gaul and Brittany, the Marne took its name from Matrona – all-mother – who was said to live beneath its surface, and the name of the Seine is derived from Sequana who dwelt at the source of the river and was supposed to have healing abilities. Consequently, in the ancient world, the waters of the Seine were alleged to have therapeutic properties. The sanctuary of the goddess at Fontes Sequaine, in the northwest of Dijon in Burgundy, was later taken over by the Romans as a healing spring.

In some cases, the offerings of human life were made to placate the river and lake-gods and prevent flooding. The Irish *Annals of the Four Masters* noted that a child was sacrificed each year to the River Bann at a ritual site near present-day Coleraine to prevent the river from bursting its banks. The site of the confluence of rivers was almost invariably a sacred spot. At the confluence of the large rivers Rhône and Soane outside Lugdunium – near Lyon – the Imperial Cult of Rome and of Augustus was established in AD 12. A large altar was set up directly beside the confluence and was inscribed with the names of sixty Gaulish tribes. The ceremony of establishment itself was, interestingly, presided over by a Celt – the chief priest of the Aedui – and the date of the ceremony coincided with the Celtic festival of Lughnasa.

The ritual drowning among the Celts of vanquished enemy leaders also suggests offerings to lake and river gods. It was, reputedly, a greater gift if the vanquished leader came from another race or creed, such as the 'death by submersion' of the Viking leader Turgeis by the High King of Ireland in the mid-ninth century. There are suggestions that Vikings might, infrequently, have carried out ritual drownings. The drowning in a bog of one of the O'Flynn chieftains of the Shiel Casuthaigh – a tribal group with territories in north Antrim – by 'black foreigners', perhaps Danes, early in the eighth century was a case in point. (see: William Adams, *The Kingdom of Dalriada*, 1906).

Spirits of Earth and Air

Wells, too were sacred places. Firstly they were associated with underground deities, and it was thought that they were a way of communicating with the underworld. They formed a bridge between this world and the spirit world, as did the tree, but led to the underworld. Secondly, it was believed that water contained its own supernatural forces, and that these were amplified within the confines of the well.

As with rivers and lakes, votive offerings would be cast into wells. Some of these appear to have been effigies or wooden figures. A well at Kelvedon, in Essex, was found to contain a ritual chalk figurine while another at Caerwent in Wales held a small stone image of a Mother-goddess. In another Caerwent well, the skeletons of five dogs were found which suggested some form of ritual sacrifice. It is worth noting that in an extremely deep well at Muntham Court in Sussex, large numbers of canine remains were also found. The sacrifice of hounds at well-sites might therefore have been widespread throughout Britain and Wales.

It is quite difficult to establish truly Celtic patterns of well-worship since many of the sites were later used for Roman ritual and offering, displaying evidence of both strands of worship. An example of this is the well at Carrawborough, the ritual site of the Romano-Celtic goddess Covenanta; the offerings there suggest her dual-racial status. Primitive arrows and cult objects, such as statues, together with coins and jewellery from the Roman period have all been found there.

The suggestion of the underground Otherworld was strong at such places. To drink from certain wells was to acquire the dark and diabolical wisdom of the subterranean sphere, and there are a number of references to characters who had done just that. Fionn MacCumhaill, the Irish warrior, received supernatural knowledge and powers while drinking from a well on the side of Slieve Gullion in County Armagh.

In Christian times, wells retained their legendary potency but were associated with Christian saints. Through the power of its saint, a well was deemed to be a healing or curing place. Recalling the Celtic practice of displaying the severed heads of enemies at sacred wells, a saint's head or skull would be displayed at the well. Such holy heads were believed to benefit the waters and the disintegrating head of Saint Mellor of Cornwall and Brittany was displayed at a Breton well that depended on this grisly artefact for its healing powers. If any unworthy person drank from the well, or washed either themselves or their clothes in it, the well might either lose its powers, dry up or else relocate.

Celtic Mythology

Again, the serpent made an appearance as a symbol at sacred wells and there are a number of stories of gigantic snakes guarding hidden treasure or submerged artefacts. These stories persisted well into medieval times. Geraldus Cambrensis told of snakes that guarded a submerged treasure in a well in Pembrokeshire, and ultimately entered the realms of children's fairy tales and hero-fiction.

Tribal Totems

The landscape was not the only source of awe for the ancient Celts. Originally hunter-gatherers, they were dependent on the abundant stocks of wild life that thronged the ancient world. It was imperative that such stocks of prey animals remained constant and that the Celtic hunters were able to catch and kill them. The Celts admired hunting animals, and warriors wished for the hunting prowess of a wolf or the strength and fearlessness of a bull. These desires became incorporated into tribal worship, as clan groupings adopted these creatures as their totems or associated spirits, hoping that the characteristics of that animal would be conferred upon the group itself.

Such a belief appears to have come down from prehistoric times. Cave paintings and later metalwork from the early to late prehistoric period depict either hunting scenes

Roman coins used in Britain

DIAS

VANO·C

DVRNACO

XIIII AR

XIIII AR

XV AR

ORCETI

TASCIA VICI

CVNO

XVI AR

XVII AR

XVIII AR

or representations of animals that were undoubtedly venerated in some way. It is known that animals served as favoured sacrifices to a number of spirits in many ancient religions.

The sacrifice of hounds at wells has been mentioned but other sites contain a mixture of human and animal bones. Aulnay-aux-Planches used in the tenth century BC, and the third-century BC site at Libenice, in the Czech Republic, are such places. Although separated by over seven hundred years and by a huge distance, they share certain characteristics of ritual worship. Both have similarly-shaped earthworks of equal length that contain a similar mix of animal and human remains.

In Ireland it was common practice, even within living memory, to bury animal bones at the corners of houses or under the hearthstone in order to bring good luck to the dwelling, surely a remembrance of pagan ceremonies (see: Kevin Danaher, *The Year in Ireland,* 1972). Most of these ritualised burials involved horses, sheep, deer and pigs, but even chickens, rats, voles and frogs have been found. Such practices were current in the Celtic west long before the coming of the Romans; coins and vessels from the Romano-Celtic period often bear stylised designs of animals such as the boar and the horse.

Celtic Mythology

In some artwork and metalwork, the figures of animals and humans are placed side by side. Wild beasts accompany the various Celtic hunter-gods as in Gaul, in a desire for continued good hunting, or to display the mastery of the human over the brute. In Romano-Celtic art, the god Mercury is sometimes portrayed accompanied by a ram as a symbol of fertility. Over the years animal and human characteristics merged creating a deity or spirit who could shape-shift between animal and human forms. Gods and goddesses most frequently took on the aspects of stags, boars and hares – probably because of these animals' strength, ferocity and speed. Even Geraldus Cambrensis, writing in the 12th century, stated that it was a common belief among the Normans that all old Irish women could turn themselves into hares at will (see: Cambrensis, *A History and Topography of Ireland*).

Cernunnos, meaning 'horned or peaked one', was a famous shape-shifting god, who combined the attributes of a stag and balding, bearded man. There is little doubt that this deity was pre-Roman and that, in various incarnations, he may have been worshipped across the Celtic world. The name Cernunnos appeared on only one monument, in Rheims, dedicated by Gaulish sailors to the Emperor Tiberius. The name might then have been used to describe a number of antler-headed deities elsewhere.

A depiction of an antlered god appears on a fourth-century BC rock carving at Paspardo in Northern Italy. A ram-horned snake, possibly a symbol of wisdom and fertility, accompanies the god. In other depictions, he is accompanied by stags and further ram-headed serpents. His most well-known incarnation comes from Britain where he is identified with the god Herne. This is possibly a part-medieval connection, as Herne was believed to have been a hunter, killed at Windsor Great Park in the early medieval period. An older representation of the god at Cirencester suggests that Britons were worshipping him from a very early time.

Cernunnos/Herne was a spirit of the woodlands and closely associated with fertility and fecundity. In many representations he was shown holding a bowl spilling out the bounty of the earth – fruits, grain and sometimes even money. He is also the lord of all animals – the embodiment of wild and unfettered nature. In this incarnation, he was sometimes denoted in folklore as Master of the Wild Hunt. This was probably a Christian invention, of the medieval period and was supposedly a madcap, and often purposeless, chase through the heavens comprising demons, ghosts, tormented souls and a whole host of supernatural creatures. At its head was the antlered Herne/Cernunnos, urging his followers on to greater efforts by holding out a long wand to direct the Hunt. The wand was also the symbol of growing wildlife and fertility, very much in the style of the later Wand of Mercury. Often those who took part in the Hunt were the souls of the dead or the damned who were condemned to wander endlessly across the skies – in the almost symbolic form of a travelling windstorm. It was not a great leap of early monkish imagination to equate Herne with the Devil and his followers with diabolical worshippers. The figure of Cernunnos, then, embodied a number of elements valued in the Celtic world – man, god and beast. Folklorists have suggested that the legend of the werewolf arose from this belief.

Spirits of Earth and Air

Other gods were purely animal and worshipped as such. Both wild and domesticated creatures were revered and often regarded as the embodiments of spirits or divinities. In the Celtic mind there was no distinction between the gods and the animals that represented them.

Domestic animal gods embodied the attributes that their votaries found most desirable. The bull was worshipped for its aggression and sexual potency; the horse for its speed; the dog was associated with healing, because its spittle was believed to have curative properties, and with the underworld, because of its digging and scavenging. Among wild animals, stags and boars were clearly venerated at a number of shrines. The boar was admired for its ferocity, making it a natural war-symbol while the stag was worshipped for its virility and swiftness of foot. The boar was associated with the gods of the underworld, for Welsh legend states that the pig was one of the gifts given to Pwyll by Arawn, King of the Nether Regions, in return for a favour. In the Romano-Celtic world such creatures began to appear in paintings and bronzes as companions to the Roman gods - perhaps demonstrating a link between the Roman and Celtic worlds and belief-systems.

One of the foremost Celtic animal-goddesses was Epona, the name derived from the Celtic word for horse. She was especially revered in both Gaul and the Rhineland but there might have been instances of British and Irish worship too. There is evidence of her veneration in North Africa, where Celts had entered the Egyptian army as mercenary corps, in the Czech Republic and even in Rome itself. In her earliest

Statue of Epona, the Gallo-Roman horse goddess, found in Alesia, France

Previous page: Detail of Cernunnos on first-century silver cauldron

incarnation, Epona may have been worshipped in horse-form but, probably under Roman influence, she soon took on classical female form. Even so, she was never seen without the horse as her constant companion. Some depictions showed the goddess riding side-saddle on a gigantic horse while others showed her straddling two or more horses, usually of different sexes, and with baskets of fruit and grain illustrating her fertility aspect. Sometimes, she is even displayed in triple-form.

Epona's symbolism and function is incredibly complex. Sometimes she was portrayed as the swift horse; that in itself made her the object of worship since horses were greatly prized among the ancient Celts. She was depicted as a sorceress and ruler of the dead and the Otherworld.

In the Welsh *Mabinogi* she appears as Rhiannon, the witch and 'wronged wife', possibly a fusion with Rigantona, a traditional goddess of the Welsh kingdom of Dyfed. Even here there is horse imagery for, according to Welsh legend, Rhiannon was forced to ride through the countryside, offering to carry anyone who wished to go to the royal palace. Taking revenge on her husband, Pwyll, she afflicted his family with ailments and illnesses, earning the sobriquets 'enchantress' and 'mistress of the night'.

Bulls were also widely worshipped across the Celtic world and were kept domestically as a symbol of wealth. They started appearing as little devotional bronze figurines from around the seventh century BC onwards and have been found in Austrian graves. It might be that these were worshipped as war or fertility gods. Bulls were widely sacrificed to the gods in many Celtic countries and there is a much evidence of the burial of weak or elderly cattle as, perhaps, offerings to underground deities. The majority of these animals had been allowed to die naturally and had then been buried whole. Formalised bull sacrifice in Gaul is recorded by the Roman writer Pliny, when two white animals were offered to the Moon Goddess at an official *Spirits of Earth* mistletoe-cutting ceremony (see **The Druidic Tradition**). In Classical and eastern *and Air* societies, bulls were associated with sky gods and the heavens and in the Celtic world connected with the Moon.

During Ireland's Celtic occupation, cattle featured significantly in its pastoral economy. The status of a chieftain was judged by the number of beasts that he possessed, so, not surprisingly, bulls featured heavily in Irish folklore and mythology. The most famous of all such tales is the *Táin Bó Cuailnge – The Cattle Raid of Cooley*. It was one of the foremost tales of The Ulster Cycle – which described a war between Ulster and Connacht over the theft of the Brown Bull of Ulster, the major rival to the White Horned Bull of Connacht. It was to this war that the great Ulster hero Cú Chulainn made a significant contribution. Peace returned only after both animals had been killed. Though maybe referring to a real war, the story is largely symbolic with the ferocity and aggression of the bull a major feature.

The most important animal totem of the Celts was, arguably, the boar. The animal served a dual purpose central to the Celtic way of life. It represented the ferocity of the hunt and the pleasures of feasting, companionship and hospitality. Pork seemed to have been widely consumed by the Celts and boars and stags were popular prey of Celtic hunters. Boars were also a symbol of warfare and slaughter among the Celts and appeared on Celtic war-bosses and helmets. Boar-headed horns, known as carnyxes, were perhaps used to signal the start of battle or sounded to terrify an enemy. With its dorsal bristles raised, the boar must have been a frightening spectacle for any hunter and, in placing this symbol on shields and armour, Celtic warriors

The bull was kept as a symbol of wealth by Celts. This primitive cave painting was discovered at Les Eyzies, France.

hoped to transfer that fear to the enemy. But it was not only on armour and weaponry that depictions of the boar were to be found. Celtic coins showing boars with their dorsal crest raised in an attacking mode appear to have been common but might have been issued only in times of war.

More common were the small figurines representing boars with elaborate crests, some from Hungary and Romania. A tiny representation of a boar has also been found on a neck-pin found at Woodendean in Sussex, England. A panel of the Gundestrupp Cauldron shows boar-shaped helmet crests and it has been suggested that the charging boar, with bristles extended, might have been part of the crest of a ruling Celtic household. (see: 'The Symbolism of Boars' in Bently (ed), *Heroes of the Dawn: Celtic Myth*, 1998). The boar-cult and boar-symbolism seems to have been widespread among the ancient Celts.

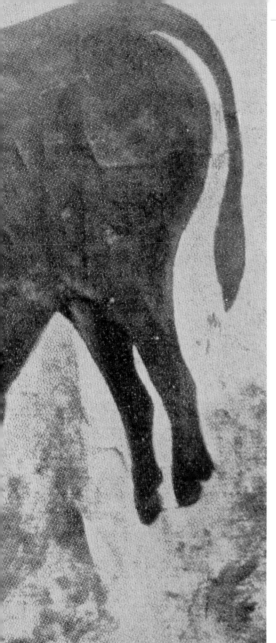

The association of boar-meat with feasting is well established – pork was central to most banquets in Celtic life and Afterlife. *The Feast of Bricriu* told of squabbling over 'the Champion's portion' among the heroes gathered there. The custom, where the largest, choicest, piece of meat was given to the greatest warrior or mightiest hero present, was mentioned in the annals of Diodorus Siculus (VI, 28). Offerings of pork or boar meat were left at shrines or were buried with great warriors to sustain them after death. The lords of Otherworld banquets were frequently depicted with the bodies of dead boars slung across their shoulders or with pigs at their side.

In tales, boars took the form of ferocious magical creatures that had to be defeated as part of a hero's quest. In the Welsh legend of Culwch and Olwen, the magical boar Twrch Trwyth is a transformed evil king, whom Culwch had to overcome as one of his tasks for Yspaddaden Pencawr. The Irish hero Diarmaid hunted down a half-brother who had been changed into the shape of a wild boar, and the boar-brother killed Diarmaid in some versions of the tale.

Spirits of Earth and Air

The god Mercury Moccus, worshipped at sites in Gaul, was associated with the hunting of wild boar. *Moccus* is a Gaulish word meaning pig or hog and the god is thought to have protected the hunters of the Lingones tribe.

Gradually, tribal totems were incorporated into Roman worship but secondary to the Roman gods and goddesses. They were seen as companions to the deities of Classical mythology, in the background of many reliefs and paintings but still a potent symbol of the Celtic world.

Triplism

Unquestionably, numbers played a very important role in both the ancient Roman and Celtic worlds and there is no doubt that the most sacred or magical of all was the number 'three'. The idea of 'the triple' had its roots in Indo-European belief.

Earlier civilisations had been structured in 'threes' - artisans, agriculturists and warriors or else as warriors, priests and farmers.

Knowledge was passed down in 'concept clusters', each concept containing three truths. In vernacular literature there were many references to triplication – the Irish goddess of war and death, had three distinctive aspects: Macha, Badhbh and Morrigu, all unified in one supernatural being. There were three sons of Uisneach, although only one had any real identity; four Children of Lir, of which three were male; three sons of Tuireen who all combined into the Three Great Sorrows of Irish Story-telling.

In other tales, there are three tasks, three wishes, three parts to a quest. In Irish mythology, the Ulster hero Cú Chulainn had his hair tied in triple braids while in the Welsh *Mabinogi*, Branwen appeared as one of three matriarchs. In early Gaulish and British folklore the mysterious Genius Cucullatus – Hooded Spirit – appeared as a triadic entity concerned with fertility, well being and abundance. Throughout the Celtic world, triple-faced images of gods and goddesses appear with astonishing frequency. Many were simply representations of the all-seeing mother-goddess who was said to look out upon past, present and future ages. In some instances, they are taken to mean the three ages of human existence – youth, maturity and old age.

Although triplication can certainly be found in the Celtic religious iconography of Ireland and Wales, it was in Germany, Gaul and Britain, during the period of Roman

OENGUS

Oengus of the Birds (also rendered as Aonghus) was the god of love. He also appears in Scottish mythology and is frequently described in fable as one of the leading members of the Tuatha Dé Danann who, according to the '*Book of Invasions*' settled in Ireland during the Dim Time, before formally recorded history.

The name comes from the ancient Irish *mac óg* or Young Son, linking him to the Daghdha. According to legend, he was the product of an illicit union between the Father-God and the goddess Bóinn. The Daghdha tried to conceal Bóinn's pregnancy by causing the sun to stand still for the nine months of her confinement so, strictly speaking, Oengus was conceived and born on the same day. He is portrayed as both a lover and a poet, demonstrating the strong connection between the two elements in the Celtic mind.

In the ancient Irish poem *Aislinge Oengaso* – The Dream or Vision of Oenghus – deemed one of the greatest Otherworld narratives, the god was smitten with a great passion for a young girl whom he does not recognise. He could think of none but her and wrote many ballads in her honour. He fell sick with love for her – an illness that no druid could heal. Eventually, he learnt that her name was Caer Iobharmhéith – Yew Berry – and, on searching for her, found her with her companions beside a lake. He had also learned that Caer was one of the Sidhe, and a shape-changer, and that every other year she must renounce human form and take on that of a swan.

Oengus approached his friend King Ailill of Connacht to intercede for him with the girl's father Eathal Anbhuail of Sidh Uamhain. The king had no success, but learnt that the only time Caer could be taken was when she was in her swan guise. Oenghus waited for the great Celtic feast of Samhain on 1 November, when her metamorphosis was to occur. He approached Caer and flew off with her, having transformed himself into a swan by the power of his poetry. They circled the lake three times, singing a magical song that enchanted all who heard it. Oengus took Caer to live with him in his palace at Brugh na Bóinne where he continued to provide inspiration for poets and bards. It wass said that while he lived in the Brugh, Oengus never aged, and his poems and ballads were as clear and fresh as the day on which he wrote them.

In accordance with the frequent triplication of Celtic deities, Oengus also appears as one of the three sons of the Daghdha. Thus he commanded divine status and was one of the leaders of the Tuatha Dé Danann.

In essence, Oengus portrayed the constant theme of love within the Celtic mythological cycles. He also served as a symbol of the divine and idealistic young man – the eternal appeal of youth. He represented creativity in the Celtic world and was looked on with great favour by the bards and filí. He appears in the Northern British counterpart, Maponos and in the Welsh Mabon, both of whom appear as 'divine sons'.

rule, that it was most evident. While there were undoubtedly triple-entities prior to Roman occupation, they seemed to have taken on a Classical 'flowering' during the high point of the Empire. The triplication came in two main forms: multiplying the entire body or just a part of the body, usually the head or face. Triple-headed deities appear on stonework in such places as Corleck, County Cavan and on Boa Island, County Fermanagh as well as in the southern reaches of Scotland. Other, more Romanised, examples are to be found in Belgium and in the Czech Republic. There, certain Romano-Celtic fertility deities are given the addition of a triple phallus or a triple vagina, no doubt to emphasise their inherent potency and virility. The idea of a triple deity seems to have been wide spread across Western Europe.

Although triplism among humanoid deities usually took the form of three heads or faces, animal gods took on an additional appendage, usually a horn or tusk. Within many of the bull-worshipping cults, a third horn was added to the animal's forehead, and probably gave it greater supernatural significance. It might also have symbolised the phallus to combine strength, aggression and sexual prowess. Figurines of bulls and boars have been found at several grave-sites, possibly there to ensure the buried chieftain's continued status in the next world. Most of the triple-horned bull bronzes and clay figures have been found in Gaul although a number have also appeared in Britain. A figurine found at Maiden Castle in Dorset shows the heads of three female deities on its back. It might have been a representation of two Romano-Celtic sculptures, from Paris and Trier, dedicated to the god Mercury, known as Tarvustrigarnus – The Bull with Three Cranes, a stylised bull with three wading birds. Horse cults – particularly those depicted at the shrines dedicated to the goddess Epona – displayed some triplism. On some representations, a three-faced goddess was shown astride a rampaging stallion, in others, a human-looking female figure straddled three horses. The latter may simply be a Roman addition to the cult of the horse.

Spirits of Earth and Air

A Celtic Pantheon?

While there is no real evidence of a 'godly family' among the early Celts, prolonged contact with Greece and Rome had a pronounced effect on Celtic belief, especially in areas of Roman occupation. Here a succession of hybrid deities was created. In places like Gaul, a godly pantheon quite unlike that of the Classical world might have evolved. In Irish mythology the Daghdha approximated to a tribal father-god and was chieftain of the magical Tuatha Dé Danann. The Daghdha was their 'all-father' and leader and was venerated as a Supreme Being by some of the early Irish. He was a frustratingly complex character: on the one hand extremely wise and learned, while on the other, an uncouth, lecherous, drunken glutton. The word 'Daghdha' means 'good god' and he was regarded as being beneficent to his worshippers in a drunken, loutish sort of way. He was associated with magic and abundance and was considered lavish in his largesse and terrifying in his anger.

Daghdha wielded a large club, which he pulled around on wheels behind him, one end of which could kill and the other could raise the dead. In representations he wears an incredibly short tunic that did nothing to hide his modesty, probably

THE BANSHEE

One of the most famous supernatural beings of Ireland is the Banshee. This female spirit's cry heralds the death of a member of certain Irish families. Her name means 'woman of the fairy', or Otherworld being, and she is a solitary figure. Her wailing, described as plaintive, almost eerie, resembles the ancient Irish keen, which women would utter upon the death of a loved one. Usually heard near the dwelling of the person about to die, it occurs even when the person involved is far away in another country. Those who have seen her describe her either as a sweet young maiden or as a sturdy matron or, in many cases, a horrid, screeching hag.

The notion of the banshee is peculiar to the Celtic world and must have sprung from belief in a generalised goddess or in localised or family spirits. Such general goddesses might have been those of warfare and slaughter - Macha, the Badhbh and the Morrigu, the Gaelic Triple-goddess. The banshee is often associated with the birds symbolic of this three-fold being – the scaldcrow or roystencrow, the hooded or grey-backed crow. This connection would also explain the three aspects of the Banshee, representing the three ages of womanhood – youth, maturity and old age. In Carlow, Wexford, south Wicklow and south Kildare, the Banshee is simply known as Badhbh -pronounced 'bow', further emphasising her link with the Triple-Goddess, while in Kilkenny and south Laois she is referred to as badhbh chaointe – keening badhbh, pronounced boheenta.

Nor is the banshee exclusively associated with warnings of death. In some very ancient tales she is described as a Muse, appearing to inspire poets and writers. In this incarnation, she also appears to mourn, in poetic verse, the death of a mighty leader in the style of the Celtic Bards. This inextricably linked her to poetry, particularly funereal poetry of which the Celtic tribes seem to have been fond.

The Banshee may have been a mortal woman inspired by the gods with the power of prophecy. Her name 'woman of the fairy' may refer to her role as conduit through which messages from the spirits were passed, someone akin to an oracle. One of the earliest references to the banshee refers to a person called Aoibheall who was the banshee or soothsayer to the Royal House of Munster. Aoibheall also appears in a tale concerning the Battle of Clontarf in 1014. She was said to have offered the champion Dúnlaing Ó Hartagái, whom she loved, and his sons two hundred years of life if they put off fighting in the battle. They refused, were all killed and Aoibheall took herself off to Lough Derg where she continually cried for the Gaelic nobles fallen at Clontarf. Some variations of the tale suggest that Aoibheall was a mortal woman with supernatural powers and strong connections with the Sidhe.

A banshee appeared in Scotland to warn King James I of his impending murder in 1437 by the Earl of Atholl. She approached the king as he processed into St John's Town, and shouted to him that if he were to enter the town, he would not live for another year. The king was advised to ignore her, as she was a drunk. Later that night, she came to his 'chamber door' and asked for admission. When she was refused, she issued her prophecy again and departed. In both cases, she is described as a banshee or Irish prophetess, but almost certainly she was a mortal woman. Her prophecy soon came true as, several months afterwards, the king was murdered at Perth.

A final banshee is recorded in the 19th century. The German travel writer Johann Kohl visited Ireland in 1842 and while in County Clare was taken to see a woman who was able to predict death within her own family. He gives her name as Cosidine and she told him that she was able to see Death, leaning on two crutches, at the foot of the meadow by her house when any family member was to die. She had not seen her own death yet, she told him. (See: Johann Kohl, Travels in Ireland, 1844; partly reprinted in The Stranger's Gaze by the Clare Local Studies Project, 1998). Because of her specialised powers, her neighbours considered this woman as something of a banshee.

Such people would have been viewed as intimately connected to the spirits of their locality and, through them, fragments of arcane knowledge including glimpses of the future could be made manifest. This knowledge would be regarded as coming from the fairies or the spirit world. In some cases, they were seen as embodiments of the spirits themselves and boasted wider supernatural powers than that of prophecy.

At some stage in history, the banshee took on the folkloric aspect that she enjoys today - that is, as the wailing prognosticator of approaching death. It was not long before she became associated with a family's patron goddess, warning of an approaching demise among its members. It is difficult to date precisely when this change occurred, but it seems reasonable to suppose that the incursions of the English into Ireland placed a stress upon Gaelic families, and that they amended their folklore accordingly. The Norman English first settled in Ireland in the mid-12th century, invited into the country by Dermot MacMurrough, King of Leinster.

The new aspect of the banshee seems to have developed in the south Leinster area, where the seizure of old Gaelic lands by the English government during the 16th and 17th centuries was particularly severe. It is thought that during the Penal Times the idea spread to other areas, and gradually the idea of the keening banshee – the harbinger of death, destruction and loss – gained wider acceptance. Gradually, too, the idea that she was a protective spirit or goddess, attached only to old Gaelic families – those with O' and Mac as prefixes to their names – became much wider and her predictions of death extended to all Irish people. The belief in the banshee has survived all over Ireland up to the present time; interestingly, in urban as well as rural areas.

A curious tradition has attached itself to her – that she uses a golden comb to arrange her tangled locks and that if any man should steal it, the banshee will take great revenge on him. There are a number stories concerning men who took the comb and then had to return it by placing it in a pair of tongs and pushing it under a door while the banshee raged outside. The tongs were invariably returned twisted and broken, demonstrating the ferocious and Otherworldly strength of the spirit. A further tradition, very prevalent in the north of Ireland, states that the banshee is represented by three knocks on the door or the window – a definite sign of approaching death.

In Ireland today, the banshee or beansidhe is still feared. This woman follows ancient royal Irish families. Her screeching cry heralds the death of a family member.

deliberately stressing his attribute of fertility, and displays a gross paunch from which abundance was supposed to flow. Most tales concerning him concentrated upon his capacity to overeat. His primary consort is the goddess Bóinn - a river-goddess from which the Boyne takes its name. She was considered incredibly fertile, bearing children with amazing rapidity. The union of the two deities was symbolic of the union between the tribe and Nature in the cosmic scheme of things.

Daghdha also mates with the fearsome war-goddess Morrigan, thus ensuring her protection for his people. The goddess Brigit (Saint Brigid – see **Legends of Saints and Holy Men**) was the daughter of the Daghdha and was believed to command supernatural powers. Associated with this family of deities were a number of other gods, such as Lúgh the god of light, who made up a minor pantheon but whose addition seem to have been made much later and under Roman influence. It could very well be argued that in this, the Celts were trying to ape the great Classical mythological structures of Greece and Rome. Many of the gods that made up the pantheons were little more than local spirits which were later Hellenised – most of the stories concerning them can also be traced back to both Roman and Greek sources.

Essentially, the gods of the Celts remained what they had always been – the fundamental and elemental forces of Nature that the ancient peoples held in awe. Such forces were contained in, and sometimes restrained by, the landscape and the animal world all around them. In the Celtic mind they demanded, and were deserving of, worship and offering.

This uneasy partnership between deity and votary was the only way that man and spirit could co-exist in the developing world of ancient times.

Spirits of Earth and Air

SHRINES AND SACRED SITES

Places of Healing and Holiness

'Nobody dared enter this grove except the priest; and even he kept out
at midday and between dusk and dawn – for fear that the gods
might be abroad at such hours.'
(Lucan: *Pharsalia III*)

Celtic Mythology

Classical writers such as Caesar, Ptolemy and Tacitus, especially those who had travelled in Gaul and parts of Britain, made direct links between sacred groves and mounds and localised worship and priesthood. Other sites of worship probably included clusters of oak-trees, individual trees, lakes, river-crossings, the sites of springs or wells and any part of the landscape that was considered to be possessed by, or the home of, a spirit.

The Gaulish word for a grove was *nemeton* – *nemed* in Irish. This has been incorporated into the names of relevant deities such as Nemetona and Aremetia. Much Celtic worship appears to have been carried out in the open air and few of the Classical writers made specific reference to religious buildings or temples. It must be remembered that writers from the Roman world wished to show their Celtic neighbours as primitive and were presenting a contrast to the soaring columns and lavish temples that characterised Classical religious architecture.

No archaeological evidence has been found of Celtic holy buildings dating from an early period. This would coincide with the Celts' close connections with the land on which they lived. Religious structures would start to emerge only under Roman influence as shrines and minor temples were built. This does not mean that there were no specified sacred sites in this early period and that they were not marked in a significant way.

Space itself was regarded as sacred within Celtic religion and the druids took care to enclose especially sacred areas. Within this area the god or spirit was supposed to focus its powers. The enclosures might have been surrounded by a stone wall, thick hedge or deliberate growth of trees, by a ditch or a simple wooden palisade or by a combination of any of these.

Such fortifications were designed to cut off the sacred from the profane and to concentrate the powers of the particular spirit within a specified locality, the enclosed ground then becoming holy. Islands, being self-enclosed by water, were important sites.

There are many Classical references to sacred islands around the coastlines of Britain and Gaul. Some of these were burial grounds on which cults of the dead flourished – it was believed that the spirits of the dead could not cross water. Some were the abodes of dark forces that demanded veneration from afar. Later, many of these sites would become churches and hermit cells during the early Christian period.

In Celtic folklore, boundaries are significant and this might stem from the demarcation between holy and profane ground. In both Scottish and Irish folklore an effective curse against an individual could only be made on a boundary line; it symbolised the separation of the mortal world from the mystical, supernatural Otherworld. To step across such a boundary was to venture from one world into the other; from the world of men into the realm of gods and spirits. The priests themselves might have lived close to land boundaries as did the hermit monks and learned men of the later Christian period.

Bogs, rivers and lakes were also places of worship. Here, the nature of the ground and space changed significantly and, in the early mind, this marked a difference between one type of existence and another. For the Celt, the borders of the Otherworld were very close and the places where the gods came and went were exceptionally sacred. The Celts also viewed the land itself in a special way and this vision played a decisive part in their psyche regarding the notion of sanctity.

Shrines and Sacred Sites

The Soul of the Earth

Traditional Celtic teaching informs us that the earth was not viewed by the Celts as simply dead matter but as a living, breathing thing. Furthermore, the material of which it was composed was inextricably bound, like a reflection, to the spirits of those who dwelt on it. Material was therefore filled with spirit and that spirit revealed itself through material. Later commentators would refer to this belief as *anima loci* – the place-soul or the spirit of place. Acknowledging the sanctity of a place was little more than an acknowledgement of the reflection of that spirit.

The best northern European understanding of the notion of *anima loci* is to be found, not in the recognised Celtic world but in the *Landnamabok – The Book of Settlement* – in Iceland and its contemporaneous texts. First discovered by Vikings and then by voyaging Irish and Scottish Celtic monks, the land appears to have been settled sometime during the ninth and tenth centuries. The first settlers in Iceland were acutely aware of the 'personalities' of places and set areas of the landscape aside to acknowledge and respect them. Certain areas and landholdings were kept aside specially for the *landvettir* – land-wights or earth spirits – as their own special property. These lands were to be held by the spirits forever. Places of worship in Iceland were developed using geomantic techniques that respected the notions of *anima loci*; not to do so would have been to invite disaster upon the settlers. Such techniques must have mirrored the activities of the first Celtic settlers when they came to the largely empty and unexplored lands of the West.

People directing prayers to sacred mountains, trees or rivers, for example Helgafell, the sacred Icelandic mountain, were often required to wash their faces, put on clean clothes and fast for a day, out of respect for the spirit who dwelt there. Similarly when passing great stones, it was customary for people to raise their caps or make some other sign of obeisance. So common was the practice that Thomas Pennant remarked that there was hardly any large stone in Scotland where the country people did not salute or leave some kind of offering. These small acts of worship gradually inculcated a healthy and general respect for the environment into those who dwelt on the land.

Celtic Mythology

The connection to the spiritual aspect of the earth sometimes extended even to the physical appearance of landholders. No king or noble should have a physical blemish or imperfection lest this reflect back on the lands that he owned or the people that he governed. Many of the old tales – e.g. the tale of the able and wise king, Conn of the Hundred Battles who was forced to relinquish the throne after losing an eye – relate the physical appearance of the land to the actions of those who lived on it. This symbiotic relationship meant that disfigured nobles were usually forced to give up their lands in case they brought famine or drought on their community or in case their arrogance offended the land-spirit. During the English occupancy of Ireland, land would be given away by the authorities as payment for services. Cornwall's administration, bankrupt after the English Civil War was notorious for the parcelling out of Irish land as payment to troops, garrisoned in the country.

This English idea of land as a commodity was beyond the comprehension of the Irish whose belief in a deep relationship between living earth and living people, saw the 'given away lands' as living, breathing extensions of themselves. It was this love for, and association with, the land that was to fuel the various land-wars in Ireland during the 18th and 19th centuries. Throughout the generations, the Celts tried to keep faith with the land and to respect it as an entity in its own right. Places were usually named after some geological feature or trait of the land and this gave the location a sense of distinction, even of individuality and personality, adding to the sense of 'being alive'. Its soul, as manifested through the animistic spirits that dwelt within its confines, was inextricably linked with the existence of the people who lived on it. Its special places were their special places as well.

Places of the Gods

It was well known that many spirits lived in high and often inaccessible places. Remote and aloof from their worshippers on the ground, any devotional ritual at their 'home' had to be carried out after a long journey or pilgrimage. Throughout the Celtic world, inscriptions and dedications to aerial spirits and sky gods are to be found scattered throughout mountainous regions. Later associated with the Roman Jupiter, suffixes denoted regional variations. Thus, Jupiter Brixianus at Brescia in Cisalpine Gaul was certainly a local god. Jupiter Ladicus in the mountains of north-west Spain was taken to be the spirit of the mountain and was assimilated into the Roman-Celtic notion of Jupiter. The same practice occurs in Hungary, Dalmatia, Bulgaria, Scotland and Ireland.

THE FAIRY THORN

Merlin and Vivian

The importance of trees in the Celtic world was reflected in the bardic tradition and many forms of worship until relatively late times. Solitary growths, in particular, had a special, mystical significance. Many species of trees and bushes featured as a centrepiece for a sacred site and the type of tree could signify the type of worship that took place there. Oaks were associated with permanence and wisdom. Drawing on this tradition, William of Waynefleet founded Magdalene College, Oxford, near the site of a great oak that had been worshipped in Celtic times, in the hope that the tree-spirit would give supernatural inspiration to the scholars who studied there. This tree survived until 1788.

In the Welsh poem *Afallanau*, Merlin – fleeing from the aftermath of a battle in which his liege lord had been killed by the forces of Rydderch Hael – entered the great wood of Caledon and, becoming a wild man, hid in an apple tree from his pursuers who passed him by. As a mage, Merlin ultimately became an oak tree himself, following his rejection by his lover Vivian.

History mirrored myth in the 17th century when King Charles hid in an oak tree following his defeat by Parliamentarian forces during the English Civil War. On many pub signs thereafter, the King's Head was portrayed as peering out from leaves in the manner of the Green Man or a forest spirit. Sacred trees and 'gentle bushes' were an important part of the early Celtic faith. It was thought that specific types of spirit dwelt within them. In Cornwall, it was said that anyone who buried treasure always planted a hawthorn over the spot to protect it. Spirits of hawthorn trees were considered especially vicious and ferocious and it was unwise and unlucky to bring hawthorn blossom into a house 'in case the spirit would follow it'. Even early Celtic Christianity was not above taking note of former pagan tree-worship and it became incorporated into mainstream Christian belief. In Brittany, at Notre-Dame-de-la-Tronchaye in Rochefort-en-Terre, a tree stump was for many years the centre of Christian rites, because of an image of a Black Madonna that was found there in medieval times. Another image was found in a rose bush near Josselin, also in Brittany, and the bush itself became revered with a great festival known as 'The Feast of Our Lady of the Rosebush'. A small shrine, erected there, gained a reputation throughout France for the cure of epileptics. French revolutionaries eventually demolished it in 1793 and the statue of Our Lady there was destroyed.

Several saints were associated with trees. In County Laois in Ireland, a former pagan well that appeared halfway up a tree became known as Saint Fintan's well, though its origins were said to stretch back into druidic antiquity. During Christian times, votive offerings were left at the foot of certain trees all over Ireland, Wales and parts of England. These were left in honour of local saints, but were probably associated with pagan tree-worship.

Gradually, the spirits of the trees and bushes became transformed into the 'fairy folk' and their trees became 'fairy bushes and trees'. The widespread taboo against cutting down such a tree persists even today, especially in Ireland.

Carnac, the alignments of Menhirs at Kermario, France

Croaghpatrick in County Mayo – the most holy mountain in Ireland – was formerly *Cruachan Aighle* – or *Aickle* – the seat of an important spirit to which men frequently prayed and made pilgrimage. This later became a Christian site with a pilgrimage up its slopes in honour of the saint, following in the tradition of the pagans. According to Julian of Furness, it was from this mountain that Patrick expelled the serpents and crawling-creatures from Ireland, surely symbolic of the rooting-out of paganism and pagan shrines on the mountain.

Mountain/sky gods were often linked with fertility, through the sun and the rain that nourished Celtic crops. It was not enough to worship them from afar; offerings and

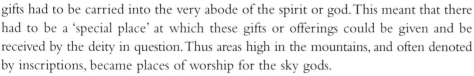

gifts had to be carried into the very abode of the spirit or god. This meant that there had to be a 'special place' at which these gifts or offerings could be given and be received by the deity in question. Thus areas high in the mountains, and often denoted by inscriptions, became places of worship for the sky gods.

Similar treatment was accorded to water-gods. While there is widespread archaeological and iconographic evidence of sky-god worship among the early Celts, there are also many examples of the worship of water spirits/gods. Rivers, lakes, wells and bogs were all centres of worship and some assumed even greater importance during Roman occupation.

The Romans, like the Christian saints and monks, had a special affinity towards water which they, together with countless other ancient peoples, viewed as the source of all life, and deserving of worship. It was a healing element serving as a sure defence against evil, since no unclean thing could cross running water. Local well and water deities filled Roman-Celtic mythology and folklore. Open-air votive sites were upgraded to Roman shrines with covered temples and porticoes. The most famous example was at Roman Bath in England but was originally little more than an uncovered site of a pagan healing spring.

In accordance with Celtic belief in the 'living earth', many rivers and lakes of the Celtic world had their own distinctive personalities. These river/lake spirits usually gave their name to the stretches of water with which they were associated – for example, the Aisne in France, from the goddess Axona, and the Boyne and the Bann in Ireland from the goddesses Bóinn and Banna. Galloway, Scotland is named after its patron Celtic goddess Deva, a goddess that might have predated the Celts. Many of these rivers and lakes were treated with awe and reverence as the dwelling places of the spirits. Gifts and offerings were thrown into the water in return for favours from the deity. Numerous Celtic artefacts have been found beneath the waters of Lake Neuchatel in Switzerland and of Lake Geneva. Many of these offerings consist of weaponry and armour, perhaps signifying a request for victory in battle. Strabo also tells of many items of weaponry and treasures being thrown by Gaulish tribes into a sacred lake near Toulouse. If these treasures were to have been stolen, he alleged, disaster would have ensued.

MÓR-RÍ

In Scotland, the Protestant Reformers in the Lowlands and the Clearances in the Highlands did not totally eradicate old beliefs and old ways of life. Literary evidence of votive sites after this time is thin but anecdotal accounts tell of the continuation of old worship well into the early-19th century. In isolated parts, such worship and practices might arguably have lingered longer than anywhere else in the Celtic West.

One of the predominant divinities worshipped in several parts of Scotland was the spirit Mór-Rí – Great King. This might not have been a formal divinity but the ancestral spirit of a famous warrior or tribal warlord elevated to divine status (see **In Search of Ancient Heroes**).

The 'old rites of Mór-Rí' were conducted in the region of Gairloch into the late-19th/early-20th century. The rituals, usually conducted in isolated places, concerned the sacrifice of cattle, usually bulls, and were supposedly unchanged since the days of the druids. These rites were dedicated to a number of supernatural figures – Mourie, Mari, and Saint Mourie – all of which were linked to the original pagan god. As far as we know, there never was a Saint Mourie; this linking of old deity to saint was simply an attempt to Christianise the pagan spirit

An account written in the mid-1860s told of a hill in the Gairloch area called *Claodh Maree*. It was referred to as 'the gods' holy hill', and was worshipped in the same way as were the gods that dwelt on Helgafell Mountain in Iceland – i.e. with tremendous respect and cleanliness. It was believed that no one could commit suicide or injure himself within view of this spot.

Mór-Rí was associated with a number of standing stones and wells scattered throughout the West of Scotland. Thomas Pennant, visiting Loch Maree in 1774, witnessed a ritual in which the derilans – the unofficial priests of Mór-Rí – gave water from a certain well to ill and disabled people before 'dipping them thrice in the lake' in the hope of effecting a cure. He went on to state that on the island of Maelrubha in the centre of the Loch, where this well was situated, grew an ancient tree dedicated to the god. It was hung with rags, cloths and ribbons and studded with nails – probably in place of regular votive offerings.

Those suffering from insanity were brought, from all over Scotland, to this tree in the hope that the god would cure them. So widespread was the belief in Mór-Rí, that Alexander Mitchell, writing in 1859 states 'people of many places ... speak of Loch Mauree'. And, from the mid-1600s onwards, the people of Gairloch were frequently condemned as pagans for their practices around the Loch.

The notion of lake-worship might have persisted into early medieval times with the legend of the death of Arthur (see **In Search of Ancient Heroes**) that was popular throughout Britain during the 12th and 13th centuries. In one of the main fables of the Middle Ages, Arthur received the sword Excalibur from the hand of the Lady of the Lake, but must return the miraculous weapon to the water-gods before his death after the battle of Camlan. Some legends say that the lake was Dozmary Pool in Cornwall and Camlan, the 'crooked or blind glen', has been tentatively identified as being near Hadrian's Wall in northern England. Arthur had quite a journey before him!

Even as late as the mid-19th century we have numerous accounts of both Scottish and Irish people gathering at lough shores to observe some kind of festival. At Lough Owel in County Westmeath, John O'Donovan remarked that the people gathered for what he called 'Lake Sunday'. Unfortunately he omits to give the date of this festival. Lough Owel was the site to which the captured Viking king Turgeis, ruler of Armagh and Meath in the ninth century, was taken and ritually drowned by the High King of Ireland. Another account, given by a Mr O'Connor in his *Ordnance Survey Letters* mentions people's observing Garland Sunday at Loughbarrow that perhaps hints at a folk-memory of ritual animal sacrifice in the lough waters:

> 'The people . . . swim their horses in the lake on that day to defend (protect) them against accidental ills during the year and they throw spancels and halters into it which they leave there . . . they are also accustomed to throw butter into it.'
> (*Ordnance Survey Letter, 1820*)

Shrines and Sacred Sites

Similar festivals took place at a well on the shores of Lough Neagh in which sticks and coins were thrown into both the well and the Lough to protect against or to cure disease. The same ritual is mentioned in *The Statistical Survey of Scotland* 1845.

On the last Sunday in June, the country people of south Fermanagh and some parts of north Cavan met on the top of Binaughlin Mountain, near Florencecourt, to celebrate Bilberry Sunday. This, according to tradition, was the time when romantic matches were made and any troth plighted on that day was sure to last. The day ended with much drinking, dancing and general merriment. Of course, the festival sprang from the tradition of Irish fertility rituals but the fact that it was held on a mountaintop suggests that it was carried out under the gaze of a beneficent sky-god. It might have been thought, in former times, that the god was part of the celebration; the locals brought their festival to the very 'house of the spirit'. The places at which these festivals were held then became sacred sites. One local claimed that a small cairn of stones used to exist halfway up Binaughlin Mountain, each stone laid there by lovers who wished to have their union blessed by the spirit of the mountain.

Further stories grew up around the site such as it was a doorway to fairyland and was inhabited by a spirit named Don Binn Maguire – the fusion of *anima loci* and an his-

Roman baths at Bath, England, where pagan pilgrims came to be cured in the healing water

torical figure. The tale of a magical horse appearing there to issue prophecies for the coming year could be linked to the worship of Epona – (see **Spirits of Earth and Air**).

Thus, special locations became either the habitation of a local deity or a place to which the god came to join in the merriment of festivals. In both instances, this lent the site a certain sanctity that the people respected.

The Isle of the Dead

Spirits of any description, it was widely reputed, could not cross clear or moving water. Therefore islands were the ideal place for wicked or vengeful spirits to dwell,

restraining their powers and affording the surrounding communities a measure of protection from their dark and malicious ways. It was prudent to stay away from such places in case the spirit manifested its wrath on some unfortunate interloper within its confinement.

In his book on the occult, Colin Wilson describes how the writer T.C. Lethbridge experienced the presence of one such spirit during a visit to the remote Skellig Michael, off the Kerry coast. While making his way back to the boat down dangerous cliff-steps, after visiting the monastic ruins on top of the Skellig, Lethbridge was almost pushed to his doom by an invisible force. This was not, he claims, simply his imagination running riot in the loneliness of the place. It was, he believes, a genuine attempt to kill him. Lethbridge was not the only person to experience something unnatural on this remote island; many other visitors to the place have remarked on a sense of presence there. Skellig Michael was the site of one of the early and most spectacular of the Christian anchorite settlements, allegedly founded by Saint Fionnán in the seventh or eighth century. Prior to the coming of the monks, it was believed to have been the abode of frightful demons that clung to the sheer sides of its rockface – the name 'Skellig' comes from the ancient Irish *sceilg* meaning 'rock'. These demons were confined there but could attack anyone who attempted to land. The arrival of the holy men was said to have purged the site of this evil presence, but evidently it did not.

Islands, particularly to the west, were closely connected with death and the dead. It was commonly believed among the Celts (see **The Otherworld**), that the Afterlife lay somewhere in the West and that this was where the spirits of the dead went. The sun set in the west, symbolising the end of life for another day and such a connection was not lost on the Celtic peoples. In British mythology, this was the location of the mystic Isle of Avalon to which King Arthur was taken after his death on the battlefield. Avalon, in medieval romance was described as The Isle of Apples. It also has an older Celtic name Ynyswitrin, meaning Isle of Glass, alluding to a mysterious crystalline Otherworld, described in several of the myth-quests of great Irish, Scottish and Welsh heroes and inhabited by spiritual beings. It is as Ynyswitrin that it is associated with Glastonbury.

Celtic Mythology

The custom of burying the dead on islands served a threefold purpose. It speeded them on their journey to the Isles of the Blest – the Celtic Afterlife – in the Far West and, since they could not cross water, it prevented their spirits from returning to torment the living. More practically, it prevented scavengers such as wolves from digging up or desecrating the bodies once they had been laid to rest.

In the larger lakes and all around the coasts of Britain, Ireland and Brittany lie a number of tiny islands and islets that have been used for burial purposes. Inis Chonáin – Saint Conan's Island – in the middle of Loch Awe for example, has been used from ancient times. Ancient graves have also been found on Rathlin Island, close to the north Antrim coast. This island was a centre for tomb building and, perhaps, for ancestor worship. The Isle of Lismore off the Benderloch coast was originally an exclusive burial site for the early Pictish kings of that region. The name Lismore signifies 'great garden' and was reputed to be an unearthly garden paradise. The connections with the 'garden or pleasant' Isle of Avalon in British myth are obvious. Even Iona – the cradle and centre of Celtic Christianity – had pagan origins. As the Island of Hii or Hu, it was believed to be the site on which the Celtic god of light, Lúgh, held his court. It had several important pagan shrines dedicated to the god. It might also have been a pagan burial site before Columcille's arrival, because it rapidly became the place where the majority of Scotland's kings chose to be interred. More than 48 of them, dating from Fergus II to MacBeth, are said to lie in Iona's soil at the cemetery of Reilig Odhran. A few foreign kings, mainly French and Norwegian, also lie there, making a royal total of about 60. In 1994, the Scottish Labour leader, John Smith, was also laid to rest on Iona. The sacredness of this island as a place of the dead cannot be overemphasised.

Other islands became associated with mythical figures. Bardsey Island, otherwise known as Bangor Gadfan or Ymys Enlii, was said to be the home of the Arthurian wizard Merlin. According to legend, the magician lies slumbering there, waiting until Wales is in danger and needful of his magical services. In 516, the island became a religious settlement, founded by Saint Cadfan, but no trace of the subterranean cavern in which the wizard was said to lie was ever found. The holy settlement that Cadfan and his brethren founded on the island was considered to be very mystical, supposedly drawing this tradition from the powers that had once inhabited the place.

GLASTONBURY

Wherever you stand on the Somerset Levels, Glastonbury Tor can be seen. It is topped by a high tower, all that remains of the 15th-century Abbey of Saint Michael, which fell down during a great earthquake in the 1600s, and which serves as a beacon for lost travellers on the flat lands below. The Tor itself seems to have been a centre for religious ritual and worship from earliest times. Investigators, as diverse as the Elizabethan mage John Dee and the modern-day historian and folklorist Katherine Maltwood, have recognised its ancient druidical significance. It is probable that, with its terraced sides, Glastonbury was an important site for Celtic religious practices. The site forms the centre of a large terrestrial zodiac, shaped from the land, following ancient tracks, farm roads and pathways and using even medieval farm boundaries. This suggests that, even in the Middle Ages, the mystical sense of such a place was being observed.

Recent research has shown that the sides of the Tor may have formed a pre-Christian processional route to the top. If correct, this would associate the site with the early Celtic druids. They may have made their way up the hill to some form of stone or shrine that had been erected at its summit. If there was a standing stone at the top of the Tor, no trace of it now remains, although the foundation of the Church of Saint

John Dee

Michael suggests that there is a pagan site underneath; early Christians were positively encouraged to build their churches in such places. The high elevation of the site conforms to pagan Celtic ritual areas, close to both the sky and the sun and looking out over the surrounding land for miles.

The fact that the Abbey and Church on the summit of the Tor were dedicated to Saint Michael might not be a coincidence. The powerful and war-like Archangel Michael was also the patron saint of fairies, ancient spirits and forces. As such, he would have had immense power over them and been able to keep them in check. Therefore, dedicating a church to him on an important pagan site would have the effect of limiting the dark powers the Tor contained, and of dispelling or restraining whatever forces the ancient druidic worship had summoned.

Folklorists, such as Nigel Pennick, have suggested that the Tor was the sacred mount and place of ritual worship of a god known as *Gwynn ap Nudd* – 'the White One, Son of Darkness' regarded as the ultimate king or Emperor of the fairies. The site was reputedly Christianised by an especially holy anchorite, Saint Collen, who caused the pagan shrine and a fairy castle to disappear by throwing consecrated water over them.

Saint Lleuddad ap Dingad, Cadfan's successor, was reputedly visited by an angel, who granted him numerous requests as long as they were in the purview or gift of God. One of the saint's requests was that the soul of anyone buried on the island should not be condemned to the torments of Hell. Consequently there were said to be between 20,000 and 30,000 saints buried in the four-acre graveyard on Bardsey – undoubtedly a gross exaggeration that added to its sanctity. As a result Bardsey became known as The Holy Island or the Iona of Wales and was a popular place of pilgrimage in the early Middle Ages. Much of its reputation might come from long before Christianity when the island was an important and magical pagan shrine.

Many of the islands formerly dedicated to ancient and primal gods, became the homes of fearsome monsters and giants. Some Orkney and Shetland isles were believed to be home to flesh-eating titans such as Gorm the Grim – although in his original incarnation as a god, Gorm might have owed more to Viking belief than Celtic imagination. Tory Island, off the coast of Donegal in Ireland, was said to be the home of the fearsome giant, Balor of the Evil Eye (see **Giants, Monsters and Fairies**). Other islands were believed to be inhabited by dark magicians and witches. Even huge and awful dragons supposedly made their nests on many of these remote rocks, adding to the pagan emphasis of the places. Some early Christians settled on them specifically to drive out evil forces by the power of their holy presence. While many appeared to have been successful in establishing Christian traditions, some islands retained pagan associations, albeit in a slightly modified form.

Celtic Mythology

Other islands became important as sites where kings and leaders would make important decisions or resolve difficult problems. If such places were the abodes of patron gods or spirits, it was argued, then surely those forces would guide the decisions of their followers. It was, to some extent, a means of consulting with the island spirit or god. A king or warlord would retire with his advisers to a Council Island to submit to the guiding influence of the local spirit. This was practical since, isolated on an island, they could devote their full attention to the matters in hand. Such Council Islands were usually linked to the mainland by an artificial causeway, sometimes submerged, in case a speedy return was necessary. Two islands in the middle of Loch Finlaggan on the Isle of Islay demonstrate the importance of such places to the Celtic peoples. The largest of them – *Eileán Mór* – was a burial site in former times while the name of the smaller – *Eileán na Comhairle* – suggests that it might have been a council centre where decisions were made and problems debated away from prying eyes. Rival claimants for leadership probably settled the matter in such places. Combat islands existed in Viking culture – the Norse word for formal, single combat – *Holmganga,* literally meant 'going to an island' – and might have existed among the Celts. The idea was that local gods and spirits would preside over the combat and ensure that the proper victor emerged. According to legend, Canute, the Norse son of King Sweyn Forkbeard of Denmark, and the Saxon Edmund Ironside retired in 1016 to the Isle of Alney in Gloucestershire to determine which of them would rule Britain. Even in those relatively Christian times, the fate of a country was given to a

Face urn 4th c.
York cemetery

Face on Roman urn, 4th–5th century, Britain

Spirit of Place to decide. In consultation with the spirit, the leaders of the community would make their decisions.

Islands, particularly remote or inaccessible ones, gradually became imbued with awe and mystery becoming natural abodes for the spirits, forces and gods that embodied the landscape. Their isolation added to their sacredness and many pagan islands were subsequently taken over by the Christian Fathers as their own holy places.

Sacred Sanctuaries and Enclosures

There were many areas of the countryside in which the gods were supposed to have their houses or homes. These 'special areas' were extremely holy and not for the common people. Throughout Iron Age Europe, ditches and banks often provided lines of demarcation, marking the distinction between the sacred world and that of the profane. References are made in the Old Testament to special sanctuaries holy to the Hebraic faith and other pagan religions. Similarly in the Celtic world the sacredness of islands was extended to areas of isolated ground and the very space that they contained.

Celtic Mythology

Many of these places occurred at boundaries. Harlow in Britain was a territorial boundary between the lands of two Celtic tribes – the Catuvellauni and the Trinovantes – so a special enclosure to a local deity was erected there. Similar enclosures appeared in Gournay, in the Oise region of France, which lay at the land boundaries of three tribes – the Ambiani, the Viromandui and the Suessiones.

Early enclosures were simple affairs – a ditch or depression to separate the sacred sector from the lands around. This also served as a means of defence if enemies attacked the site. Others were stands of trees, groves and small spinneys in which rites could take place. Sometimes, a ditch surrounded them, though this was not essential since the reputation of the god might serve to keep attackers away. Later the enclosures became more formal with rough stone walls rising protectively around them. The walls fulfilled the dual aspects of creating an air of separateness and sanctity within the enclosure and of providing some form of military fortification against outside forces. They added to the illusion of the House of the God by providing at least a structural basis for such a habitation. Some structures were incredibly complicated with both outer and inner walls. The outer wall provided a perimeter to the entire site while the inner encircled the 'holy ground' itself. This feature, perhaps primarily constructed for greater defence, had the effect of adding a further layer of complexity to the form of religious worship practised within. Where there was an inner and an outer sanctuary the devotees probably gathered in the outer area to worship while the inner sanctum was the dwelling place of the god and the preserve of his or her priest alone. The priests then adopted a new role; they were mediators between the deity and the people. They were also the only ones entitled to cross the final boundary between the human world and that of the gods. This gave them increased power and status in the eyes of their followers. It was the priest, only, who carried individual requests into the Holy of Holies. Enclosed sites co-existed beside open-air places of worship across the Celtic world.

It was a simple matter to develop these enclosures by covering them with a roof; the notion of a Godly House was then complete in the ancient mind. Mostly this was not done until the Roman period and was largely a result of occupation by Roman forces. The Mediterranean 'god's house' was a splendid, formal structure, reflecting the majesty of their own gods. Many such buildings were covered with votive inscriptions but not one of these inscriptions mention the purely Celtic holy men, the Druids, but rather use the word *flamen*, a latin word for a priest. Clergy, as well as architecture, had become more Romanised.

A good example of the development from open site to formal temple is that of the healing springs beside the River Avon in Britain. Probably an open-air place of worship for the Celts, geological forces pumped hot water out of the earth at 46ºC at the rate of 250,000 gallons a day. The extent of their devotion to the gushing water is not known but they constructed a rudimentary causeway across the surrounding marshy areas and left an offering of 18 pre-Roman coins to Sulis, the goddess of the water. Because of the curative properties associated with water in the ancient mind, this might have been a healing centre, although its importance can only be guessed at.

Shrines and Sacred Sites

Early in the Roman occupation of Britain, moves were made by the invading forces to enclose the place in classical architectural style. The Romans called the locality *Aquae Sulis* – The Waters of Sulis – celebrating what was, by then, a predominant Roman-Celtic water cult. Probably the original enclosure was around the main spring, turning it into a kind of reservoir, but gradually the facility became increasingly complex. An altar was erected, as were a number of supplementary and ancillary buildings, some enclosing other springs. The shrine of Sulis would eventually change its name and become an important military centre in Roman Britain. The name adopted came from the springs themselves – Bath. By the middle Roman period in Britain, the area had been turned into public baths, although many traces of the former religious site remained.

The jewellery, coins and personal objects that were dumped into the main spring as offerings, provided evidence that invocations to the goddess continued into a relatively late period. Over 12,000 of them have been uncovered. A number of small pewter tablets, each bearing a curse against an enemy were also found. These 'curse tablets' were actual requests to the goddess, to take terrible vengeance on those named and promised her offerings if the requested misfortune was granted. Despite this rather sinister aside, the main purpose of visiting the shrine at Bath was to take the healing waters and many pilgrims flocked there, hoping to be 'cured'.

Bath was widely known as an important healing centre and the evidence of the offerings and the 'cursing tablets' strongly suggests that an organised priesthood dwelt at the shrine and oversaw the worship. At least one priest, Calpurnius Receptus, lived and officiated at the sacred place for almost 60 years. Other finds in the Bath area – a moon-shaped pendant and what is probably part of a sceptre – might indicate greater numbers of clerics at the shrine. These finds suggest a Roman-style religion greatly influenced by Celtic belief.

The life-size pewter mask found in a culvert near the central baths shows a stylised Roman face with Celtic features and hair arranged in a recognisably Celtic manner. This might have represented a deity worshipped at the site or, more probably, the face of an officiating priest. What was simply a hot geyser, set amid mud flats and worshipped as a nature goddess by early Celts, quickly became one of the most formal and important religious centres of Roman Britain.

Another similar religious site that developed from relatively insignificant origins is Harlow in Essex. There is evidence that the area was the site of early Celtic religious and ritual activity connected to ancestor worship since the crest of one of the hills was certainly used as a very early graveyard. Immediately prior to the arrival of the Romans, the site was enclosed although it was little more than a bank and ditch. It is thought to have enclosed a wooden shrine, possibly dedicated to death or a warrior cult. Around AD 80-90 a small rectangular temple was built on the site of the earlier shrine. A later addition was a courtyard with an enclosing wall that surrounded the temple. An open-air altar was erected at one end, in front of the entrance to the temple itself. Two inner walls were constructed at this time; each connected to a number of smaller buildings some, perhaps, shops at which sacrifices were sold and some living accommodation for the clergy who officiated at the site. There is no inscription to a specific god but indications are that it was a war-deity. A carving showing a head, surmounted by a large helmet, together with the discovery of four metal daggers and a bronze sheath would seem to suggest a god or goddess closely linked with warfare and conflict.

Under the floors of several sanctuaries, a wealth of fascinating objects have been found which, it is assumed, were calculated to protect or enhance the sacredness of the place. Buried weapons have been found at several sites in Eastern Europe, suggesting offerings to the god for victory in battle or even for supernatural defence of the sanctuary. Interestingly, at sites like Harlow, the bones of ritually slaughtered animals have been found, from feasts within sanctuary precincts, when a portion of their meat would have been offered to the god. In Eastern Europe, these animal bones are alarmingly mixed with human remains, demonstrating that in parts of the Roman-Celtic world, old practices dating from the time of the Druids had not been entirely forgotten.

The dead were frequently believed to be extremely hostile towards the living. It seems likely that the enclosures not only lent sanctity to the ground and air within them but protected the people who lived outside them. In other words, the enclosures were made to restrain spirits which, if allowed, would cause harm to mortals.

Celtic Mythology

Where possible, Celtic communities buried their dead on islands so that moving water would protect them from the unquiet spirits. Those who lived away from available islands had to take other measures to protect themselves and one was to segregate the area in which the dead lay. They buried their dead on high hilltops and on mountainsides, well away from the communities of which they had once been a part - and to which they might return. In addition they encircled the burial sites with deep ditches filled with water, thorns and protective objects that the spirits would have to cross to return to the world of the living. It was imagined that the hostile spirit would give up any attack, rather than combat such obstacles.

Later, drystone walls were used to encircle burying grounds, both to keep in the ghosts and, from a more practical point of view, to keep out scavenging animals. A number of old folktales from Ireland and Scotland such as *Teig O'Kane and the Corpse* speak of phantoms that are trapped behind, and cannot cross, an unseen wall of fire that surrounds the graveyard.

Not only ancestral ghosts were restrained by such enclosures. There was, in early Celtic belief, a strong veneration for chthonic – underworld – deities. In order to make due offerings, dry wells and holy shafts were sunk into the earth. These created a contact point between an underworld of spirits and the day-to-day world of mortals. Through these connections, the powers of the god could often be manifest, exuding beneficence or malignant powers. If the latter, it was as important to be protected against the powers as to worship them. Consequently restraining walls were raised to limit the extent of the forces that seeped from the votive shafts.

Shrines and Sacred Sites

In Britain, as in most of the Celtic West, many of these wells or shafts are of Roman date. This does not mean that they were part of Roman religion or that the Romans even used them; it is more probable that they were used by native Celts at the time of the Roman occupation. This assumption is strengthened by the fact that several of the enclosed shafts were tiled and had crow skeletons imbedded in their walls – crows being the symbols of Underworld deities.

Healing Springs and Pools

From very earliest times there has been a close association between water and healing. It was supposed, according to earliest belief, to wash away both disease and physical afflictions and to purify the skin and body. Under Roman influence, great baths and water-pools were created all through the civilised world, yet even these were associated with rudimentary spirits and forces. One of Christ's miracles was performed at the healing Pool of Beth-said where an angel or spirit 'ruffled the waters with its wings' and the first person that entered the pool afterwards was cured of their affliction.

The great water-healing shrines of the Celtic world did not fully flourish until the Roman–Celtic period. In Roman Britain and in Gaul there were a number of curative cults who made regular pilgrimages to the great centres at places such as Bath, Lydney and Source des Roches de Chamalières in the hope of being healed.

Not all of these sites were temples in the grand style of Bath. Some were merely ornamented pools based around springs or natural clefts through which healing waters ran. Pilgrims flocked to these centres, some bearing wooden or clay representations of themselves in their distressed state believing that the deity would replace these with better models and so cure them.

In earliest times, there were local spirits or forces that performed healing in return for supplication and worship. Over the years, recognisable deities began to evolve, largely due to classical influences. In northern Britain there were a number of identifiable aquatic deities, the most important being the goddess Coventina who presided over a site near Carrawburgh. Similarly Verbeia was worshipped at the rivers Wharfe and Tees while a number of other water-nymphs were the object of veneration at sites along the Humber. A name that occurs time and again is that of *Latis*. This might have been a generalised term since it means 'goddess of the Pool'. Another virtually nameless incarnation of the same goddess may be found at the healing springs at Buxton where the name *Aquae Arnemetiae* means 'the waters of the goddess who lived in the sacred grove' – a concept that united two sacred Celtic sites.

Celtic Mythology

Water was associated not only with healing. In the Celtic mind it was also associated with fertility and renewed life. After all, water was necessary to make crops grow and to restore vitality to parched earth – and people. Some deities might have combined the attributes of healing and fertility, becoming important entities closely connected to the source and creation of life. Along the River Boyne in Ireland, a number of early Celtic tribes believed that they had sprung from the loins of the river goddess Bóinn. The mating of the supreme god Daghdha and the river-goddess Bóinn (see

LOWBURY HILL

Lowbury Hill in Oxfordshire might once have been the site of an important Celtic sanctuary or shrine. The earthworks at the top of this hill suggest a rectangular enclosure, and an underground round barrow hints at some form of chthonic worship.

The site was first excavated in 1913–14 and further work was carried out much later, using a geophysical survey and a limited programme of excavations. It yielded a number of very interesting finds. It is suggested that the original site might have been a systematically and deliberately planted holy grove, dated around the first century AD. The spacing of tree holes seems to indicate that the grove might have formed a boundary against the outside world. Some time around the second century AD the ring of trees was replaced with a wall. The grove then became a much more formal enclosure and the basis of a simple temple.

Within the confines of the enclosure, several other interesting discoveries were made, including a number of spears, some ritually damaged and deliberately bent. A number of coins and other artefacts had also been buried, probably as offerings. This suggests a prolonged period of consistent use as a sacred site.

The second discovery was the grave of a woman whose face had been deliberately mutilated. There is no explanation for the disfigurement and it is impossible to tell to which era the body belongs. It might be that the woman was a priestess, seeress or witch whose corpse had been ritually deposited within the temple precincts, an offering to underground forces believed to inhabit the region.

The temple's hilltop situation, the long history of occupation and the construction of an artificial grove suggests that the ground at that site was extremely sacred. Its continued existence, even into the Roman period, emphasises its importance. The burial of the spear and ritually damaged weapons hints of a deity connected with battle and warfare.

The whole Lowbury Hill excavation shows just how difficult it is for us today to come to grips with the thought-processes of our ancestors, and how incredibly difficult it is to identify the exact nature of Celtic ritual sites.

Spirits of Earth and Air) is symbolic of the union between the fertile land and the river-water that brought about growth and irrigated crops. The marriage between a river-spirit and a tribal god was not uncommon among the Celts. The river ensured the well being, fertility and rejuvenation of land and people. At many sites, such as Bath and Buxton, offerings of money and jewellery are to be found – symbols of hope and requests for good health and well being.

For the ancient Celts, water was a powerful symbol and the number of water-shrines and sacred pools that flowered during the Roman occupation of Western Europe bears testament to this. Although the major aquatic shrines date from that period, there is no doubt that springs and pools were being enclosed as sacred sites through-out Europe long before the Romans arrived.

Ground, bog, lake, mountain, grove and pool – all were the embodiment of the land-scape as well as the home of the gods. As such they were places of veneration, areas that needed to be 'sectioned off' from the rest of the world. Surely this is the origin of temples and churches even today.

Shrines and Sacred Sites

IN SEARCH OF ANCIENT HEROES

Weapons, Warriors and War-Gods

By all the evidence, the Celts enjoyed fighting. Classical writers such as Polybius and Strabo, refer to their fearsome reputation as warriors. They were so ferocious that even the mighty Roman Empire was wary of engaging them until 225 BC, when the myth of their invincibility was exploded at Cape Telamon. The ancient mythological cycles speak of individual feats of valour, military skill and magical and splendid weapons that were used to great effect. Some writers describe elite warrior cults for whom fighting and battle was a distinct way of life with warrior-schools that trained young men to be great fighters with a love of conflict. Descriptions of Celtic feasts contain accounts of contests of strength and 'mock battles', some of which appear to have been frightening in their intensity. An air of competition existing within the fragmented society of the Celtic world came to the fore during such gatherings. It was a mark of honour for a tribe to boast the best warrior in the region and he was usually accorded special status.

Celtic Mythology

Folk tales and legends tell of many heroes and mighty warriors who might not have enjoyed much existence outside the imaginations of bards and storytellers. Some might be the human representations of ancient war gods; others might be the fusion of lesser warriors, into a central character who then became, through the years, a quasi-historical figure. One such figure might have been the greatest of all British heroes, King Arthur. But this exaggeration and combination of attributes is characteristic of most of the great heroes of Celtic myth. The roots of the warrior-hero stretch back to the very dawn of Celtic society and beyond.

Early War-Gods and Warriors

Warrior deities in Western Europe originated in prehistoric times, before the arrival of the Celts. Bronze Age people worshipped some form of fighting or war-god as exemplified by carvings on menhirs or standing stones like those at Puech-Real in France. Such stones were clearly venerated and were probably the physical embodiments of spirits of conflict, showing figures in fighting attitudes or carrying weapons. Rock carvings such as those at Val Camonica had religious significance and show ancient types of daggers and spears. Consequently, some historians suggest that the weapons themselves might have been venerated or that the warrior was considered merely an extension of a specially powerful or enchanted armament. This has some significance to Arthur's famous sword, Excalibur. Similar weapons are associated with other legendary and historical figures.

William Millaton of Pengersick Castle in Breage, Cornwall, during the reign of Henry VIII, was said to have a magic sword – given to him by a 'foreign princess' – which ensured victory for its user in battle (see: Robert Hunt '*Popular Romances in the West of England*').

Carvings in northern Italy, an important early Celtic area, and parts of Scandinavia, where some Celtic-style peoples had settled, show pitched battles between groups of warriors carrying mighty and potent weaponry. Italian carvings are believed to date from the second or third millennium BC and are certainly Celtic or pre-Celtic. As Gelling and Davidson have suggested, this depiction shows delight in and respect for the weaponry that is used (see: P. Gelling and H.E. Davidson: '*The Chariot of the Sun*', Dent 1969).

Just as stones and trees became physical embodiments of the natural forces lurking in the landscape, so the warrior became the embodiment of the power that resided in his own weapon. The armament itself gave him his potency in battle. The worship of weapons was reflected in the burial of weapons in certain areas and was distinct from the aquatic rituals that formed part of the worship of river-deities.

In Search of Ancient Heroes

In places such as South Cadbury in England, the burial of weaponry appears to have been quite common. Here, at a small, enclosed shrine, weapons were separated from animal sacrifice conducted there and placed in another grouping for burial. Caesar mentions that, among the Celts, weapons that had been captured in battle, even if broken or damaged, were placed in distinct heaps as an offering to the gods of the victors.

Armour and protective dress were just as venerated as weapons, hence offerings of body armour and decorative war-harnesses left at such river sites as the Severn and the Thames in England. Many of these might have been talismans, used magically to protect the warrior in the heat of battle.

Traditionally, according to several Classical writers, the early Celts often fought naked, but helmets, shields and harnesses, together with pieces of armour, were sometimes employed and there is evidence for a type of chain-mail as protection against sword attacks. The elaborate detail inscribed on some of the armour that has been recovered, suggests that these were far from mere functional items of equipment; many might have held supposed magical properties or, at least, been of symbolic importance to the wearer.

Some helmets from central Germany had stylised bronze horns attached to them, suggesting ferocity and aggression. Other helmets had been fashioned in the shape of boars' heads, presumably for the same purpose. By wearing these, the warrior claimed allegiance to the gods represented and invoked their aid during the ensuing conflict. He might have imagined that he became one with the deity and that supernatural power flowed through him. This was known as the *'riastradh'*, or 'battle spasm' among the ancient Irish and was strongly associated with great warriors or heroes such as Cú Chulainn.

A frightening description of the warrior in a state of riastradh is described in the great Irish epic, the *Táin Bó Cuailnge* – The Cattle Raid of Cooley. He shakes from

BRIAN BORU

Death of Brian Boru after Battle at Clontarf, 1014

Arguably no other historical figure in Ireland is better known than Brian Boru. So famous has he become that many of the stories concerning him are little more than folk-tales, part of an overall mythology. He is, for instance, reputed to be the only man in Ireland who could sit astride the Pooka – a ferocious fairy horse which had terrified the Irish countryside. He obtained from the monster the promise that it would never attack another Irishman (except those in the throes of intoxication). Brian is also credited with the killing of several giants in the West of Ireland but his name is probably used in all these instances to cover a number of heroes or to refer to the overall concept of the hero. Brian, however, certainly existed.

The name Brian is thought to have been the adaptation of the earlier *Briun*, or even a Breton title *Brien*. From 976-

1014, he was leader of the *Dal gCais* sept of Thomond (County Clare) and also High King of Ireland from 1002 until his death. He is the first of the factious Munster kings to have had such an impact upon Irish history. His sobriquet, *Boru*, is suggested as a derivation of *boraimhe*, meaning a cattle tribute, thus giving him the nickname 'Brian of the Tributes'. However, some historians render the title as 'Boramha' referring to Béal Boramha, on the right bank of the Shannon near Killaloe. This, they claim was Brian's birthplace.

Brian came to the leadership of the *Dal gCais* in 976 after the assassination of his elder brother during the internecine wars which characterised the Munster dynasties. He proved to be a strong and able leader, restoring some measure of stability to politically-fractured Munster. He launched a campaign against certain Viking settlements in Ireland – particularly the settlement of Limerick. In fact he became one of the first known native kings to successfully defeat the Vikings on Irish soil.

As his reputation and military prowess increased, Brian became more ambitious. He threatened the reigning Ui Niall High King of Ireland – Mael macDomhaill – that if he did not relinquish the throne, Brian would take it by force. The High King, not wishing such a confrontation, immediately vacated the throne and Brian became Ard Rí (High King). From this position, he increased his attacks against the Vikings and the 'foreign Gaels' (a king of half-Norse/half-Irish hybrid people) with unremitting savagery. He was greatly hated by the Irish Norse, even though he was married to a woman who had previously been espoused to Olafr the White, Norse king of Dublin.

The final conflict between the Norse and Celtic worlds in Ireland took place at Cluain Tairbh (Clontarf) on Good Friday 1014. The two spheres of influence hurled themselves at each other in bloody battle and by the end of the day, Norse power in Ireland had been largely broken. However, Brian himself was dead – killed by an axe thrown by a Manx Norseman Brodr, as he stood in the doorway of his tent awaiting news of victory (at the age of 72, he had taken no active part in the battle himself). Thus, he passed into history as one of the greatest of the Munster kings.

head to toe and revolves within his skin that becomes red and hot to touch. His features become bestial – one eye becoming large and bloodshot while the other becomes extremely small and menacing. His mouth becomes impossibly large and emits both fire and sparks, while his hair becomes spiked and emits further flame. The 'warrior light' shines on his brow, temporarily blinding all that come near him. In this state, he is uncontrollable but also invincible. He seems to be little more than a magical killing machine that cannot be harmed. When the *riastradh* has abated, Cú Chulainn is left drained and weakened.

There seems little doubt that the Celts considered this frenzy to be possession by the warrior-gods or spirits and it might have been channelled through a weapon or talisman – in Cú Chulainn's case, it might have been his *gae bolga* or great war-spear. Nor was Cú Chulainn the only warrior to experience the *riastradh* because, according to classical accounts, battle-frenzy seemed common among the Celtic armies, turning them into formidable and almost invincible fighters. When in this state, the warrior was at one with the god and seemed divine, becoming a physical representation of an elemental force.

The iconographic representation of battle-gods in this early period is relatively sparse. It might be that the Celts had little conception of how the deity should look, or that they felt no need to represent what was essentially an insubstantial battle-force. Where iconography exists, it is difficult to know whether those represented are gods or people overcome by supernatural frenzy. Celtic coins, probably issued during times of conflict, often depicted acts of warfare. Individual warriors, cavalry, chariots and groups of infantry were all represented, as was the total rout of an enemy. Coins issued by the Andecavi, a tribe based around Angiers in France, show the horses of a charioteer trampling a fallen foe who lies supine beneath their hooves, complete with shield and spear. Interestingly, a number of coins from Britain and Gaul depicted a warrior with a great crow perched on his back. This is clearly indicative of the three-fold goddess – Morrigan, Macha and the Badhbh – who represented war, slaughter and death. It appears that this goddess possessed the warrior and granted him victory on the battlefield. We know too, of the British war-goddess, Andraste, clan-patroness of the war-like Iceni and mentioned by the writer Dio Cassius.

In early iconography, chain mail or body armour was sometimes depicted as bearing a severed head on the breastplate. This might have been to terrify a warrior's enemies with the promise of their inevitable

In Search of Ancient Heroes

Warrior on Celtic coin, between 1st century BC and 1st century AD, Britain

fate and is to be found in artwork from Celtic Gaul and parts of Britain. Accounts by Classical writers speak of severed heads hanging from the saddlebows of Celtic horses as a warning to their foes.

The preponderance of magical weapons and personalised talismans does not detract from the fighting skill of the warrior and there are indications that the Celts worked hard to develop battle techniques among their young men. From earliest times, the most formidable warrior or most successful hunter must have enjoyed a special status within his community. The nature of that status, however, is unclear. The warrior/hunter might have been individually praised for his skill, or he might have been regarded as a channel for the tribal deity who gave him those powers. This gave him an almost god-like status in the eyes of his contemporaries and it is possible that he might have been worshipped either as a god himself or as the physical embodiment of one. The concept of the 'hero', as we understand the term, did not appear until medieval times, with the rise of romantic literature. The great and well-known stories concerning the heroes or heroic warriors of old were not written until the 12th and 13th centuries, at the earliest, when they were committed to paper by learned scribes and monks. Yet, even those acknowledged the 'god-connections' of heroes by making them either the children of gods or the offspring of a mortal and Otherworld entity. Later writers were to embellish the basic legends even further by creating more Otherworld connections or by providing the hero with an enchanted weapon or sending him on a mystical quest. These stories belong to a post-Celtic age but, ironically, have come to embody the heroic Celtic ethos.

Celtic Mythology

Ritually Damaged Weapons

Before meeting the ancient heroes of the Celtic world, we must consider the occurrence of ritual damage – particularly of weaponry. Such damage was not confined to armaments of war; ritually broken pots and jars have been unearthed at a number of sites, such as Flag Fen in Cambridgeshire. The act of breaking, bending or cracking an object was its symbolic death, severing its connections with the real, physical world before it could be offered it to the gods or forces of the Otherworld. It might also have symbolised the returning of weapons to the entities that had given them to human warriors. A common way of offering ritually broken swords, spears or axes was to deposit them in a river or lake. At the Flag Fen site, 300–400 bent or otherwise damaged swords, daggers and other items of martial equipment have been found.

From this evidence, historians have argued that the ritual desecration of weapons was probably widespread in the late Neolithic period and continued well into the early Iron Age. The practice of dumping broken weapons into lakes was common in the majority of Celtic lands but seems to have been particularly prevalent in Cornwall and Wales. Large deposits of ritually smashed weapons have been found in the lake of Llyn Cerrig Bach on the island of Anglesey, famed as a centre of ritualised worship (see **The Druidic Tradition**). This legend-motif appears in the story of King Arthur's death when the magic sword Excalibur is returned to the waters when Arthur no longer needs it.

Ritualised damage was also carried out at a number of pre-Roman shrines. Broken and deliberately bent swords have been found at sanctuaries in Oise, France, and at Harlow, England (see **Shrines and Sacred Sites**). The practice was not as common in the Roman period, it seems; perhaps because the adopted Roman gods did not condone that form of worship or perhaps the need to 'pacify' weaponry was not so strong. It may also mean that the belief in magical armaments was already dying but the notion of the individual hero, personally skilled in combat, was already taking shape.

Arthur

The most widely known and most mysterious of the great Celtic heroes was Arthur, King of Britain. Though his name and hero-status is widely recalled, we cannot say when he lived or, indeed, who he was. He might have been a British king who unified the feuding British kingdoms under one banner and who established order and a code of chivalry. He might simply have been a local warlord who was able to seize

ROBIN HOOD

Whether or not Robin Hood actually existed, there is little doubt that his legend owes a debt to Celtic mythology. Apart from any historical arguments as to the veracity of Robin Hood, we can identify elements of nature-folklore in the common tale. Some folklorists have suggested that Robin Hood is merely another name for Herne the Hunter, Master of the Wild Hunt and his Merry Men devotees or ghosts of the dead. The strong connection between the outlaw and the deep woodlands, home to many medieval outlaws who became the 'wild men' of popular imagination, gave credence to such a belief. He was linked to Windsor Great Park in Berkshire, where he was supposed to be the ghost of a huntsman, whose body was reanimated through the sorcery of local wizard Phillip Urwicke. Herne, or Cernunnos, as

Robin Hood, Maid Marion and Friar Tuck on a 17th-century woodcut

a nature spirit, was widely associated with woodlands throughout early and medieval England.

A number of references strengthen Robin Hood's ties with nature gods. A variant of his name, *Rob Hoode* derived from *Hob* or *Hod*, the name of a Celtic spirit associated mainly with the home and hearth but sometimes also with the outdoors. Hob embodied plenty and fertility and was worshipped with libations of milk, either left by the fireside at night or poured out on the doorstep just as the sun went down. In return, Hob showed his pleasure to the household by ensuring that it had enough to live on. This may be a variant of the idea of 'robbing the rich to give to the poor', a trait of Robin Hood and his men. In medieval England, very few outlaws gave to the poor.

The second clue to the outlaw's Celtic origins is in the colour of the garments worn by himself and his followers. This is described in children's stories as Lincoln green, the colour of nature. The figure of Herne is sometimes described as being cloaked in a green robe and wearing a cowl, like a monk. Many pub signs for 'The Green Man', as Herne was commonly known, show a bearded face peering out from under a green cowl or hood.

The outlaw's name could, therefore come from the idea of Robin in a Hood. Certain types of woodland fertility spirits went about cowled and hooded and wore long, flowing green cloaks. Perhaps this was the true mythological origin of Robin Hood.

vant gilles voit que
faire li couuient. sire
uient arriere la ou les
pre estoit li la prent ⁊ la recome
ce a regarder ⁊ a plaindre mlt
durement ⁊ dist tot en plorant.
ha. estre bone ⁊ bele plus que nu
le autre tant est siis damages

large tracts of land and outmanoeuvre other chieftains in battle. If so, his 'kingdom' could have been in Southern England, Ireland, Scotland or Wales. Perhaps he was the last defender of Celtic Britain against the hordes of invading Saxons. We wonder about the folkloric trappings that attend his legend, about Excalibur that was pulled from a stone and about Merlin his adviser.

The first concern is the name Arthur, which is certainly not Celtic. Although subsequent British Celts speak of 'great Arthur', the origin of the title is *Artorius* a standard Roman name. It was not reported in Britain until around the seventh century, about fifty years after Arthur was supposed to have died, when the last lowland British armies were destroyed by advancing Saxons and were gloriously described as 'the heirs of great Arthur' – thus making a purely Celtic connection. Around the same time, a number of local kings took the name and more named their children Arthur. After that it was dropped from use and did not resurface until the Norman period when the early medieval romances gave it certain popularity. Thus, for about 600 years, the name of Arthur was virtually unknown anywhere in Britain.

The sixth century, when Arthur is said to have lived, is part of a period known as 'The Dark Ages', for little written material remains from that era. There are references to a great number of texts, written by monks, but not many seem to have survived. Only one relatively contemporary source refers to a ruler who might be Arthur. This is found in the writings of a monk named Gildas who, around AD 540, penned a scathing attack on the chieftains, princes and bishops of his day. Gildas knew the Bible thoroughly; he had also read some Classical texts and he knew something of the literature of the late Roman Empire. But he had no historical sources to hand and, like many of his monkish contemporaries, he relied heavily upon the memories of men who were very old when he himself was young. This led to great gaps in both his argument and knowledge of history. For example, 'from the time of the (Roman) Emperors', he mentioned only two major events – the 'revolt of the unclean lioness' (Boudicca) in AD 60 and the rebellion of Maximus in 388. This did not stop him citing references to former rulers.

In Search of Ancient Heroes

One of those whom Gildas held up as an example of valour and stable government was a chieftain whom he does not name – he names nobody at all in the previous eighty years, except Ambrosius Aurelius – but from his hints, this could only be a ruler such as Arthur. As far as the ardently conservative Gildas was concerned, the rule of Arthur had but one aim – to create a British version of the fallen Roman Empire. He was, in effect, a Roman monarch.

But although nothing was written about Arthur, oral tales survived during the sixth, seventh and eighth centuries, particularly in Wales. These would later form the core of a number of Welsh poems that eventually found their way into writing. Saint Ninian of Whithorn related an old poetic fragment about the deeds of a king who is surely Arthur, while eighth-century Welsh poetry is rich in allusions to lost verses

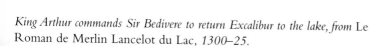

King Arthur commands Sir Bedivere to return Excalibur to the lake, from Le Roman de Merlin Lancelot du Lac*, 1300–25.*

about this king. By the ninth century, however, much of the interest in Arthur had died out – the British and the Irish only remembered his name and a few tales about him might have remained along the Welsh borders. Yet some references must have survived – probably in an oral tradition – for the medieval Norman writers seized on it and turned it into a full-blown mythology that has survived to this day. These romances had little to do with the Celtic period but more with political propaganda, given the increasing enmity between France and England in the 12th, 13th and subsequent centuries.

The Arthur of folklore took on some of Gildas's exposition. That viewpoint was personal and quite political; Gildas disliked the corrupt political and ecclesiastical institutions of his day and was, through his writings, determined to change them and perhaps advance himself at the same time. His interpretation of Arthur was not objective. He was calling for fair and stable government and was using Arthur to exemplify this.

Gildas's 'historical' Arthur upheld the 'restraints of truth and justice'. He headed a strong and orderly government that suggested a Golden Age long before the bloodshed, confusion, turbulence and internecine warfare that characterised Gildas's time. His reign was short but effective. According to tradition, he rebuilt, albeit briefly, the institutions and governmental structures that had collapsed following the Roman withdrawal. He brought stability to a land torn by striving warlords who attempted to fill the power vacuum left by the vanished Roman administration.

Celtic Mythology

The legend of Arthur as we know it developed many hundreds of years after the supposed life of the monarch. It was probably based on a number of Arthur-like figures that existed in Wales, Cornwall and Brittany. When considering these romances, we must remember that not all of the stories come from the one source or refer to the same man. Arthur is an amalgam of figures, possibly centred round one historical character about whom very little is known. This did not prevent the romanticists from developing the figure but, in the process, they created a great deal of confusion. We have difficulty in placing Arthur within the Celtic realm and in locating his kingdom in Wales, Cornwall or Scotland. This confusion might have arisen from all the different sources cobbled together by the medieval writers and the attempts to integrate other myths with the central tale.

Stories of Arthur-like warriors existed in Wales, Cornwall and Brittany, long before the medieval writers adapted them but it is from Norman sources that most of our legends have derived. Such stories were not written as history but to serve the specific purposes of the writers – just as Gildas had used them many centuries earlier. Geoffrey of Monmouth, writing in the 12th century, portrayed Arthur as a fearless champion of the Celtic peoples who drove the invading Saxons and others from British shores and who led forays and expeditions against Europe which the British subsequently subdued under his guidance. Geoffrey's account was directed to serve the ambition of the Plantagenet kings of England and to ingratiate himself at Court.

Onsideratū q̄ par les triūphalles
et glorieuses oeuures que les
vaillans hommes a nobles che
ualiers anciennement firent en
fait de cheualerie acquirent en leurs vi
es louenges a gloire de perpetuelle me

moire. Je vostre treshumble et tresobeis
sāt seruiteur a l'honeur a louēge de vo'mō
tresredoubte a souuerain seigue² chief de
toute noblesse a cheualerie. Charles huiti
esme de ce nō trescrestiē roy de frāce. Affin
q̄ vostre cheualereux couraige a des ieu

The original source was probably a Breton poem, *Mailière de Bretagne,* that might not have been about a British ruler. The tale was taken up with enthusiasm, not only by the Court, but also by the King's subjects. It was amalgamated with other folktales from the British countryside and the mighty Celtic hero Peredur of York, killed in AD 580, was transformed into Sir Perceval.

The tales had changed. Writers such as Geoffrey had adapted them to suit contemporary tastes. They no longer wrote about wild Celtic chieftains, riding out from their fortified strongholds to raid their neighbours. They portrayed what a medieval audience would know and recognise - kings, knights, squires and stately castles. To appeal to the English Court, the elements of chivalry and courtly love were introduced.

The classic English version of the legend is Malory's *Morte d'Arthur* written in the 15th century (almost a thousand years after Arthur's reign). Other renderings of the legend with added folkloristic detail followed. They claimed that Arthur travelled all over Britain, conquered the Welsh and the Scots and brought peace wherever he went. By then he had a mystical sword, Excalibur that he alone, in all England, had drawn from a rock in his youth. Loyal and chivalrous followers, the Knights of the Round Table surrounded him, the epitome of courtly service. All this suited 14th and 15th century notions of manners and propriety.

In Search of
Ancient Heroes

But we do not know if Excalibur existed and if it was Arthur's mighty sword. It is possible that Excalibur was a remembrance of the enchanted weapons that prehistoric warriors had wielded and through which the Celtic gods channelled their powers. The idea of Arthur's drawing it from a stone might have come from the mistranslation of a medieval monk. Geoffrey of Monmouth magnified Arthur's greatness, implying that he was the only ruler who could take the sword 'from out of the Saxons' – ex Saxon – i.e. the only British ruler who could defeat them. A monk copying the text later, might have wrongly copied it as 'from out of the stone' – ex saxa – evolving a whole legend from this single error. Parallels could be drawn between the mythical Arthur and the historical Rhydderch Hael, the powerful king of Strathclyde. He supposedly had a sword named Dyrnwyn that only he could draw from its scabbard. The weapon would burst into flames from hilt to point and destroy anyone else who attempted to withdraw it. A number of common tales linked the person of Arthur to the Strathclyde king, the most prominent concerning Merlin who, according to folktale, was Rhydderch Hael's brother-in-law. Whatever its literary origins, Excalibur was a gift from the gods and had to be returned as soon as Arthur died.

Merlin's connection with the Arthur stories is thought to be a fusion of two distinct myth types in medieval France by writers of the period. There are a number of other additions. There is the enigma of Camelot, Arthur's palace and the centre of his administration; if it existed and where it was. Many places have staked a claim to the site of Arthur's court, Glastonbury in Somerset, Tintagel in Cornwall to name but

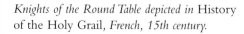

Knights of the Round Table depicted in History of the Holy Grail, *French, 15th century.*

two. Possibly, Camelot is a variation of the pagan Otherworld myth. It is an imagined realm where goodness and order forever hold sway and in which righteousness prevails. Descriptions of the kingdom do not refer to churches or abbeys and there is no mention of a hierarchical church structure. The nearest person to the bishop-figure is Merlin who has more than a hint of the druid. The Knights of the Round Table were probably local warlords some of whose legends were contemporaneous with those of Arthur. To ensure their immortality, they were incorporated into the Arthur-legend as lesser but valiant figures. Sir Bors is almost certainly the Welsh hero Bedwyr who appears in the famous tale of Culwch and Olwen while Lancelot appears to be a variant of several French legends about local champions. The local interests fed into the Arthur-myth have served to keep the tradition alive through the ages and surrounded the Knights of the Round Table with romance throughout the Celtic world. The table, of course, was round so that no hero could sit at its head making them all of equal importance. Arthur was not invariably depicted as gentle and chivalrous. In Scottish legend, he was sometimes described as a tyrant and a ferocious military commander who showed no mercy to his prisoners. A poem, penned by Saint Nennius, referred to several battles in the Cheviot region north of Hadrian's Wall in which Arthur's troops were involved. These wars were perhaps to unite the kingdom of Strathclyde with the rest of Britain. The genealogies named the king as Dynfnwal who was honoured above his contemporaries and who reputedly made several raids into Lothian. He was regarded as a mighty ruler who supported a stable, Roman-style government within his own kingdom and in those that he conquered. Perhaps King Dynfnwal aided Arthur in his campaigns in the north and was rewarded with a large territory as a trustworthy guardian of the northern frontier. Some legends about Dynfnwal might have been incorporated into the overall Arthur legend and the characters of the two kings might have merged.

Celtic Mythology

Before the end in the narrow glen at Camlan – the blind or crooked glen – Arthur's Celtic roots re-emerged slightly. He was forced to return Excalibur to the mystical forces and was carried off to the Isle of Avalon, symbolic of the Celtic Otherworld. The three maidens who bore him there were symbolic of the triple-goddess of the early Celts. His apparent slaying by his own illegitimate son, Mordred, might symbolise the passing of the old chieftain at the hands of his more vigorous offspring. Only at his death does Arthur become a Celtic hero in any recognisable sense.

Perhaps Arthur was little more than a local warlord who had the vision and military might to unite his fragmented people under a quasi-Roman system of government. Perhaps he was, as Gildas has portrayed him, a noble and wise monarch who ushered in a brief period of stability in the midst of the post-Roman turmoil. Maybe he was a combination of a number of rulers – Dynfnwal, Rhydderch Hael – who both advanced and consolidated their own kingdoms and passed into legend. These are only suppositions and the figure of Arthur remains as romantic and as enigmatic as ever, a shadow swathed in mystery and legend.

Cú Chulainn

The only other Celtic warrior-figure who rivals Arthur in legend and mythology is the Irish champion Cú Chulainn who appears within what is known as the Ulster Cycle of myths.

The name means, 'The Hound of Culann' although the prefix 'Cú' was a common designation for a warrior in early Irish literature. The title was used as late as the 12th century to denote a fearsome warrior – as in Cú Ultach O'Flynn, Lord of the Northern Shíol Cathasaigh, defeated near the mouth of the River Bush by the Norman knight John de Courcy in 1170. No evidence is given for the meaning of his second name, although several legends attempt to explain it. It is clear that he had his origins in a Celtic cult that venerated military prowess.

It is possible that Cú Chulainn might not be a name but a title. The hero's real name is given in the earliest legends as *Setanta*, corresponding to the Celtic Setantii tribe in Britain. His favoured weapon is a mighty spear or javelin that is referred to as the *ga*, or *gae*, *bolg* (*bolga*) vaguely reminiscent of the Belgae, a well-known tribe in Western Europe. The name of his father-in-law, *Forgall Manach*, reflected the Menapii of Gaul. They, in turn, were supposed to have given their name to County Fermanagh in Ireland, *Fir Manapii*, the men of the Manapii. His birthplace was stated to be County Louth although this might have been only the site of his cult.

THE FIANNA

The Fianna were a number of great Irish heroes of the later mythological period. So famous were they and so many stories were told about them that they have acquired a mythological cycle all to themselves – the *Fionn Cycle*. The name is taken from their leader Fionn (or Finn) MacCumhaill (who was later turned into the giant Finn Mac Cool – see **Giants, Monsters and Fairies**).

Fionn himself deserves the status of hero. He was, according to the Cycle, born after the murder of his father Cumhaill and was raised by a druidess. As a result of her teachings he developed a great affinity with the natural world. When he reached early manhood, he ousted his father's murderer, Goll, from the leadership of the elite Fianna. In the process, he acquired a magic bag made of crane skin which contained a spear, a helmet and a pigskin belt. In order to further himself and his prospects, Fionn went to the bard Finnegas in order to learn poetry. Whilst there, Finnegas managed to catch the enchanted Salmon of Knowledge and gave it to his young pupil to cook. Whilst it was cooking, Fionn burnt his thumb on its skin and as he sucked the blister, acquired supernatural knowledge.

Returning to Tara, Fionn found it in great uproar. Every Samhain night (at the end of October. See **The Great Wheel of Existence**), the fortress was burnt to the ground by a malignant goblin named Aillen who first enchanted the court and then set fire to it. Fionn slept with his cheek against the enchanted spear which he had found in the crane-bag and thus was able to stay awake and kill Aillen before he could burn down the fortress. For this act, he was given leadership of the Fianna.

Under Fionn's guidance, the Fianna prospered. In order to join them, a warrior had to undergo several severe and testing initiation rituals. They performed many supernatural deeds all across Ireland including the killing of a five-headed giant and several gigantic and terrifying boars and hounds. Fionn even managed to challenge the Tuatha de Danann god Nuadu in battle and overcame him. This seems to suggest that Fionn was already semi-divine.

In his old age, Fionn seems to have become very bitter and jealous. With an old man's passion, he became infatuated by the beautiful Gráinne. She rejected his advances in favour of Diarmaid, with whom she eloped. Fionn hurried off in hot pursuit and subsequently dishonoured himself as a hero by treacherously arranging Diarmaid's death. Gráinne prophesied that Fionn would die as soon as he drank from a drinking-horn. According to one story, Fionn was abandoned by the rest of the Fianna for his part in Diarmaid's death. Old and alone, he challenged some strangers to a contest of strength, in which he had to leap the River Boyne. He took a drink from a horn, obviously forgetting Gráinne's prophecy. He made the leap but fell short and was drowned in the river. Without his leadership, the Fianna ultimately scattered and became nothing more than a legend.

The collection of seventh to ninth century additions to the central tale of Cú Chulainn was obviously thought necessary to provide some history for the hero. In creating this background, the ancient scribes caused great confusion by creating different myths about the hero's character and origins. The compiler of the first rendition of the *Táin*, which is a collection of oral tales relating to a war between Ulster and invaders from the Irish Midlands, faced the task of bringing these differing strands into a coherent whole. This explains many inconsistencies in stories surrounding Cú Chulainn's birth and boyhood and the ambiguity about his kinship to King Conchobar.

The main ancient Irish text referring to the exploits of Cú Chulainn is the *Táin Bó Cuailnge* – The Cattle Raid of Cooley – and the hero's entrance into the narrative dated from around the seventh or eighth century. Early forms of the text attempt to link Cú Chulainn to the royal household of Ulster and to the Otherworld. His mother, the Ulster king's sister, supposedly slept in the house of an Otherworld being at *Brugh na Bóinne*. Here she gave birth at the same time as a mare dropped two foals. The baby later became ill and died but was reborn again as Cú Chulainn. The true father of the child was revealed as Lúgh, God of Light. If he was of royal blood, then the latter tale was a fabrication designed to disguise King Conchobar's alleged incestuous relationship with his sister.

*In Search of
Ancient Heroes*

Almost from infancy, the young Setanta displayed superior skills at hunting, athletics and war-craft. He could throw his famous javelin, the *gae bolga*, and catch it before it touched the ground. In one tale, an unspecified enemy surprised the Ulster men while the infant hero lay sleeping. On waking Setanta grabbed a hurley-stick and went to the battlefield where Conchobar and his men were being held prisoner. Belabouring the enemy, the child released the king and his son Cormac and brought them safely home.

Additions to the texts in the late-eighth/early-ninth centuries seek to explain the origins of his name. While an infant, Cú Chulainn was unaccountably given in fosterage to a smith named Culann whose hound he accidentally killed. In a fit of remorse, he declared 'I will be your hound', hence the pre-fix 'Cú' – hound - and the name 'Hound of Culann'. The title is taken to mean Warrior of Culann although just who or what Culann is unclear.

The tale of the child's slaying the monstrous hound of the smith Culann coincided with the monkish notion of monsters and giants that represented the forces of paganism (see **Giants, Monsters and Fairies**). It was crafted on to the central tales at a much later period, perhaps during the 10th or 11th centuries, probably to assert Man's superiority over the wildness of Nature. Some late medieval sources render the name as *Cú na Ceirde*, the 'Hound of the Craftsman (or the Smith)'.

Some folklorists suggest that the slaying of the beast might have marked an initiation rite that the young Setanta, in common with other young warriors, had to endure to

Cú Chulainn goes into battle

CONALL CEARNACH

One of the few Irish heroes who could equal Cú Chulainn was Conall Cearnach. He appears as a mythical warrior in the Ulster Cycle and seemed to have been an ancestor-hero of the Conailli, a tribe that inhabited parts of Counties Louth, Down and Armagh. His name is thought to derive from *Cuno-valos* – Strong, Like a Wolf – and his nickname is frequently given as 'Triumphant'.

He appeared in Irish literature around the eighth or ninth century and the stories about him are probably an amalgam of old hero-tales from the Irish midlands. His origin is unclear – from Ulster or Connacht. During the early medieval period, Connall Cearnach was a supporting character in much of the Ulster Cycle, who gave cohesion and sequence to many of the tales. Portrayed as one of the great warrior-heroes among the Ulster men, he was also a mercenary who was promoted to captain in the army of Eochaidh Feidhleach, High King of Ireland around the time of Julius Caesar. In this capacity, he performed mighty deeds, including attacking a castle or fortress deep in the Alps that was guarded by a monstrous serpent. This story is probably derived from earlier Christian mythology concerning the Breton saint Samson of Dol, who allegedly charmed a terrible serpent out of a fortress in the mountains and tamed it.

An ancient Irish text, written around AD 800, proclaimed Conall Cearnach as the foremost hero in Ulster. This title – claimed by a number of other warriors – led to the unfortunate incident at Bricriú's Feast in which Cú Chulainn superseded Conall as a great hero. No real enmity or jealousy between the two warriors is evident, and Conall becomes a firm friend to the young Cú Chulainn.

Tales of Conall Cearnach were so well known throughout the medieval period in Ireland that several Irish septs claimed descent from him. The name MacConnell, prevalent in parts of Down and in the Irish midlands, may have been derived from this association. Tales of his martial prowess were legion – he supposedly journeyed all over the ancient world to perform wonderful feats.

Legend states that he once owned the fort of Dunseverick on the bleak north Antrim coast, before it fell into the hands of the ancestors of the O'Caháns. From here, he was said to have travelled to Rome and fought in the arena before the Emperor Tiberius. The Emperor was so impressed with him that he immediately created him an officer of the Roman army. Conall did not remain in Rome but wandered east, arriving in the Holy Land around the time of the Crucifixion. Irish Christian legend suggests that he was one of the Roman soldiers at the foot of the Cross and that a drop of Christ's blood fell on his brow, giving him the first Christian baptism. That, it was alleged, had a profound influence on Conall's life. He became a Christian, teaching and preaching throughout the east. There are references to a Conall the Celt, an early Christian saint, who taught in Turkey but whether this is Conall Cearnach is open to question.

join a Celtic warrior-cult. In the *Táin*, he successfully passed the test and became the ultimate warrior – excelling in athletic prowess and skills and an expert in weaponry. The very sound of his voice was so authoritative that it could strike terror into the soul of any foe.

What these texts seem to suggest is that Cú Chulainn might have been Lúgh in another guise or, that a fundamental connection existed between the two. There was a strong Lúgh-cult in County Louth during the first and second centuries AD and the stories relating to Cú Chulainn, which are County Louth based, might reflect diversification among the worshippers. The distinctive warrior-bias of the Cú Chulainn myth seems to suggest this.

Another medieval text in which Cú Chulainn appears is a very ancient poem entitled *Tochmarc Emire* (The Wooing of Eimhear). This epic was probably originally written around the eighth century but enjoyed periodic expansions and reworking of its text until the tenth or eleventh century. Encouraged to look for a suitable wife by all the other champions of Ireland, who had grown tired of the number of eligible girls thronging around the great hero, he searched all Ireland for a suitable girl. Eventually, he settled on Eimhear, the daughter of Forgall Manach who ruled lands to the south of the River Boyne in County Louth. She laid down conditions for the winning of her hand and Cú Chulainn had to perform 'the feat of the salmon leap' in battle. This meant killing hundreds of men in a particular way. He had to perform a special leap

Conall Cearnach, one of the Roman soldiers who stood below the cross at Christ's crucifixion.

while delivering a single sword-stroke so that his blow would kill certain men but leave others untouched. He was also to go without sleep from November to August. Cú Chulainn agreed to these tests and returned to Eamhain Macha - the seat of the Ulster kings. Eimhear's father, was strongly opposed to the union and followed the hero, in disguise, to the royal court where he advised Cú Chulainn to go to Scotland to study under the noted female warrior Scathach. The hero went, but first studied for a time with a warrior named Domhnall. Then he went to meet Scathach and her warriors who had been bribed to kill him. He defeated this army by performing the salmon leap. From this account came the first mention of the battle frenzy for which he was to become famous. Much impressed by his fighting prowess, Scathach took him as a lover and he helped her in her campaigns while learning about war-craft. Later Cú Chulainn returned to Ireland to claim his bride but found Eimhear's house so well guarded that he could not take it for a whole year. In one attack, he killed over three hundred men before performing the salmon-leap over the ramparts and taking the stronghold. Having performed all the feats required of him, he claimed Eimhear as his wife and took her back with him to Eamhain Macha.

Stories about the champion's death were already in circulation by the 10th century. It appears in the Ulster Cycle, and in a number of tales from around that time. The circumstances of his death are linked with an invasion of south Ulster by the forces of Meadhbh, Queen of Connacht. Meadhbh's existence as a real person is questioned because one of the translations of her name is 'She Who Intoxicates' and she might have been a warrior-goddess of the Irish Midlands who inspired her followers into battle. They swept into Cuailnge, the Cooley area of County Louth, and a war between Ulster and Connacht began in earnest.

Cú Chulainn at this time had grown weary of battle and had withdrawn to the Valley of the Deaf where no sound or news from the outside world could reach him. The great hero had many enemies – three of whom were the children of Cailitín, a warrior whom Cú Chulainn had slain, all of them great sorcerers. By magic they created the illusion that Eamhain Macha were being attacked and one of them, Niamh – a young lady for whom Cú Chulainn had a particular affection – came and told him that he was sorely needed in battle.

On his way to the battle, he and his warriors passed three old women – a representation of the triple-goddess, signifying death – who were washing the corslets of the fallen in a river. As he passed one held up a gore-stained garment that the hero recognised as his own. He knew, then, that would be his last battle.

And so it proved, for the three sorcerers were waiting to fight him. One threw a javelin that killed Cú Chulainn's charioteer Laogh and the second lodged in the side of the hero's favourite horse. The third javelin, thrown by Lughaidh, the son of Cú Roí, struck Cú Chulainn himself. The hero's intestines fell out but, gathering them up, he staggered to a nearby lake to drink. Then he used the intestines to tie himself to a great standing stone and there he stood sword in hand. For three days, his foes did not dare to approach but in the end Niamh herself, in the guise of a crow flew over and, lighting on his shoulder, confirmed he was dead. As he tried to remove the sword from the dead fingers, Lughhaidh caused the blade to slip and lopped off his own hand.

The medieval tales concerning Cú Chulainn – and there is a large repository of them – were seized on by the romantic Irish writers of the late 19th century. Writers such as Standish James O'Grady, Lady Augusta Gregory, W.B. Yeats and Pádraig Pearse turned him into a popular figure, vastly distanced from the original oral tales, but more symbolic of Irish culture and nationhood. The trend continues to this day when The Hound of Cullen is still regarded as one of the foremost Irish icons.

Mabinogi

Medieval Welsh literature has many parallels with that of Britain and Ireland. Most of the great heroic stories are to be found in a collection of tales known as *Mabinogi* or *The Four Branches of the Mabinogion* taken from the Welsh oral tradition. The tales have been preserved in two distinct sources: *The White Book of Rhydderch* (collected and written 1300-25) and *The Red Book of Hergest* (collected and written 1375-25). The tales thus collected are of a much earlier origin.

The origin of the term *mabinogi* has created a slight controversy among folklorists and historians. Sir John Rhys, writing in 1887 as a preface to *The Red Book of Hergest*, stated that its source lay in the literary and artistic training of the *Mabinogi*, apprentice rhymers 'who had not yet acquired the art of making verse but had received instruction from a qualified bard'. Others, such as Cecile O'Rahilly and T. Gwynn Jones saw links between the Irish bardic schools and those of the Welsh and traced the word to Irish mythology. The origin is the Irish *mac ind oc*, which relates to *Oengus Óg*, in his incarnation as the son of the Daghdha, 'the ever young'.

In Search of Ancient Heroes

The tales were not translated into English from the original Welsh until the 19th century. Lady Elizabeth Guest (1812-95) produced several volumes between 1838 and 1849. She differentiated between *Four Branches of the Mabinogion* and common *Native Welsh Tales*. A third grouping consisted of three Arthurian romances of comparatively late origin.

One of the most famous of all the *Mabinogi* tales is that of Culwch and Olwen probably written down in the 11th century. The story owes something to both British and Irish tales since it holds a number of themes in common with both types of folklore. It is also the oldest of the Welsh tales to mention King Arthur of Britain.

Culhwch was the son of King Cilydd, a minor Welsh king (although he seems to appear again as one of Culhwch's companions) and cousin to Arthur, King of the Britons. Although of royal birth, he was accidentally born in a pigsty – the name Culhwch means 'pig run' – and was afterwards abandoned by his mother.

Raised by a swineherd, Culhwch eventually learned of his true heritage and made his way to Cilydd's court. There he found his mother dying. Fearing that her husband the king would marry again and dispossess her son, she made Cilydd promise that he would not re-marry until a briar with two heads grew on her grave. Cilydd promised and appointed a monk to watch the grave for this strange event. After seven years, the monk grew lax in his duties and forgot to tend the grave. Cilydd also forgot his promise and remarried.

Culhwch's stepmother had a daughter by a previous marriage and decided to cement the royal relationship by demanding that the two should marry. Culhwch refused, saying that the girl was far too young to marry him. In a fit of rage, his stepmother, a powerful witch, placed a curse on him, saying that the only girl that he was fit to marry was Olwen, the daughter of Yspaddaden Pencawr, the monstrous, flesh-eating giant-king and that he should wed her right away. On hearing Olwen's name, Culhwch fell in love with her and resolved to win her from her terrible father. Pencawr would not give up his only daughter lightly, especially because of the well-known prophecy that his own grandson would kill him.

To help his son, King Cilyyd sent him to his cousin Arthur in Britain to ask for help in his quest. Culhwch travelled to Arthur's court where he reputedly performed many superhuman feats of strength to impress the warriors. Arthur was hesitant in joining the Welsh hero. The matter was settled when Culhwch threatened to shout so loudly that the sound of his voice would cause every pregnant woman in Arthur's domain to miscarry. Arthur gave his cousin several of his best warriors and they set out on the quest.

Celtic Mythology

Culhwch found Olwen and declared his love for her. She admitted that she was attracted to him but said that they could never marry because of the prophecy that hung over her father, Yspaddaden Pencawr. He would never allow the marriage and would do all in his power to stop it. Backed by his warrior-companions, Culhwch went to the giant and asked him for his daughter's hand in marriage.

Pencawr, like most of the very ancient giants, was a sly creature and, while not refusing the request outright, he tried to put the hero off the idea. He made several attempts to kill him but, on each occasion, Culhwch was saved by one of his companions. Eventually, the giant gave him a list of virtually impossible tasks to perform before he could win the hand of Olwen. These tasks included obtaining a pair of magical birds that were the property of Rhiannon, the Welsh Queen of the Dead; stealing a magic cauldron laden with treasures from Ireland and retrieving a pair of scissors from between the ears of the magic boar Twrch Trwyth. In these quests, Culhwch was aided by a variety of supernatural figures from Celtic myth. They included Mabon, a divine hunter who had been imprisoned in a fortress at Gloucester, the Blackbird of Kilgowry and the Salmon of Llyn. The final labour was the most fearsome and was performed in the tale by Arthur himself – obtaining a drop of blood from the Hag of Hell. Having completed the tasks, Culhwch returned and demanded the hand of Olwen and Pencawr could hardly refuse. In some variants of the tale, the strain proved too much for the ancient monster and he collapsed and died as Olwen was handed over, thus negating the prophecy.

The tale was taken from a number of sources and added to across the years. Medieval elements were introduced, for example, the Hag or Queen of Hell. A number of medieval supernatural or wonder-tale elements are featured in the story, particularly in relation to Twrch Trwyth, an evil king in the guise of a boar. Culhwch himself is a pig and he seemed to have used transforming magic to overcome the monster. In the Celtic world throughout the Middle Ages, the idea of the shape-shifter, werewolf, magical hare, etc., was extremely strong in folk-belief.

There are some stock Irish elements in the story, probably because of the original sources involved. At times, the character of Culhwch vacillated between that of an ordinary mortal and that of a god, very much in the style of Cú Chulainn. The character and appearance of the monstrous, one-eyed Pencawr obviously parallels the Irish ogre, Balor of the Evil Eye (see: Insert Box **Giants, Monsters and Fairies**). Probably many of the stories in *Mabinogi* were derived or adapted from Irish traditions.

In Search of Ancient Heroes

Over the generations, such figures as Arthur, Culhwch and Cú Chulainn have assumed an identity of their own and have been added to the mythology of ancient heroes. Perhaps the tales of their fortitude and heroism have made them such enduring icons.

THE GREAT WHEEL OF EXISTENCE

The Cycle of the Celtic Year

Time was as important to the Celtic farmers as the land, linked as both were to the cycle of life manifest in the countryside. There was a time for planting, a time for harvesting, a time when the earth was hard and infertile, a time when it was abundantly fertile. As the Celts became dependent upon agriculture as a way of life, so the notion of time coupled with the concomitant notion of fertility became increasingly important.

Celtic Mythology

They noticed one important factor about the land – everything appeared to be cyclic. Crops planted at a certain time would flourish at another and though the ground was iron-hard during one season, it would become lush and verdant in the next. As they observed this cycle repeated time and time again, the agricultural Celts began to conceive time and existence as a great wheel constantly turning and structured their lives accordingly.

For the Celtic farmer, existence was governed by the changing seasons and the concept of fertility so important to the Celtic people. The fertility of the land varied with

REBIRTH AND REGENERATION

The concept of regeneration and rebirth is a continuing theme throughout Celtic mythology. In the Celtic mind, there was an underlying certainty that death was not the end. Whether individual consciousness passed into the Otherworld or into a vague Afterlife, it survived physical demise. The Celtic druids were probably the first holy men to argue for the existence of a soul.

Caesar, in *De Bello Gallico*, argues that the druids encouraged Celtic warriors not to be afraid of death in battle by promulgating the idea of an immortal force within each individual. These soul-forces, the soldiers were told, would pass directly into the realm of the gods on the destruction of the body.

After a period of living in the next world, they would probably return to the living world in another body. The theme of rebirth was in accord with the changing of the seasons and the turning of the Great Wheel. If it was so in the rest of Nature, it should be so among human kind, ran the argument in Celtic minds. A man who was buried in the darkness of the earth might burst forth just as easily as the corn-seed or the tree-leaf.

In both Irish and Welsh vernacular mythology, there are references to cauldrons that resurrect the dead. In the *Second Branch of the Mabinogi*, the Irish invaders possessed a great cauldron into which they threw their dead at the end of each battle, causing them to spring up alive by the next morning. This theme is mentioned in the Irish *Book of Invasions* during battles between the Fomorians and the Tuatha Dé Danann. Here, a wonder-worker of the Tuatha threw fallen warriors into a sacred well and the dead rose up to fight in the next battle.

There are also vernacular tales about the regeneration of limbs lost in battle, recalling natural regeneration again: stags shed their antlers at one season's end and grew them again at the next. Here the connection with Herne, in his role as a forest god, is evident. There are some stories of warriors who buried broken limbs hoping that they would grow again and be rejoined to the rest of the body. This all was part of the main theme of Celtic life: the cyclical nature of events.

the seasons, affecting the lives of those who dwelt on it. The crops grew and were harvested at specific times of the year and livestock gave birth in their time. The superior supernatural being was the Mother Goddess or Matres, the ultimate deification of fecundity and well being. Many divine couples in Celtic mythology demonstrated the sexual and reproductive essentials on which people depended. Such gods and beings were regularly invoked at certain times of the year. Most of the gods and goddesses embodied aspects of fertility and sexuality. Even those deities who embodied war embraced at least an element of the idea of fertility. These two aspects – the rotation of time and the ideas of fertility – gradually became ingrained into the very fabric of Celtic consciousness and, quite naturally, emerged in their most basic beliefs and folklore.

The Great Cauldron of Rebirth

The cauldron played a significant part in both Celtic life and belief. As a symbol of well being, it pre-dated the Celts by many thousands of years; from the early Bronze Age of pre-Celtic Europe, bronze vessels were used in both feasting and ritual and appear to have been specifically associated with the dead. From about the second millennium BC, they were used as cook-pots, perhaps for boiling meat and for heating water or drink. The feasts would probably have been great tribal occasions, as the cauldron would have produced such large quantities. Some cauldrons unearthed hold between 14 and 17 gallons – hardly a family cooking pot. Many of the monstrous pots have been found in Ireland, Scotland and in Brittany. Such mighty cauldrons were also associated with the dead and seem to have formed an important part of Irish funerary rites. Some seem to have been used as vehicles, perhaps for transporting the dead from one world into the other. Carried on a cart mounted on wheels, as in representations of the Urnfield vessels, these massive containers carried the remains of the dead, sometimes burned and charred, out of the mortal sphere. In parts of Iron Age Scandinavia, the vessels were located primarily in watery contexts, such as Gunstrap and Bra.

The Great Wheel of Existence

In other parts of the Celtic world particularly in Eastern Europe, cauldrons were filled with jewellery and expensive gifts, perhaps denoting the personal wealth of the interred. The treasure would pass over into the Otherworld to support him there as it had done in the human world.

The burial of cauldrons containing ashes or human remains might have had yet another meaning linked to fertility. Celtic farmers associated the earth with rebirth and renewal. Tribal belief imagined that the dead, planted in the fertile earth, might return, renewed and revivified. Corpses buried in their cauldrons might suddenly spring to life, particularly if they were semi-divine warriors or wise men. The notions of the burial-cauldron and of fertility and rebirth became intertwined in Celtic mythology and folklore where cauldrons, or great pots, of rebirth and revitalisation appear in Classical and vernacular tales.

In the Second branch of the Classic Welsh epic the *Mabinogi*, the Irish king Matholwch possessed a magical cauldron. He cast his dead warriors into the cauldron each night and, boiling them up, restored them to fighting fitness on the following day. Though the warriors were healthy and had severed limbs miraculously restored, they had lost the power of speech. Using this supernatural artefact, the Irish threaten the Welsh with invasion. The Welsh King, Bendigeidfran, had to destroy the cauldron before the Irish could be repulsed. Ironically, the cauldron had originally belonged to Bendigeidfran who had lent it to Matholwch before hostilities broke out between Ireland and Wales. Irish myth states that the cauldron originated in Ireland and therefore rightfully belonged to the Irish king. A gigantic man, accompanied by his even

more titanic spouse, had carried it on his back from a site known as 'The Lake of the Cauldron'.

The magic cauldron of immortality features in the tale of Culhwch and Olwen, also to be found in the *Mabinogi*. The retrieval of the cauldron was one of the quests of the hero Culhwch before he could marry Olwen, the daughter of the monstrous giant Yspaddadan Pencawr (see **In Search of Ancient Heroes**). Culhwch had to travel to Ireland to wrest the enchanted artefact from the druid Diwrnach, chief adviser to the Irish High King. He failed and his cousin, Arthur of Britain, won the cauldron, that was reputedly full of all the treasures of Ireland, for him.

The symbol of the cauldron, both as representation of rebirth and as source of continuous abundance, looms large in Irish mythology. Each Irish '*bruidhean*' – Otherworld hostel or 'house of the god' – had its own magical pot that could easily feed one hundred warriors and never became empty. Such inexhaustible cauldrons also regenerated dead warriors. This accorded with the dual notions of feasting and revitalisation, believed common among Celtic warrior cults. In Irish mythology, the Daghdha, the father of all the gods in the Irish pantheon (see **Spirits of Earth and Air**), was supposed to own a cauldron that overflowed with foodstuffs, beer and whiskey. The Daghdha was widely regarded as a god of fecundity and plenteous living; his cauldron was a symbol of this and also conformed to the Irish idea of hospitality. The club that the Daghdha reputedly carried, that could raise the dead, corresponded to the notion of the cauldron and warfare.

The Great Wheel of Existence

Celtic scholars such as Miranda Green have suggested that the Daghdha with his club and cauldron might be another representation of the Roman-Celtic god Sucellus who carried a hammer and pot, perhaps signifying death and resurrection. The Daghdha's pot was so large that it could make a porridge that contained the whole carcasses of sheep, pigs and goats and eighty measures of milk and fat. It was regarded as the Celtic equivalent of the Viking 'Horn of Plenty', which the supreme Norse god Odin and his son Thor alternately held.

Quests for such magic cauldrons in both Classical and vernacular tales might have formed the basis for the later medieval romances, such as the quest for the Water of Life or, more importantly, the Search for the Holy Grail. The Grail Myth might have been a Christian representation of earlier cauldron-quests. In some Irish Classical versions of the story, the hungry Cú Chulainn and his friend Cú Roí, whom he later kills, went on a hunt for Muirias, the legendary cauldron of the Daghdha. They managed to steal it from a mysterious castle: a foretaste of the later Arthurian quest with its eerie castle of the Fisher King. Another Celtic monarch known as Midir the Proud owned a magic cauldron that he was supposed to have brought back from the Otherworld after a similar quest. Journeys of discovery involving supernatural cooking pots are to be found in vernacular Welsh sagas such as *The Spoils of Annwn*.

Celtic Mythology

The cauldron held a special place in Celtic society and was therefore often invested with supernatural properties. It was also an essential part of the stereotypical witch's magical baggage. Within the cauldron, all kinds of powers ebbed and flowed, lending a mystical force to whatever was cooked or mixed in it. As the symbol of mystery and death, it was emblazoned on the Celtic mind.

Festivals and Feast Days

Two aspects dominated the Celts' view of the passing of the year. One was the natural, visible change in the seasons; the other was the long-term position of the sun in the sky. With the greening of the countryside came life and vitality: Nature at her most abundant. Green was the colour of rebirth and regeneration. Legends of the Green Man reflect this.

When the ground was hard and nothing would grow it was regarded as a dark or sterile time. When life was verdant, the sun blazed, high and vigorous, in the sky but when the season changed, it was low and feeble. When the sun was at its height, the days were warm and bright; when it was at its lowest, they were cold and miserable. To the Celts, this was a sign that in winter the gods were weak and might even die. But they knew that the Great Wheel of Existence would turn once more, that the sun would be restored and that growth and plenty would return. That was the way of things; life was cyclic. Everything died to be reborn in the fullness of time.

Around key points in the turn of the Wheel of Life, they held a number of celebrations, some for specific purposes. During the great feast of Yule in the depths

Thor, son of Odin, battles against the Jøtune

of winter, logs were burned to restore heat and warmth to the ailing sun and to the frozen earth. Other festivals marked events in natural and communal life such as the gathering in of the harvest; the Celts needed no special excuse to celebrate. Later, many pagan festivals would become part of the Christian calendar.

Many feasts and celebrations had only local significance but there were a number of major festivals that were also observed.

Imbolc (or Imbolg)

As winter loosened its grip on the countryside, days began to grow longer and the first stirrings of spring were observed. The sun began to rise higher in the sky and migrating birds returned. The ground that had been hard and cold became ready for planting. Ewes became heavy with lamb and their lactation increased. The agricultural Celts celebrated the returning vitality and fertility in the land with a great festival called Imbolc, which means 'in the belly' and stressed both the renewal and rebirth of the land. This festival was held around February, as the lengthening of daylight became noticeable, and was closely associated with the Celtic fertility goddess Brigit – a mother-goddess and protector of women in childbirth. At this time, in parts of the Celtic world, the first-born of the year was sacrificed to dark gods, the Crom Cruach, for example. Blood was allowed to flow into the ground to restore it and to ensure ample crops for the coming year. Great fires were lit to add extra strength to the sun so that it could support the crops across the coming months. Nothing would be thrown out of a Celtic household until after the feast of Imbolc for fear of losing 'the luck' for the rest of the year. This was a common superstition in Ireland within living memory.

The Great Wheel of Existence

The Spring Equinox

At spring and autumn Equinox, the forces of light and darkness were in perfect balance, according to Celtic traditional belief. It was therefore necessary to strengthen

SUN WORSHIP

The later Celtic religion was centred on Nature, perceiving the vital forces as moving through, and manifesting themselves in, the living world. One of the most important was the sun. It was the source of growth, fertility and healing and demanded the worship of its followers if it was to function effectively.

Rock carvings all over Europe, but especially in the north, show solar images and depictions and early metalwork, dating from the first millennium BC, show mounted figures presumed to be aspects of sun gods.

The sun was a protector who drove away evil as it drove away winter's cold and terrifying darkness. Amulets, bearing solar representations and formed in the shape of a great wheel have been found in Austria and ornaments and coins bearing images of the risen sun have been found in tombs and elsewhere. It is possible that the Celtic peoples thought that the soul might have needed the sun's protection while it made its long, difficult journey towards rebirth.

Wheels appear on head-dresses worn by priests and priestesses who officiated at sun-worshipping rituals, as can be seen by those found on the site of an ancient temple at Wanborough in Surrey together with a necklace or pendant that symbolised the great wheel.

Even within early Celtic Christianity, the symbolism of the sun and the wheel was recognised. Stylised Celtic crosses show the wheel at their summit, allowing the sun to shine through their spokes. Thus, worshippers could kneel before the Christian Cross while worshipping the sun that shone directly through it.

There is little mention of the sun or sun gods in vernacular Celtic literature and it could be that all references to sun gods were expunged by the monks who copied down the tales. It is thought, though, that the Irish god Lúgh might have been a solar god and the goddess Eriu, who drank each day from a shining golden goblet, might have been a sun goddess.

Sucellos and Nantosuelta, Celtic underworld gods

the light while holding the darkness in check. The festival on 21 March invoked the gods of light and was one of the festivals centred on the early year. The most important festival was that of the Moon Goddess Eostre who was also a fertility goddess. Her symbol was the fecund rabbit or hare – the mad March hare. At her revelry, her priests would hold up a barley cake marked with four quarters, to symbolise the quarters of the Moon, as a token of plenty for the year to come. It eventually became the holiest period in the Christian calendar, Easter. The cake of the pagan priest became the Hot Cross Bun, still marked with the Moon's four quarters but now assuming a Christian symbolism.

A minor festival around 18 March honoured the clover, to call for good luck throughout the coming time. Clover was considered a very lucky plant, believed to repel both demons and venomous reptiles. The four-leafed variety was especially effective with its wheel-like appearance, signifying the wheel of life and providing a powerful *apotropaic* – sign against evil. The festival became the Feast of Saint Patrick on 17 March and the clover became shamrock. The three leaves of the 'immortal leaf of bard and chief' representing the three-fold goddess, now symbolises the Trinity. The legend of Saint Patrick's use of the plant to explain the Christian Mystery to the pagan Irish was developed. There is no mention of the shamrock in any of the various 'Lives' of the saint.

The egg demonstrated the fertility of the Spring Equinox. To the Celts, the egg represented the womb of the Earth Mother that was split open by the penetrating rays of the sun to give life and vigour to creation. This perspective also underlay the notion of the Druid's Egg (see **The Druidic Tradition**) supposedly created from the

Sucellos

foam generated by two mating serpents. This is the origin of our present day Easter Egg and the ancient custom of painting eggs: originally the only colour permitted was scarlet, the colour of the sun. The rolling of eggs signified contact with the earth and suggested the movement of the Great Wheel.

Bealtane

As the sun became higher in the sky, so the days grew warmer, and kinder. They were now almost at their longest and nature was at its most lush. In the Celtic farming year, it was time to turn the cattle onto fresh pasture to fatten them for the winter.

The name *Bealtane* means 'bright or good fire' and the festival was held on 1 May. It signalled the real beginning of summer and welcomed the health-giving rays of the sun. Many bonfires were lit to ward off the spirits of disease and as a sympathetic gesture to strengthen the heat of the sun so it would penetrate the womb of the earth. The fires attracted great superstition and magical lore. Within living memory in Ireland, herds of cattle were driven between two sacred Bealtane fires to protect them from fluke and other bovine diseases. This had its origin as early as the ninth century but the Irish scribe Cormac, writing in the late 800s, said that it was primarily for fertility reasons.

In Roman times, the festival was associated with the Roman-Celtic healer-god Belenus and possibly with the Phoenician god Baal, since all these 'bel' names have links with light and fertility.

Bealtane was a particularly Irish festival and was characterised by the Irish Ard Rí or High King lighting the first Bealtane fire on the Hill at Royal Tara. It was here that Saint Patrick is said to have challenged King Laoghaire and his druids by lighting the first fire on the Hill of Slane (see **Legends of Saints and Holy Men**). Saint David is said to have made a similar gesture in Wales.

A feature of the Bealtane fire in many parts of the Celtic world was the leaping by young men and warriors over the flames. This emphasised their prowess and might have been to ensure success in hunting or in battle. Fire was a particularly mystical element, conferring special attributes upon those who venerated it. The fire-leaping exercises might also have served as tests of strength and courage among the warriors.

Celtic Mythology

Bealtane had its dark-side too, for the forces of the dark and the supernatural were not far away, even at this bright time of the year. May-Eve (30 April) was still regarded, along with Hallowe'en, as a time when fairy power and the might of the evil dead were at their highest. Sprigs of mountain ash were tied to doors, windows and chimneys to ward off witches and malignant spirits on this day.

Midsummer

With the sun at its brightest and strongest everyone enjoyed the full flood of its light and warmth. There was still much growth left in the fields and Nature ran wild. As the Greek scholar, Heraclitus, put it: *Panta rhei, ouden menei* ('everything flows, nothing is static'). The Midsummer festival was the great celebratory festival of fertility and good things; fire and water were its representations, both highly sacred elements that represented the male/female aspects of regeneration and vitality. The festival is sometimes called Bealtane or Little Bealtane in Ireland because it was thought that Saint Patrick moved the Irish 'bonfire night' to Saint John's night on 23 June, to overcome the pagan implications of May Eve. In doing so, he moved it to the lesser festival of Midsummer on 22 June, though some traditions hold that it was moved to 28 June, the feast of Saints Peter and Paul. It was a feast for intoxication and a time to enjoy the fruits of the earth. Great fires were lit and it is still widely believed in Ireland that a burnt sod from Saint John's Eve is a charm against the Devil and his minions.

Lugnasadh (Lugnasad)

The word *Lugnasadh* or *Lunasad* is the Irish/Scots Gaelic for the month of August. It was one of the major festivals of the Celtic agricultural year and traditionally the festivities lasted from about 15 July to about 15 August.

THE IMPORTANCE OF FIRE

Saint Vincent

There was a strong link between Celtic religion and the element of fire. To the early Celts flames were an expression of the sun, so beneficial to the land. Fire was a supernatural element; while its destructive powers were recognised, its ability to warm the land and illuminate the darkness along with its purifying and cleansing qualities were also acknowledged. In many old non-Celtic tales, fire was considered a gift to humanity from the sun.

Many great bonfires were lit during long, gloomy European winters to reinvigorate the sun for the coming year or to restore heat to the frozen earth. In Midsummer, fires were lit as a celebration of the sunlight and to emulate the vigour of the summer sun. The word *bonfire* might derive from 'bone-fires. In the mid-fourth century, it is believed, fires were lit in pagan lands to commemorate the burning of the bones of Christian saints by the Emperor Julian the Apostate

Ritual bonfires served a dual purpose: to celebrate the power of the sun or to restore heat to its failing incarnation. Ash from the fires fertilised the land and trampled into the ground around a ritual fire provided a bed for young seeds allowing them to germinate and grow.

Gradually, the ritual pagan bonfires were taken over by the Church and turned into Christian festivals. Great fires were lit in Midsummer, theoretically to celebrate the birth of Saint John the Baptist but in fact, allowing the Celtic midsummer festivals to continue.

Wheel rolling was popular at many of these festivals, symbolising the turning of the year. In fourth-century Aquitaine, Saint Vincent observed a pagan ceremony where a burning wheel was rolled down a slope and into a river. The place then became the shrine of the sun god that was supposed to provide goodness and light for the year. An almost identical practice is detailed on Saint John's Eve in parts of England, except that an overall sky-god was venerated rather than just the sun.

Fire also provided for the destruction of enemies or criminals, who were ritually burnt. The symbolic and well-known Wicker Man was used for this. A monstrous humanoid shape made from wicker was filled with men and animals and set alight. A commentary on Lucan's *Pharsalia*, written around the ninth century, attributed this rite to a god named Taranis who appears to have been a thunder/sky deity. The ritual seems to have continued into early modern times with the burning of 'straw men' in both England and in parts of Ireland.

The Wicker Man

As its name suggests, the Lugnasadh festival was connected to the god of light, Lúgh, who gave his name to several locations across the Celtic realm. The most famous was at Lugdunum – the 'fort of Lúgh' – near Lyon in France where, in AD 12, the Emperor Augustus established his own cult. The date he chose was, significantly, 1 August, to coincide with the height of the Gaulish Lugnasadh.

The festival, with attendant fair and sporting events, was believed to have been inaugurated by the god Lúgh himself in honour of his foster-mother Tailtu. Other sources claim that it was to celebrate one of the god's many marriages. The festival was widespread throughout Ireland and continued there in its original state, long after its demise elsewhere. In Ulster, it was celebrated at Eamhain Macha and the High King officiated at a grand festival for the whole of Ireland at Tara.

The feast was strongly associated with the coming harvest. When it had been collected, a portion was left outside for the gods or else baked into an offering cake for the fertility deities in exchange for favour the following year.

Gradually Christianity took over this festival transforming it into 'the Loaf-Mass' or Lammas, a festival held later in the year, to God for the safe harvest. Churches were built where Lugnasadh dancing had taken place and T.C. Lethbridge in *Witches: Investigating the Ancient Religion* demonstrates that many parish churches dedicated to Saint Michael are on such sites.

The Great Wheel of Existence

The fairs and the games continued, however. Tom Graves in *Needles of Stone* has pointed out that various Irish wake-games, played during a wake for the dead, come from this festival. Many of the fairs became horse fairs and one of the most famous in Ireland continues – the Lammas Fair in Ballycastle, County Antrim.

The Autumn Equinox

If Lugnasadh marked the beginning of the harvest, then the Autumn Equinox marked its completion. The crops had to be gathered in before the forces of darkness and cold returned to haunt the world. The sun was sinking in the sky and appeared to grow smaller.

The festival might have been to protect the community against the dark forces crawling back across the world. It was held around 21 September and, with its harvest theme, might have been the forerunner of our harvest thanksgiving services; it, too, gave thanks for the gathering of crops before they could be snatched away by evil. Any crops not harvested by the Autumn Equinox were left to rot in the field, in case bad luck attended the gatherer.

In Celtic Christian mythology, this was the first time that the Devil stepped out after the bright days of summer and his passing could be seen in the changing colours of the berries in the hedgerows. No berries could be eaten at this time as they were 'marked with the Devil's spittle'. Summer was practically over and the dark days of winter were almost at hand.

Samhain

With the festival of Samhain – pronounced 'sow-en' – celebrated on 31 October, summer finally ended and the Celtic winter officially began. On a strictly agricultural level, it was time to bring in the livestock from the fields when some beasts were chosen for slaughter and others marked out as stud – or brood-animals for the New Year. It was a time for feats of strength and fighting prowess, but it was also a time to mourn the passing of summer.

On a supernatural level, this was an important time. The old year was dying, while the young year was waiting to be born. The Veil between the mortal world and the Otherwold was very thin and often creatures passed between the two spheres. It was a time when the gods granted the dead a chance to return to the world of the living, to contact their kin. In Ireland, it was the time of *Féile Na Marbh* – the great Feast of the Dead – at which the deceased were welcomed back into their homes. Whiskey and bread were often left in houses to refresh the dead and fine ash was scattered around the fireplace for them to leave their tracks for the wondering gaze of their descendants the next morning.

Celtic Mythology

The sidh-mounds and raths were opened and the fairies roamed freely through the countryside, unbound by any holy restrictions. Sometimes the fairies and the dead travelled together and householders were well advised to stay indoors to avoid meeting such a procession. With fairy agreement, and the cost of the sight of one eye, one could see the shades of those who would die within the coming year as they processed along the midnight roads under fairy supervision. At that price, it was well to leave such things alone.

As Christianity spread, the nature of Samhain changed. It became a Christian festival, though its connections with the Otherworld and the dead were not completely severed. The following day, 1 November, became known in the Christian calendar as The Feast of All Hallows, or All Souls' Day, when the dead were specifically remembered with prayers and Masses. Samhain became All Hallows' Eve or Hallowe'en and is still regarded as a time when ghosts, witches and other evil creatures have free reign across the world of the living. In the Celtic era, Hallowe'en must have been a very frightening time and one when everyone stayed indoors for fear of what they might encounter.

Yule

In a sense, the great festival of Yule on 22 December summed up the cycle of the Celtic year. The word Yule, according to the Venerable Bede, came from the Norse word *Iul* meaning 'wheel' and suggested that this was the time when the Great Wheel of Existence had completed its circle. By the time the festival came around, the countryside was firmly in the grip of winter; the sun was low in the sky, trees were bare and leafless and the ground was cold, iron-hard and sterile. The early Celts worried that their gods were dying and that darkness would remain forever. It was important that heat and vitality were returned both to the sky and the ground; thus all over Celtic Europe, great fires were lit.

In later Celtic folk-belief, Yule had a dual meaning, it symbolised the death of the old year and heralded the birth of the new. Although the ground was cold, it would soon be warm again and Nature would burst forth at the festival of *Imbolc*. The low-point of the period of Yule became the central festival of a number of formal religions, one of which was Christianity. Before the Church accepted 25 December as the Christ Mass, it had been the symbolic festival of the Persian sun god Attis and his son Mithras – the festival was known as The Feast of the Unconquered Sun. Many of the Mithras legends – for example, virgin birth in lowly circumstances - Mithras was born in a cave – were incorporated into the Christian message. The date of Christ's birthday, placed in the depths of winter to coincide with the Celtic Yule festival, is highly significant.

After Yule, the Great Wheel began to turn again, bringing the festival of *Imbolc* around once more. Gradually some festivals assumed less importance and four great functional festivals – Imbolc, Bealtane, Lughnasadh and Samhain dominated the Celtic year. Many of these became major Christian holy days - Imbolc became Candlemas (2 February) with its own rhyme: 'On Candlemas Day, Throw a candle away'.

The Great Wheel of Existence

In Ireland, because of its close association with the goddess Brigit, it became Saint *Brigid's* Day. Where the festivals of local deities persisted, they became 'pattern days'– the feast of a local or patron saint. Until very recently the tradition of pagan-festival-become-Christian-holiday persisted in many country areas – particularly in Ireland and in parts of Scotland and Cornwall.

The Dark Time

The dark side of the Great Wheel was a dreadful time; these were dark days indeed, with little sunshine and overcast skies. The wind was chill and the ground frequently buried under snow. It was believed that the forces of light hid their faces and the powers of evil had free reign in the world. It was the time of the Leprous White Lady, a death goddess who walked the countryside, taking the young and old under her cloak. Carried in the folds of her cloak were disease and illness that she dispensed with a liberal hand. She might have been an incarnation of the Welsh Death Goddess Rhiannon or the Badhbh or Morrigan of Irish myth.

In the fields, there was not much work for the ground was hard and no crops could be planted. Livestock was kept indoors and the men and women of the Celtic world kept close to the fires and watched the dark days and even darker nights with trepidation. It was a time for story telling, particularly legends of the dead or of fearful monsters. The Christmas ghost story is a tradition that stretches back to the Celtic past.

The darkness would pass as the Great Wheel turned and the cold and dark moved away. The days would brighten and grow longer, the sun's strength would be restored as it climbed higher in the sky and soon it would be *Imbolc* again. This was how it was for the Celts. Everything was cyclic; all things died and were reborn. Everything turned like a great wheel.

Celtic Mythology

BIBLIOGRAPHY

Alcock, L., *Arthur's Britain*, Harmondsworth, 1971
Annyle, *Celtic Religion*, Constable, 1906
Ashe, G., *The Mythology of the British Isles*, Methuen, 1990
Ashe, G., *The Quest for Arthur's Britain*, Pall Mall Press, 1966

Barley, M.W. and Hanson, R., *Christianity in Britain AD 300–700*, Leicester University
        Press, 1968
Beresford-Ellis, P., *Wales: A Nation Again*, Constable, 1987
Beresford-Ellis, P., *The Celtic Empire: The First Millennium of Celtic History
        1000BC–51AD*, Constable, 1990
Beresford-Ellis, P., *A Dictionary of Celtic Mythology*, Constable, 1992
Beresford-Ellis, P., *Celt and Saxon: The Struggle for Britain AD 410 – 937*, Constable, 1993
Beresford-Ellis, P., *The Druids*, Constable, 1994
Bottrell, W., *Hearthside Tales of Cornwall*, Penzance, (reprinted) 1997
Bowen, E.G., *The Settlement of the Celtic Saints in Wales*, University of Wales Press, 1956
Briggs, K., *A Dictionary of Fairies*, Penguin, 1977

Carr-Gom, P., *The Druidic Tradition*, Element Books, 1991
Chadwick, N., *The Druids,* Cardiff, University of Wales Press, 1966
Croker, T.C. and Lover, S., *Ireland,* (Senate Reprint), 1995
Crossley-Holland, K., (ed.), *Folk Tales of The British Isles,* Faber, 1985
Curtin, J., *Hero Tales of Ireland*, London, 1894

Danaher, K., *Gentle Places, Simple Things,* Mercier, 1964
Danaher, K., *Irish Country People*, Mercier, 1966
Danaher, K., *Folk Tales of the Irish Countryside*, Mercier, 1967
Danaher, K., *The Year in Ireland,* Mercier, 1972
Davidson, H.E., *The Lost Beliefs of Northern Europe*, Routledge, 1993
Delehaye, H., *Legends of the Saints,* (Crawford Tr.), London, 1907
De Poer, *Saint Patrick's World: The Christian Culture of Ireland's Apostolic Age*, Four
        Courts Press, 1993
Dillon, M., and Chadwick, N., *The Celtic Realms*, Wiedenfeld and Nicholson, 1967

Ellis, T.P. and Lloyd, J., *The Mabinogion*, OUP, 1929
Evens-Wentz, W.Y., *Fairy Faith in Celtic Countries*, (reprinted Colin Smythe), 1977

Filip, J., *Celtic Civilization and Heritage*, Prague, 1960

Glassie, H., *Irish Folk Tales*, Penguin, 1985
Green, M.J., *Dictionary of Celtic Myth and Legend*, Thames and Hudson, 1992

Celtic Mythology

Green, M.J., *The Celtic World*, Routledge, 1995
Gregory, Lady A., *Visions and Beliefs in the West of Ireland*, Colin Smythe, 1970
Guilleme, A., *Prophecy and Divination*, London, 1938

Van Hemmel, A.G., *Immrama: Voyages*, Dublin, 1934
Herdmans, W.A., *Manx Antiquities*, Liverpool, 1914
Higgins, G., *The Celtic Druids*, London, 1829
Howells, W., *Cambrian Superstitions*, London, 1831
Hunt, R., *Cornish Folk Tales*, Redruth, 1975

John, C.R., *The Saints of Cornwall*, Redruth, 1982
Jones, T.G., *Welsh Folklore and Folk-Custom*, Methuen, 1930
Jones, P. and Pennick, N., *A History of Pagan Europe*, Routledge, 1995

Keen, M., *The Outlaws of Medieval Legend*, Routledge, 1977
Kendrick, T.D., *The Druids: A Study in Keltic Prehistory*, Methuen, 1927

Legious, J.P., *Byways in Brittany*, Geneva, 1921
Lewis, D., *Religious Superstition Through the Ages*, Oxford, 1975

MacCollough, J.A., *The Religion of the Ancient Celts*, Edinburgh, 1911
MacCollough, J.A., *Celtic Mythology*, Boston, 1918
MacNeill, M., *The Festival of Lughnasa*, Oxford, 1962
Mackie, J., *Tales of the Highland and Islands*, Edinburgh, 1881
Martin, M., *A Description of the Western Isles of Scotland Circa 1695*, Birlinn Ltd, 1994
Merrifield, R., *The Archaeology of Ritual and Magic*, London, 1987
Meyer, K., *Death Tales of Ulster Heroes*, Dublin, 1906
Monro, D., *A Voyage to St Kilda and a Description of the Western Isles of Scotland, 1774*, Birlinn Ltd, 1994
Morris, J., *The Age of Arthur*, Weidenfeld and Nicholson, 1989
Morris, S.J., (ed.), *Nennius: British History and the Welsh Annals*, (tr. Phillimore), London, 1980
Murphy, M.J., *Now You're Talking*, Belfast, 1975
Murray, L. and C., *The Celtic Tree Oracle*, Rider, 1980

Ó hÓgáin, D., *Myth, Legend and Romance: An Encyclopaedia of Irish Folk Tradition*, Prentice Hall, 1990
O'Rahilly, T., *Early Irish History and Mythology*, Dublin, 1946
Ó Súilleabháin, S., *A Handbook of Irish Folklore*, Dublin, 1940
Ó Súilleabháin, S., *The Folklore of Ireland*, Batsford, 1974

Pascal, C. B., *The Celts of Cisalpine Gaul*, Brussels, 1964
Patch, H.R., *The Otherworld*, Harvard University Press, 1950
Pennant, T., *A Tour in Scotland and a Voyage to the Hebrides in 1769*, Chester, 1771
Piggot, S., *The Druids*, London, 1968
Powell, T.G.E., *The Celts*, London, 1968

Rafferty, J., (ed.), *The Celts*, Mercier, 1964

Bibliography

Rhys, J., *Celtic Folklore*, 2 vols, OUP, 1901

Rolleston, T.W., *Myths and Legends of the Celtic Race*, Harrap, 1911

Ross, A., *Pagan Celtic Britain*, Routledge, 1967

Saint-Leger, Gordon R., *The Witchcraft and Folklore of Dartmoor*, Peninsula Press, 1994

Scott, M., *Irish Ghosts and Hauntings*, Warner Books, 1994

Sebbilot, P.Y., *Le Folklore de France*, Paris, 1904

Severin, T., *The Brendan Voyage*, Hutchinson, 1978

Skene, W.F., *Celtic Scotland*, 3 vols, Edinburgh, 1876–1890

Spence, L., *The Magic Arts in Celtic Britain*, Rider, 1949

Stukely, W., *The History, Religion and Temples of the Druids*, London, 1729

Stukely, W., *Stonehenge: A Temple Restored to the British Druids*, London, 1740

Toulston, S., *The Celtic Year*, Element, 1998

Waite, A.E., *The Hidden Church of the Holy Grail*, Rebman, 1909

Walker, P.N., *Folk Tales from the North York Moors*, Robert Hale, 1990

Welch, R., (ed.), *W.B. Yeats: Writings on Irish Folklore, Legend and Myth*, Penguin, 1993

Wilde, Lady, *The Ancient Legends of Ireland*, London, 1888

Woodmartin, W.G., *Pagan Ireland*, London, 1895

Woodward, A., *Shrines and Sacrifice*, Batsford, 1992

Zipes, J., *Victorian Fairy Stories and Their Origins: The Revolt of the Fairies and Elves*,
    Methuen, 1987

INDEX

Entries in italics are literary works.
Location references in bold relate to special articles inset into
the main text.